W9-CBD-229

Advance praise for *Number Go Up*

"A riveting and horrifying but also endlessly entertaining investigation into the bad parts of crypto (which are most of them). This book is what happens when the funniest financial journalist in America takes on the funniest story in modern finance, and the results are as darkly hilarious as you could hope for."

—Matt Levine, *Money Stuff* columnist

"This book is ludicrously compelling. I, quite literally, couldn't put it down—and I don't even care about crypto. Zeke Faux writes about this world with such clarity, humor, and perspective that the portrait captures something even larger: a moment in time that we can't afford not to understand."

—Evan Osnos, National Book Award–winning author of *Age of Ambition*

"Business journalists are not usually lauded for their bravery, but it takes guts to gaze into the abyss of late-stage capitalism—never mind parachute directly into it—and Zeke Faux's descent into the blatantly nonsensical, blistering immoral world of cryptocurrency is a kind of hero's journey. It's a riveting, character-driven narrative in which Faux, a longtime writer for *Businessweek* and a crypto skeptic, guides readers through a vividly rendered hellscape populated by corporate lawyers, drug lords, terrorists and former child actors—among others—while nimbly telling the story of how a 'hobby for nerds,' became, in the words of its more infamous villains, 'the world's biggest Ponzi scheme.'"

—Jessica Pressler, special correspondent, *Vanity Fair;* producer, *Hustlers* and *Inventing Anna*

"This book is riveting, scary, funny, unbelievable, depressing, insane, and many other adjectives, but I'll stop here and just say: If you want a front-row seat to one of the greatest business stories of all time, you should read *Number Go Up* now. It's worth your time and Bitcoin, Ethereum, Tether, etc."

—A.J. Jacobs, *New York Times* bestselling author of *The Puzzler*

"*Number Go Up* is both a serious financial investigation and an incredibly entertaining romp through crypto's wildest days, with deep access to all the people responsible and their cadre of true believers. Over and over in the book, Zeke Faux gets the classic confession from the villain explaining how he did the crime—but in Faux's case, it's while the crime is ongoing, at over-the-top parties that are celebrating the scams, attended by your favorite celebrities, where Faux seems to be the only one asking the uncomfortable questions. This is a definitive, incisive, and revealing tale of crypto's great promise and epic crash."

—Sarah Frier, author of *No Filter:*
The Inside Story of Instagram

"Zeke Faux's *Number Go Up* does what should be impossible—it combines meticulous reporting with irresistible storytelling. The book reveals what was arguably the most brazen financial con of the twenty-first century and does so without getting mired in abstraction or hype. It is the definitive book about crypto and the only one you'll want to read."

—Max Chafkin, author of *The Contrarian*

"The only book about crypto you need to read . . . Faux has gone deeper than anyone inside a movement that aspires to replace traditional finance, but seems more likely to blow up and take the world down with it. Get ready to laugh, then cry, then scratch your head at the sheer insanity of billions of dollars being magicked out of thin air by stoned tech bros. By the end of the book, when Faux brings readers to a compound of crypto scammers working in slavery-like conditions in Cambodia, all your expectations will have shattered. *Number Go Up* is an instant-classic: *Liar's Poker* for the era of digital monkey tokens, written with a sensibility that meets our absurd moment in time."

—Kit Chellel, co-author of *Dead in the Water*

"*Number Go Up* is a dizzying safari of the surreal, hilarious, can't-make-it-up insanity of the crypto boom. Racing across the globe from the Bahamas to Italy to Cambodia, Zeke Faux takes readers behind the velvet rope and onto the mega yachts and multimillion-dollar tropical compounds of the billionaire crypto schemers, hustlers, and evangelists who may all be headed to prison—but are having a riotously good time turning the financial world upside down."

—Joshua Green, #1 *New York Times*
bestselling author of *Devil's Bargain*

"*Number Go Up* is funny, enraging, racy, and profound. We were waiting for the first great crypto book and Zeke Faux has written it."

—Oliver Bullough, author of *Moneyland*

"Before the crash, Zeke Faux set out to chronicle the rise and fall of crypto. It's lucky for us that he did, because his book, *Number Go Up,* is an almost too good to be true saga that would be impossible to reconstruct unless you were there as it was happening. It's essential reading for anyone who wants to understand the mass delusion that was crypto—and anyone who wants to understand how we can fool ourselves."

—Bethany McLean, bestselling co-author
of *The Smartest Guys in the Room*

NUMBER GO UP

NUMBER GO UP

INSIDE CRYPTO'S WILD RISE AND STAGGERING FALL

· · · · ·

ZEKE FAUX

CURRENCY

NEW YORK

Copyright © 2023 by Zeke Faux

All rights reserved.

Published in the United States by Currency, an imprint of Random House,
a division of Penguin Random House LLC, New York.

CURRENCY and its colophon are trademarks of Penguin Random House LLC.

Hardback ISBN 978-0-593-44381-1
International edition ISBN 978-0-593-72822-2
Ebook ISBN 978-0-593-44382-8

Printed in the United States of America on acid-free paper

currencybooks.com

2 4 6 8 9 7 5 3 1

First Edition

Map by Olha Bosenko

For Nikki

CONTENTS

NUMBER GO UP

PROLOGUE

Nassau, Bahamas
February 17, 2022

Total Value of All Cryptocurrencies: $2 Trillion
(Yes, Trillion with a "T")

"I'm not going to lie," Sam Bankman-Fried told me.
This was a lie.

We were in his office in the Bahamas, and I had just pulled up my chair to his desk and turned on my tape recorder. I had flown in on assignment from Bloomberg, where I worked as an investigative reporter, to see the man at the center of the cryptocurrency frenzy that was sweeping the globe.

Bankman-Fried stared ahead at his six monitors and scrolled through emails as he told me that I could always count on him to give his honest opinions about crypto. *Forbes* had recently declared him the world's richest person under thirty, but he looked like a student who'd been shaken awake after an all-nighter in the library. He was schlubby and shoeless, in blue shorts and a gray T-shirt advertising his cryptocurrency exchange, FTX. His wild curly hair was so matted down by the headphones he'd been wearing that he resembled a half-sheared sheep. On his desk I saw an open packet of chickpea korma—yesterday's lunch.

My plan was to write a profile of crypto's boy genius, the man who, at twenty-nine, seemed to have the future of money figured out. His rise had been so meteoric that it seemed plausible when he said FTX would one day take over all of Wall Street. He was worth at least $20 billion, but he claimed he'd only gotten rich so that he could give it all away. He drove a Toyota Corolla and liked to sleep at the office on a beanbag chair, which I could see next to his desk.

It was an irresistible story. The problem was that it was not true. While the media, politicians, venture capitalists, and investment bankers lauded him as a benevolent prodigy—a Warren Buffett or J. P. Morgan for the digital age—he was secretly embezzling billions of dollars of his customers' money and blowing it on bad trades, celebrity endorsements, and an island real-estate shopping spree to rival any drug kingpin's.

I'd like to tell you that I was the person who exposed it all, the heroic investigator who saw through one of history's greatest frauds. But I got tricked like everyone else. I was sitting next to the biggest con man since Bernie Madoff, with a clear view of his emails, internal chats, and trading records, and I had no idea what he was up to.

"You can use me as a resource for information," Bankman-Fried said, tapping his crew-sock-clad feet aggressively. "That's one of the biggest things I want to convey."

"That makes sense," I said to him, nodding amiably.

I DID HAVE my suspicions. From the day I started digging into the crypto world, I had seen nothing but red flags. Why were all these companies based in infamous offshore regulatory havens? What was up with all these random virtual coins that were supposedly worth tens of billions of dollars? Was that, just maybe, a precarious foundation for the future of finance? Were they all scams?

But by the time I visited Bankman-Fried's island hideaway, the logic of the financial world had broken down. Hardly anyone knew what cryptocurrencies were for. Even supposed experts couldn't explain them. It was unclear why many of the coins would be worth anything at all. But from 2020 to early 2022, the prices of Bitcoin and hundreds of other lesser coins—with ridiculous names like Dogecoin, Solana, Polkadot, and Smooth Love Potion—were going up and up. While I was in the Bahamas, people traded more than $500 billion worth of them, and the market value of all coins combined topped $2 trillion.

Crypto boosters claimed they were in the vanguard of a revolution that would democratize finance and lead to generational wealth for those who believed. The roar of the rising prices drowned out the skeptics. Incomprehensible jargon became inescapable. *Blockchain.*

DeFi. Web3. The metaverse. What these terms meant was beside the point. Newspapers, TV, and social media bombarded potential investors with stories of regular people who invested in them and got rich quick.

Crypto seemed like a giant slot machine that had been rigged to pay out almost every time. Hundreds of millions of people around the world gave in to the temptation to pull the lever. Everybody knew somebody who'd hit it big. And the more people who bought in, the higher prices rose.

None of this led to any sort of mass movement to actually use crypto in the real world. Nobody tossed their credit cards, closed their bank accounts, and abandoned the dollar or the euro in favor of, say, Cardano coins. But the hucksters, zealots, opportunists, and outright scammers who created the boom got unbelievably, unimaginably, impossibly rich.

Bankman-Fried told me that as many as five of his colleagues at FTX were billionaires. And that was just a single crypto company. Many unprofitable start-ups with questionably legal business plans were valued in the billions. Changpeng Zhao, who founded another crypto exchange called Binance, made a fortune estimated at $96 billion. The numbers got so large that even the most delusional crypto fantasies started to sound reasonable. It seemed like nothing could stop crypto's manic rise.

Until, of course, the house of cards collapsed. Starting in the summer of 2022, many companies in crypto were revealed to be frauds. The bubble popped. About $2 trillion of market value was erased. Billionaires went bankrupt. Millions of ordinary people lost their savings. The financial authorities who'd allowed scammers to run rampant finally decided it was time to lay down the law. Bankman-Fried and many of his associates were arrested. Crypto didn't disappear entirely, but the fever had broken.

THIS IS THE story of the greatest financial mania the world has ever seen. It started as an investigation of a coin called Tether that served as a kind of bank for the industry. But it morphed into a two-year journey that would stretch from Manhattan to Miami, to Switzerland, Italy, the Bahamas, El Salvador, and the Philippines. It is based on hundreds of interviews with people at every level of crypto, from gamblers to coders to promoters to billionaires. I visited their yachts and parties at the pinnacle of the frenzy and their hideouts as the authorities were closing in.

From the beginning, I thought that crypto was pretty dumb. And it turned out to be even dumber than I imagined. Never before has so much wealth been generated with such flimsy schemes. But what shocked me was not the vapidity of the crypto bros. It was how their heedlessness had devastating consequences for people across the world. By the end, I'd find myself in Cambodia, investigating how crypto fueled a vast human-trafficking scheme run by Chinese gangsters.

I PITCHED THIS book to my publisher in November 2021, near the mania's peak, on the premise that crypto would soon collapse, and I'd chronicle the catastrophic fallout. Three months later, I was sitting with Bankman-Fried at his Bahamas office and looking at the computer screens behind his fuzzy head. I was oblivious to the giant fraud happening right in front of me. In fact, by then, I was starting to worry that I would never figure out the secret behind the crypto boom.

I was still fairly certain that huge swaths of crypto were essentially a pyramid scheme, but the bubble hadn't popped. The industry was doing great. It seemed quite possible that the craze could continue far beyond my deadline. Or maybe crypto would gain so many followers that it would become unstoppable. I had no idea what the ending of the book was going to be.

After we'd spent a few hours together, I decided to ask Bankman-Fried for advice. This was half interview tactic, half genuine cry for help. I didn't expect him to tell me his whole industry was really a fraud. But I wanted to see if he might be willing to point me in the right direction. So I laid out my whole narrative dilemma. I told him my theory: that the coin called Tether, the supposedly safe crypto-bank that served as the backbone for a whole lot of other cryptocurrencies, could prove to be fraudulent, and how that could bring down the whole industry.

Bankman-Fried said that I was wrong. Crypto wasn't a scam, and neither was Tether. But he wasn't offended by my question. He said he totally understood my problem. Then he did something that didn't strike me as strange at the time. But knowing what I know now, I can't help but wonder if he was trying to make some kind of winking confession.

Bankman-Fried cut me off, nodding, as I tried to explain more. His tone turned chipper. He said: "It's like the narrative would be way sexier if it was like, 'Holy shit, this is the world's biggest Ponzi scheme,' right?"

Right.

CHAPTER ONE

"I Am Freaking Nostradamus!"

Brooklyn, New York
January 2021

In January 2021, at the depths of the pandemic malaise, my friend Jay sent a message to our group chat of high school buddies saying that he'd invested a few hundred dollars in something called "doggie coin," and that we should too. "I don't know anything about it other than its name," he wrote. "I am very bored."

He didn't even have the name right. It was called "Dogecoin," pronounced "dohj," and it was a cryptocurrency based on a meme of a Shiba Inu glancing to the side. Don't worry about how exactly a dog joke turns into a financial asset—even Dogecoin's creator didn't understand how it happened. Like most cryptocurrencies, it had no "revenue" or "profits." There was no reason why it should have any value.

I told Jay all this. I said that, as a joke, Dogecoin wasn't even funny. He didn't care. "I fully understand how stupid this is. That's why it's funny to me," Jay wrote.

It wasn't like Jay was some degenerate gambler. He was a thirty-six-year-old professional who owned a house with a pool in a nice Boston suburb and served on two charitable boards. As he read about Dogecoin on Reddit, he grew convinced that for some reason, other people would buy the dog-joke cryptocurrency too. It wasn't a crazy thing to think. During the Covid-19 lockdowns, millions of people had downloaded apps like Robinhood and Coinbase. Understimulated mentally and overstimulated monetarily, they'd started tapping the BUY button. These day traders gathered on Twitter and Reddit, where they shocked Wall Street by sending shares of left-for-dead retailer

GameStop up more than tenfold, nearly bankrupting hedge funds that bet against it. Then they took this nihilistic, buy-it-for-the-LOLs mentality to crypto.

Dogecoin replaced politics and dad jokes in the group chat. Jay texted us to say that Dogecoin had sponsored a NASCAR driver. I noticed Elon Musk was talking about it too. As the price climbed from a penny to two cents, then three cents, then five cents, I got more and more annoyed. It wasn't so much that Jay was making money and I wasn't. It was more that I knew I was right. And, okay, I was jealous.

A few days after Jay's first text, I pulled up *Drudge Report* to see a smiling Shiba Inu splashed across the news aggregator's front page: "Reddit Frenzy Pumps Up Dogecoin! Now Worth Billions!" Jay eventually sold out and made several thousand dollars. Then he taunted me by sending selfies from a trip to Walt Disney World, financed with his trading profits. "If you listened to me when I first told you to throw $10 on Dogecoin, you'd all be $500 richer right now," Jay wrote. "I am freaking Nostradamus!"

Jay wouldn't admit he'd gotten lucky. He acted like his Dogecoin score proved his astute understanding of crowd psychology. Even after he moved on, I didn't. I started seeing crypto bros everywhere. They were acting like the rising prices of the coins proved they were geniuses. And their numbers were growing.

IT SEEMED LIKE everyone but me was cashing in their stimulus checks or retirement savings and buying crypto. Whenever anyone would ask me whether they should invest, I'd tell them I thought it was risky. But no one listened. Just on my block in Brooklyn, one of my neighbors made enough to renovate her kitchen and another bought a house and moved away.

The worst part was, I was supposed to be the expert on this kind of thing. I'd spent most of my career reporting on Wall Street scammers and predatory tech companies. I wasn't exactly a hard-boiled investigator. I was a thirty-six-year-old Brooklyn dad, with three kids, a minivan, a seven-speed bicycle, and a habit of reading online reviews before buying so much as a pack of double-A batteries. A few months later, my first-ever attempt at a stakeout—of a Brooklyn loan shark's office—would go embarrassingly wrong: I shaved my facial hair to disguise my appearance, then arrived to find a neighborhood full of bushy-bearded Hasidic Jews. But in general I was good at writing about scams. I liked figuring out how con men were exploiting legal loopholes, unraveling their tricky contracts, and tracing their offshore shell corporations.

Crypto didn't hold the same appeal for me. I'd resisted the topic whenever it came up at work. It seemed so obvious. The coins were transparently useless, and people were buying them anyway. A journalist composing a painstaking exposé of a crypto scam seemed like a restaurant critic writing a takedown of Taco Bell.

But after my argument with Jay, I began to warm up to the idea. I wanted to prove him—and everybody else—wrong. So, a few months later, in May 2021, when the editor of *Bloomberg Businessweek* walked by my desk and floated a crypto assignment, I was ready.

"What do you know about stablecoins?" he asked me.

THE ANSWER WAS *Not much.* But I did know they were called "stablecoins" because, unlike coins with prices intended to go up, they were supposed to have a fixed value of one dollar. That was because each coin was supposed to be backed by one U.S. dollar. The biggest stablecoin by far was called Tether.

Tether seemed to be at the center of the crypto world: More Tethers changed hands each day than any other cryptocurrency. It was a way for traders to zap their money from exchange to exchange, and a way to park their investments in a stable asset. I was surprised to learn that by then there were 55 billion Tethers in circulation—an amount that would have made it one of the fifty largest banks in the United States. This meant that, supposedly, people had sent $55 billion in U.S. dollars to the company and received 55 billion made-up Tether coins in exchange. Tether insisted that it had parked the $55 billion in safe investments. But the thing was, no one knew where this money was.

A few hours on Google revealed that the company was incredibly sketchy. One of its top executives was an Italian plastic surgeon turned electronics importer who'd once been caught selling counterfeit Microsoft software. Among its founders was one of the child actors from the Disney ice-hockey classic *The Mighty Ducks*. In an old document I discovered on Tether's website, I found a list of the risks of buying the cryptocurrency. The company said it could go bankrupt, or the unspecified bank holding its money could, or a government could confiscate its assets. Last on the list: "We could abscond with the reserve funds." I made a note of that one.

I couldn't tell which country's authorities were overseeing Tether. On a podcast, a company representative said it was registered with the British Virgin Islands Financial Investigation Agency. But the agency's director, Errol George, told me that it didn't oversee Tether. "We don't and never have," he said.

There were plenty of critics who speculated that Tether was not actually backed by anything at all. Some argued that Tether was creating tokens out of thin air and using them to prop up the entire crypto market. If they were right, and Tether really was a Ponzi scheme backed by nothing, it would be one of the biggest frauds in history.

This wasn't just a conspiracy theory for online haters. The concerns reached the highest levels of the U.S. government. I couldn't believe it when, a few months later, I learned that Treasury Secretary Janet Yellen had summoned all the country's top financial officials—the chair of the Federal Reserve, the head of the Securities and Exchange Commission, and six others—for a meeting to discuss Tether.

The situation was absurd: Inflation was spiking, a Covid surge threatened the economic recovery, and Yellen wanted to talk about a digital currency dreamed up by a kid from *The Mighty Ducks*. To me it seemed like a playground snowball fight had gotten so out of hand that the Joint Chiefs of Staff were being called in to avert a nuclear war.

The regulators wanted to know where Tether's billions were too. But they also believed that even if Tether was real, and it did have something like $55 billion somewhere, it had gotten so large that it put the entire U.S. financial system at risk. Their fear was that Tether would suffer a bank run. If the people who owned Tether coins started worrying about whether Tether really had those billions of dollars, they might start cashing them in. Fear would grow that Tether would run out of money. A stampede could start. No one would want to be among the last ones stuck holding Tethers when it did.

If Tether had money tied up in investments, it would have to dump them at fire-sale prices. The other institutions that invested in the same things would take losses. That's what happened in the financial crisis that crashed the U.S. economy in 2008, when no one knew which funds had sunk all their money into worthless subprime mortgages. The panic rippled through the financial system, setting off runs on one bank or fund after another.

"In a panic, everything collapses and they look to the federal government to bail them out," one attendee at Yellen's meeting told me. "If the crypto market was isolated, maybe we could live with that. But hiccups in one market start to translate into other markets. These are the things we're paid to worry about."

TETHER WAS THE kind of mystery I found interesting. And it seemed possible that Tether was the mysterious force pushing crypto prices to ever higher heights. If Tether was revealed to be a fraud, I figured the entire bubble might pop, and the prices of all the coins would crash. That would include Dogecoin. Even "Nostradamus" would have to admit I was right. So I set out to look for Tether's money.

It was hard to believe that people had sent $55 billion in real U.S. dollars to a company that seemed to be practically quilted out of red flags. But every day, on cryptocurrency exchanges, traders bought and sold Tether coins as if they were just as good as dollars. The coins were traded so frequently that on some days, more than $100 billion in Tether changed hands. It seemed the people with the most at stake in the crypto markets trusted Tether, and I wanted to know why.

Luckily, in June 2021, twelve thousand crypto die-hards were gathering in Miami for what was being billed as the biggest crypto conference ever. The featured speakers would include Ron Paul, Twitter co-founder Jack Dorsey, and, inexplicably, skateboarder Tony Hawk. Who could resist?

CHAPTER TWO

Number Go Up Technology

The Florida crime novelist Carl Hiaasen once wrote of his home state, "Every scheming shitwad in America turned up here sooner or later, such were the opportunities for predation." In his books, the scheming shitwads are crooked cops, corrupt politicians, and the cocaine traffickers who financed much of Miami's skyline. But plenty of people at Bitcoin 2021, the crypto conference I'd come to attend, met the description.

I was deeply skeptical about cryptocurrency before I arrived, and what I had been learning about Tether wasn't doing much to dispel those doubts. In Miami, though, I would be surrounded by true believers. These were the people trying to make crypto go mainstream and attract big money from institutional and individual investors alike. They claimed the "blockchain technology" behind it would soon power everyday financial transactions.

The conference was supposed to be exclusively about Bitcoin, the first and largest cryptocurrency, but as this was one of the first large gatherings of any kind since Covid-19 vaccines became available, I figured anyone who was anyone from the entire crypto industry would be there. My plan was to listen politely to a bunch of tech bros pitching their apps, and then to ask them what they knew about Tether.

When I got to the Mana Wynwood Convention Center, the warehouse-like venue hosting the event, I saw thousands of people waiting outside in the blazing hot sun. The line to enter snaked for at least a mile, past a garish mural of a cartoon rat and another of a bug-eyed crying clown. The attendees wore T-shirts with crypto slogans, like HAVE FUN STAYING POOR or HODL, a meme about never selling crypto derived from a typo for the word "hold." Some had shirts advertising their favorite coins, whose names seemed designed to compete for attention by being as stupid as possible. During the conference, the price of one coin called CumRocket would quadruple after Elon Musk tweeted a triptych of emojis (a splash, a rocket, and a moon) that appeared to reference it.

The atmosphere was more like a carnival than a tech conference. Near the entrance, I spotted a dumpster full of Venezuelan bolivares, with the label CASH IS TRASH pasted on the side. A skate ramp had been set up for Tony Hawk to show off his tricks. Inside the doors, models walked the floor body-painted with Bitcoin's logo, past booths advertising crypto companies, luxury watches, and Miami nightclubs. Almost no one was wearing a mask. I took mine off to fit in. The acrid stench of cologne was everywhere, which was almost a relief—as long as I could smell it, I figured I probably didn't have Covid.

That Miami was playing host to this strange gathering was no coincidence. Francis Suarez, the city's forty-three-year-old mayor, was the first speaker. Techno blasted as he walked on stage in front of a giant orange Bitcoin "B" logo. He was wearing a special T-shirt of his own, emblazoned in neon Miami Vice lettering with HOW CAN I HELP.

"In this city we truly understand what it means to be the capital of capital," he said. "It means to be the capital of Bitcoin."

Suarez declared he wanted to pay city employees in Bitcoin, to accept the cryptocurrency as payment for fines and taxes, and even for the city to invest in it. FTX, Sam Bankman-Fried's crypto exchange, was paying $135 million for the naming rights to the Miami Heat's NBA arena, owned by the city, and Suarez said the money would pay for anti-gun-violence programs and summer jobs for teens.

The mayor equated Bitcoin's doubters with his city's skeptics, who liked to needle him about climate change by pointing out that streets flooded even on sunny days. As it so happened, during the week of the conference, the U.S. Army Corps of Engineers had released a report calling for a massive, twenty-foot-high seawall across Biscayne Bay, blocking the ocean views of the city's financial district. "You guys see any water here? I don't know, I don't see any water here," Suarez joked to the crowd.

The speakers who followed were so enthusiastic about Bitcoin, they made Suarez seem like a pessimist. Some said Bitcoin would allow free and instant money transfers, replacing MasterCard and Visa. Others said it would give access to the financial system to the billions of people around the world who didn't have bank accounts. There seemed to be no limit to what Bitcoin could do. One podcaster on stage called it "the first manmade incorruptible money and social institution" and said it was "potentially the most important invention in human history."

Many of the speakers railed against central banks and inflation. Their bête noire was "fiat money." That means money printed by central banks—in other words, pretty much all money in modern times. They blamed it for all of society's ills, from inflation to war to malnutrition, and called for a return to the era when money was backed by hard assets (even though nearly all economists believe this would lead to frequent financial crises). Only this time, Bitcoin would take the place of gold.

"Bitcoin changes absolutely everything," said Jack Dorsey, who was on stage in a tie-dye T-shirt, sporting a shaved head and a guru-length beard.

THE SPEAKERS IN Miami made Bitcoin sound complex and revolutionary, practically divine. Its incomprehensibility was almost a selling point. Boosters likened the moment that one finally understood Bitcoin to a religious awakening. The breathless hype made me more confused about what exactly a Bitcoin was or how the blockchain worked. I would only later figure out that crypto wasn't that complicated—at least not the important parts.

A blockchain is a database. Think of a spreadsheet with two columns: In Column A there's a list of people, and in Column B there's a number representing how much money they have.

Column A	Column B
ZEKE	0.647
SBF	1,000,000

With the Bitcoin blockchain, the numbers in Column B represent Bitcoins. And the people in Column A are identified by strings of random characters instead of names. That's it. That's what Bitcoins are—numbers in a spreadsheet. There is nothing else. Without the spreadsheet, the Bitcoins don't exist. If we were talking about the

Dogecoin blockchain, the numbers in Column B would represent Dogecoins. Tethers are just numbers in a spreadsheet like this too. (Technically, a blockchain is a list of all transactions ever made, which is compiled into something like this spreadsheet by software, but close enough.) The next section explains how this works exactly, and I promise I'll do my best to keep it interesting, but you can skip it if you want—you are now an expert on Bitcoin and the blockchain.

TWO-COLUMN LISTS LIKE the one on the previous page have always been at the core of the financial system. That's the central function of a bank: keeping track of how much money each customer has. It's a lesson I learned years earlier from an underrated source of financial wisdom: *Saturday Night Live*.

The skit in question opens with a pudgy banker sporting a vest and slicked-back hair addressing a boardroom full of employees as Beethoven's "Ode to Joy" plays on strings. One of the employees is Will Ferrell, in a handlebar mustache, trying his best not to smile. Narrowing his eyes behind his round spectacles, the banker explains that what he is saying is the most important principle of Wall Street. "We will make a list of our clients, and how much money each of them has given us," he says. "We will keep this list in a safe place." The employees nod seriously. The banker reiterates the importance of the list. "We must take special care of the list with each client's name and the amount of money he has invested," he says. "If we were to lose that list, we would be ruined." Then he adds another rule: "If my wife calls while I'm in shagging my secretary, tell her I'm at a board meeting. That way I'll be able to continue shagging my secretary without my wife knowing about it."

It's funny because it's true: It would be really bad if a bank lost the list. And while banks tend to do a pretty good job of keeping track of it, the periodic financial crises throughout history give some reason why you might prefer not to entrust your life savings to some self-interested, secretary-shagging financier.

The technical innovation of blockchain is that it lets customers get together and maintain the list themselves, with no banker involved. If I want to transfer 1,000 Bitcoins from my account to someone else's, there's no handsy banker to call. So instead, my computer broadcasts the transaction to all the computers that run the Bitcoin network, sending all the other Bitcoin people a message that says, "Hey, I'm transferring 1,000 Bitcoins to another account."

SO WHERE DID this idea come from? Bitcoin, the ur-cryptocurrency, was born on Halloween in 2008, at the climax of the subprime mortgage crisis, just after the storied investment bank Lehman Brothers failed. It began when a person or group going by the name Satoshi Nakamoto posted a message on a cryptography email list. "A purely peer-to-peer version of electronic cash would allow online payments to be sent directly from one party to another without the burdens of going through a financial institution," Nakamoto wrote.

Nakamoto's identity was a mystery. But his idea appealed to libertarians, techies, and cypherpunks, who saw a way for people to create free markets on the internet that governments couldn't control. They liked that the transactions were more or less anonymous. Nakamoto's idea spread through cryptography listservs, message boards, and other obscure corners of the internet. Coders and cryptographers volunteered to help Nakamoto develop open-source Bitcoin software. Then, in 2011, Nakamoto's communications abruptly stopped, and those volunteers took over maintaining the network. Nakamoto was never heard from again.

Bitcoin was especially dependent on volunteers because of the system Nakamoto had devised to protect the list. The problem was that someone could try to spend the same Bitcoins twice at the same time—more or less cutting and pasting money.

The solution that Bitcoin uses to prevent this "double-spending problem" is called "mining," and it's incredibly complicated and confusing. It also uses so much electricity that the White House has warned it might prevent the United States from slowing climate change. It's like something out of the world's most boring dystopian science-fiction movie.

I will attempt to explain. Here goes: Once enough messages about transactions come in, some computers in the network called miners compile the batch into what's known as a "block." They confirm that I actually have 1,000 Bitcoins and that I haven't already sent them to someone else. Then they make the block official and add it to the existing list of blocks—the blockchain.

But these miners don't just hold a vote on whether the transactions are valid. That would require trusting a vote-counting system. Instead, the miners have to compete in an impossibly hard guessing game to generate a random number—as of 2023, the odds were 75 sextillion-to-1 against a correct guess. The winning miner gets to publish the block and update the ledger, and they get a reward of six and a quarter brand-new Bitcoins, created out of the ether automatically. The difficulty of the game automatically increases when more miners enter it.

IN THE EARLY years, there wasn't much that one could do with Bitcoins other than mine them. People did it on their home computers. It was a hobby for nerds, like model trains or ham radio. The price of a Bitcoin hovered right around zero.

But in 2011, a site popped up on the dark web that took advantage of Bitcoin's apparent anonymity. It was called Silk Road, and it was a sort of eBay for drugs, where sellers listed marijuana, heroin, ecstasy, and cocaine, sold the drugs for Bitcoins, and sent them through the mail. "It kind of felt like I was in the future," one early customer told a reporter after buying 100 micrograms of acid on Silk Road for fifty Bitcoins.

Silk Road was Bitcoin's first commercial application. Drug consumers didn't set up their own mining rigs before going shopping on the dark web. They bought Bitcoins for cash on rudimentary exchanges. The demand started driving up the price.

Bitcoin was so tied to Silk Road that when the site's founder, Ross Ulbricht, was busted in October 2013, the price crashed. But a month later, Bitcoin's price mysteriously increased tenfold, past $1,000. Mentions of Bitcoin millionaires started appearing in the news. The Wall Street establishment called it an unsustainable bubble, giving Bitcoin still more attention. Years later, researchers would find that the spike was the result of fake trades and price manipulation, but by then the idea of getting rich on Bitcoin had entered the popular imagination.

By the time of the conference in Miami in 2021, a single Bitcoin cost $39,000, and it would have cost $691 billion to have all the numbers in the whole Bitcoin blockchain put into my account.

· · ·

IT WAS A tribute to Nakamoto's ingenious design and Bitcoin's volunteer coders that the system held up all this time. But the design also led to an unintended consequence: massive amounts of pollution.

The system depends on economic incentives. The miners who confirm transactions have made such a large financial investment—in buying computers to compete in the guessing game—that it wouldn't make economic sense to undermine Bitcoin by entering false transactions. But that also means it does make economic sense to run tons of computers to guess random numbers in hopes of winning the Bitcoin reward. As one person famously put it on Twitter, "Imagine if keeping your car idling 24/7 produced solved Sudokus you could trade for heroin."

That is as bad for the environment as it sounds. Once Bitcoin's price started rising, competition drove out the hobbyist miners. Within a few years, companies were selling specialized computers that were extra good at the guessing game. Miners started operating whole racks of them. Then warehouses full of racks.

Mining became an environmental disaster. Miners scoured the globe for sources of cheap power. Pretty much everywhere they set up shop, locals objected. Residents of Niagara Falls, New York, complained that Bitcoin miners' powerful cooling fans—necessary to keep the computers from overheating—were drowning out the sound of the area's massive waterfalls. China—not exactly known for its environmentalism—banned mining due to its massive energy use. (Of course it was welcomed by Texas.)

Other coins would adopt different authentication systems that used far less electricity, but Bitcoiners opposed any change to Nakamoto's mining system. There was no way to reduce mining's energy use. The difficulty of winning the guessing game—the thing that incentivizes all this energy-intensive computer use—is what kept anyone from hacking the system. Some tried to use renewable sources, but as of 2023, about 85 percent of the electricity used for Bitcoin mining came from coal and natural-gas plants. By some estimates, Bitcoin mining consumed as much energy as the entire country of Argentina, population 46 million.

If this all sounds insane to you: I know. I am with you.

. . .

THE FUNDAMENTAL ABSURDITY of all this is that the numbers in the Bitcoin blockchain don't represent dollars, or even have any inherent tie to the financial system at all. There's no reason why a Bitcoin should be worth more than a Dogecoin or any other number in any other database. Why would someone burn massive amounts of coal just to get a higher number written in the blockchain for their account?

At first, the theory was that Bitcoin's value would go up once it became part of the mainstream financial system. The idea was that if Bitcoin was a superior financial technology, then lots of people would want to use it for their financial transactions. And if lots of people wanted to use it, they would need to first buy some.

When that didn't happen, Bitcoiners started referring to the currency as "digital gold." Nakamoto's design limited the total supply of Bitcoins to 21 million. They argued that the limited supply meant the currency's price was sure to rise. But, of course, just because the supply of something is limited doesn't make it valuable—only 21 million VHS tapes of Pixar's *Toy Story* were made at first, and you can get an original on eBay for three dollars.

For Bitcoin believers, the rising price became its own justification. On stage in Miami, many of the speakers resorted to a sort of illogical reasoning: The price of Bitcoin will go up because it has gone up. They wielded this circular argument to ward off doubt and call forth a future of infinite bounty. It became a mantra: Number go up.

"NUMBER GO UP," declared Dan Held, an executive at a crypto exchange called Kraken, on stage at Bitcoin 2021. "Number go up technology is a very powerful piece of technology. It's the price. As the price goes higher, more people become aware of it, and buy it in anticipation of the price continuing to climb."

I couldn't believe what I was hearing. I am not a computer scientist, but I don't think you can just call the concept of prices going up forever, for no reason, a "technology." Thirteen years had passed since Bitcoin was invented—about as long as it took to get from the first websites to the iPhone—and the best argument anyone had for Bitcoin was that it was a financial bubble that would just keep growing forever?

But "number go up" had become a kind of cult. It helped that Satoshi Nakamoto had completely disappeared and his or her real identity had never been revealed, giving the worshippers a mysterious and absent god.

The aisles were jammed when the emcee introduced two men who seemed to be the stars of the show, judging by the riotous applause. Max Keiser, a Bitcoin podcaster, emerged first, in a white suit and purple sunglasses, to pounding EDM. "Yeah! Yeah!" he screamed, pumping his fists, as the dance music built to a drop. Elon Musk had recently said that Tesla would not accept Bitcoin due to its environmental impact, and Keiser was raging like the billionaire had run over his dog. "We're not selling! We're not selling! Fuck Elon! Fuck Elon!"

A fifty-six-year-old executive named Michael Saylor walked out, wearing an all-black outfit and black leather boots. Keiser called him a "giga-Chad," *Chad* being internet slang for an alpha male, and by the standards of the conference, in which reckless day-trading counted as manliness, he was.

A more accurate description would be that Saylor was the biggest loser in the room. He didn't mention it during his talk, but his software company, MicroStrategy, had nearly gone bust during the dot-com bubble, back when the internet counted as a hot new technology. In 2000, just before it popped, he told *The New Yorker:* "I just hope I don't get up one day and have to look at myself in the mirror and say, 'You had $15 billion and you blew it all. There's the guy who flushed $15 billion down the toilet.'" Right afterward, he lost $13.5 billion.

But MicroStrategy survived, and for years Saylor chugged away in relative anonymity. Then he'd started buying Bitcoin. Then he bought more. By the time of the conference, he'd sunk $2 billion of MicroStrategy's money into the cryptocurrency.

On Twitter, Saylor had put laser eyes on his Twitter profile pic—a culty signal of the crypto faithful, which meant one believed the price of a Bitcoin would hit $100,000—and started posting cryptic Bitcoin aphorisms, like: "Bitcoin is a swarm of cyber hornets serving the goddess of wisdom, feeding the fire of truth, exponentially growing ever smarter, faster and stronger behind a wall of encrypted energy." His philosophy sounded even more unhinged when, once the crowd died down, he delivered it in his nasal voice with a straight face.

"Bitcoin you can think of as a plant life," Saylor said on stage. "I put my monetary energy, my life force, into it, and then I let it live for the next thousand years. It's okay just to be alive for a thousand years. What's wrong with being rich forever, right?"

I was not immune to the appeal of everlasting life and money growing like kudzu. For a moment, as I sat in the darkened room among the true believers, I felt like a sucker for keeping my money in a regular old retirement account. But I had a job to do: I was there to find out about Tether.

IN ADVANCE OF the trip down to Miami, I'd looked up all of the attendees, trying to see who would have done business with the company and might know something about it, and arranged interviews with several of them. First, a colleague had invited me to tag along for a brief meeting with Sam Bankman-Fried, whose exchange FTX was reportedly a big user of Tether.

I wanted to talk with him about something called "commercial paper." Commercial paper is a Wall Street term for short-term loans to corporations, which finance routine expenses like inventory or payroll. Tether claimed to hold about $30 billion of the stuff, which would have made Tether the seventh-largest holder of such debt, right up there with Charles Schwab and Vanguard. But a few colleagues and I had canvassed Wall Street traders, and none of them had seen Tether making any investments in the commercial-paper market. "It's a small market with a lot of people who know each other," one commercial-paper specialist had told me. "If there were a new entrant, it would be usually very obvious."

Some people speculated that what Tether called "commercial paper" was really debt from exchanges like FTX. That would explain why no one on Wall Street had dealings with Tether. FTX could simply send Tether a note saying, "I promise I'll pay you $1 billion," and Tether could zap over 1 billion coins, and no one would be the wiser.

We were meeting in a crowded room designated for media. It was a zoo, packed full of reporters from crypto-focused websites. I saw a muscular crypto podcaster strut in wearing a tight black T-shirt, flanked by three similarly dressed and similarly buff helpers. Another man carried a fluffy dog as he filmed interviews.

Bankman-Fried was visiting from Hong Kong, where FTX was based. He'd come to celebrate the renaming of the Miami Heat's stadium from American Airlines Arena to FTX Arena, and, when we sat down, he seemed distracted. I had only a few minutes with him, so I launched right into the theory that Tether was issuing him coins in exchange for IOUs. He assured me the theory was not true.

"We've wired them a lot of dollars," he said. He also told me that he'd successfully cashed in Tethers, transferring the digital coins back to the company and receiving real U.S. dollars in exchange, though the process he described sounded a bit strange.

"This is going through three different jurisdictions, through intermediary banks," he said. "If you know the right banks to be at, you can avoid some of these intermediaries."

Before I could follow up, he was hustled away by his team of public relations representatives.

I'D ALSO SET up an interview with Alex Mashinsky, the founder of a company called Celsius Network. I'd read that Tether was one of Celsius's early backers, so I figured he would know a lot about stablecoins. Mashinsky seemed to be everywhere at the conference—on stage, on the floor of the convention center, and in the media room doing back-to-back-to-back interviews. We met in a small, windowless room, which was quieter.

Mashinsky, fifty-five, was raised in Israel and still spoke with a slight accent. He was tall and stocky, with close-set eyes and brown hair combed over his large forehead. His special T-shirt read UNBANK YOURSELF. To set him at ease before I got to any probing questions, I asked him an easy one: Explain your company's business model.

Mashinsky's response made no sense at all. He told me that users could deposit cryptocurrencies with Celsius and earn interest. The rates were as high as 18 percent a year—this at a time when most banks were paying almost nothing at all on savings. And he said that the company loaned out money too, but at low rates. His plan, in other words, was to buy high and sell low. It sounded like a great way to lose money, or possibly a Ponzi scheme.

I decided to move on to Tether.

"Do you deal with stablecoins yourself as part of your business?" I asked.

"We have billions of dollars in stablecoins," he said.

Celsius, it turned out, had $18 billion in assets. I couldn't believe it. Somehow Celsius had accumulated as much money as a large hedge fund with a business plan that wouldn't even work for a kid's lemon-ade stand.

"That's what I was imagining," I murmured, trying to keep a straight face.

Mashinsky said there was no reason to worry about what was backing Tether.

"Stablecoins are basically just a digital version of the U.S. dollar, right?" he said. "There's no monkey business."

But then he described what sounded very much like monkey business. Tether, in addition to investing in Celsius, had lent more than $1 billion worth of its coins to the company, which Mashinsky used to invest in other things. Mashinsky claimed this was safe because for every $1.00 worth of Tethers he borrowed, he put up about $1.50 worth of Bitcoin as collateral. If Celsius went bust, Tether could seize the Bitcoins and sell them. He told me this was a service Tether offered to other companies too.

I had thought Tether's business model was to sell each coin for a dollar and put that dollar in the bank. Mashinsky was saying that Tether was effectively printing new money—by lending out coins to him backed only by Bitcoin. That was a lot less safe. Despite the chorus of believers, there was no reason to think that the numbers would go up forever.

I asked Mashinsky whether the promises he was making about Celsius were too good to be true. He insisted they weren't. But the more he talked, the less I believed him. He said the key was that Celsius passed along most of its earnings to its users, unlike traditional banks, which invest customers' money and keep the profits for themselves. Mashinsky said banks like J.P. Morgan were dishonest when they claimed they could only afford to pay tiny interest rates to savers.

"Somebody is lying," Mashinsky said. "Either the bank is lying or Celsius is lying."

I was pretty sure I knew who was lying, and it wasn't J.P. Morgan. I made a mental note to investigate Celsius when I got back to New York.

THE STRANGEST MOMENT of the Bitcoin 2021 conference came at the end. A small, boyish man paced the stage, giggling and cursing, as he told the story of a few months he'd spent at the beach in El Salvador. He was wearing a giant white hoodie and a baseball cap, and he seemed like a high school student giving an extremely inappropriate report on what he did for summer vacation. I later learned his name was Jack Mallers, and that he was the twenty-seven-year-old head of a Bitcoin-related company called Strike.

Mallers explained that he had gone to a beach town in El Salvador because a surfer from San Diego was teaching poor people there about Bitcoin, which was somehow going to help them stop being poor. He claimed that while he was hanging out on the beach, he got a message on Twitter from the brother of the president of El Salvador. Before long, he was advising the Central American nation on monetary policy.

Then I watched in disbelief as the visage of the president of El Salvador himself, Nayib Bukele, appeared on a big screen behind Mallers. In a recorded address, he announced for the first time that El Salvador would be adopting Bitcoin as a national currency. Rather than telling his citizens first, he had chosen to reveal a major national policy to a bunch of Bitcoiners, in Miami, Florida, in English, a language most Salvadorans don't speak.

The audience went wild. Mallers got so worked up that he started to cry. For the first time, millions of people would be using Bitcoin for regular, everyday transactions. With Bitcoin powering the economy, he asserted, El Salvador's youth "won't have to resort to crime or violence," and the country "won't have immigration problems."

"I'm not launching in Europe, I'll be there. We die on this hill. I will fucking die on this fucking hill!" Mallers choked out between sobs. "Today, humanity takes a tremendous leap forward in re-instilling human freedom."

I didn't get it. There was a reason no one used Bitcoin to buy coffee—it was complicated, expensive, and slow to use. And what would happen if poor Salvadorans put their savings in crypto and then the price fell? But the audience was rapt. As I scanned the crowd, I saw that Mallers wasn't the only one wiping away tears.

NOT EVERYONE I spoke to in Miami was a Bitcoin cultist. The biggest users of Tether were professional traders at hedge funds and other large firms, and I interviewed several of them too. What they explained to me was that for all the talk of peer-to-peer currency, and the ingenuity of a way to transfer value without an intermediary, most people weren't using cryptocurrencies to buy stuff. Instead, they were sending regular money to exchanges, where they could then bet on coin prices.

The crypto exchanges, like Bankman-Fried's FTX, were essentially giant casinos. And many of them, especially in the early days of crypto and outside the United States, couldn't handle dollars because banks wouldn't open accounts for them, wary of inadvertently facilitating money laundering. This was where Tether came in. When customers wanted to place a bet, they first bought some Tethers. It was as if all the poker rooms in Monte Carlo and the mahjong parlors in Macau sent gamblers to one central cashier to buy chips.

The biggest traders made their money by facilitating countless smaller bets, like Jay's envy-inducing Dogecoin win. They needed to move big sums of money from exchange to exchange, and they did it with Tether. They said they routinely bought and sold hundreds of millions of Tethers and viewed the currency as an industry standard. Even so, many had their own conspiracy theories about Tether. It's controlled by the Chinese mafia; the CIA uses it to move money; the government has allowed it to get huge so it can track the criminals who use it. It wasn't that they trusted Tether, I realized. It was that they needed Tether to trade and they were making a lot of money doing it. There was no profit in being skeptical.

"It could be way shakier, and I wouldn't care," said Dan Matuszewski, co-founder of CMS Holdings, a cryptocurrency investment firm.

The traders told me that the people who ran Tether were secretive and likely wouldn't speak with me. But they said there was one person who had been involved with the coin who loved attention: Tether's co-founder, the former *Mighty Ducks* actor.

His name was Brock Pierce and, judging from his social media accounts, he seemed to have made a fortune on crypto. The more I learned about Pierce, the more curious I was about him. He flew around the world promoting crypto in a Gulfstream jet that he had spray-painted with Monopoly money and the Bitcoin and Ethereum logos. He had mounted a vanity presidential campaign in 2020, with the singer Akon as his chief strategist. He wore loud hats, vests, and bracelets, like Johnny Depp in *Pirates of the Caribbean,* and spoke in riddles, like Johnny Depp in *Charlie and the Chocolate Factory*. He had a tattoo of a scorpion on his right shoulder. He was, of course, a regular at Burning Man.

CHAPTER THREE

Doula for Creation

Brock Pierce was at seemingly every crypto convention, but I'd had a hard time getting his undivided attention. I figured that Tether's co-founder would know whether the company really had those billions of dollars in reserves. At least he would be able to give me a clue. While I was at Bitcoin 2021 in Miami, I texted with two of his assistants, but neither could tell me when Pierce would have time for a sit-down interview. At the next crypto convention I went to—also in Miami, of course—I heard Pierce was throwing a party at a mansion. This time, when I texted Pierce's chief of staff, he told me to head on over.

At the conference, I'd been talking with a young Bitcoiner named Dev, and he offered me a ride. He wore hexagonal sunglasses and a leather trench coat. One of his fingers was sheathed by metal, making it look like a dragon claw and him like a huge nerd. He was visiting from New York and seemed happy to find a potential friend.

In his Mercedes convertible, Dev lit a cigarette and told me he'd gotten into Bitcoin in high school, back when a coin only cost one dollar, to order drugs from Silk Road. He'd order cocaine in bulk, pay in Bitcoin, and have it shipped to his parents' house in the Bronx. He was eager to show off. As we sped past a golf course, he revved his engine and filmed a video for his Instagram. I told him I thought the heyday of the dark web was behind us.

"No, it's real. It's huge. You do any drugs?" he said.

I told him I didn't but I didn't mind if he did. At a stoplight, Dev pulled out a baggie of pink stuff he called "tusi"—which he said was cocaine for rich people—then scooped up a bit with his finger-claw and snorted it.

A few minutes later, we arrived at Pierce's mansion. It was white stucco, with palm trees out front and a Land Rover parked on the grass. I felt bad I didn't invite Dev inside, but I wasn't sure I was allowed to bring guests.

As soon as I walked in and saw the scene, I realized my mistake. Dev would have fit right in. There was no sign of Pierce. The place was filled with an assortment of curious partiers, grifters, and hangers-on.

The house was modern and impersonally furnished, with marble floors, silver appliances, and a shiny grand piano. I realized he'd probably rented it for the week. On the floor of the living room, a woman I recognized from a Netflix documentary on social media manipulation played with her baby. I overheard a hedge fund manager bragging on the phone about the "MILF" he'd had sex with the night before.

I decided to mingle and ask the guests what they knew about our absent host. A beautiful woman told me she'd spent a week with Pierce in the Colombian jungle, where he'd bought land to protect it for Indigenous people. "It's amazing what he does," she said. Another man told me Pierce was building a spaceport on an old army base in Puerto Rico. An obnoxious guy who described himself as a "futurist" told me a story about a time in Ibiza when Pierce went three days without sleeping. "He's surrounded by people who are benevolent dolphins and not sharks," he said. He then asked me to smell a pastry for him before he ate it, telling me he was allergic to raspberries.

I crossed the marble floors and passed through a glass door into the yard, where I saw a long table of preppy men and women who looked like they had wandered in from a different party. I took a seat at one end and told the people sitting next to me about my crypto reporting. One of the men across the table was an aide for the PayPal founder and investor Peter Thiel, who had become a major donor to Donald Trump's presidential campaign. Thiel had delivered a speech at the conference that day in which he called Warren Buffett a "sociopathic grandpa" for doubting Bitcoin. He did not tell the audience that the venture capital firm he co-founded, Founders Fund, had recently sold off the vast majority of its crypto holdings.

At some point, a man at the other end of the table began bragging loudly about a cryptocurrency called "Let's Go" or "Let's Go Brandon," a slogan that, through an almost inexplicable memeification process, had come to stand for "Fuck Joe Biden" among Trump supporters. The man, who I later figured out was a hedge fund manager named James

Koutoulas, announced to the table that his plan for the coin was "dumb but it's working." A month earlier, a podcaster had presented Donald Trump himself with five hundred billion of the tokens, and just that afternoon, Donald Trump Jr. had made a cryptic post on Twitter seemingly referencing the meme coin.

"Is that allowed?" someone asked.

"They're allowed to make money," Koutoulas said. "Fuck the SEC."

I wandered back inside. As the night went on, everyone got drunker and I got increasingly bored. A documentary filmmaker, his producer, and their cameraman arrived. They were looking for Pierce too. In the kitchen, an older guy with a leathery tan sneakily filled up his water bottle from a handle of whiskey. Someone complained that their shoes had been stolen. A doctor from Boise, Idaho, and a Bitcoiner were talking about the coronavirus vaccine and "medical freedom." The Bitcoiner refused to tell me his name. "Real G's move in silence," he told me, with a high-pitched laugh.

Six young women with long straightened hair wearing short skirts or sequined dresses arrived in a group. One of them sat at the piano and played a song. "Look at the rack on her," a guest said to me, not quietly enough. He then walked over and told her she sounded like a dying bird. Pierce showed up past midnight but disappeared into one of the mansion's many bedrooms before I could corner him for an interview.

A FEW WEEKS later, I was in the Bahamas at yet another crypto convention, when a seriously hungover friend told me she'd partied the night before on a superyacht moored a half mile off the coast of the island of New Providence. She said a crypto guy she didn't remember the name of had bought it from a Russian oligarch.

She showed me some videos from her Instagram. On her phone, I saw the setting sun reflecting off the side of a giant, five-level yacht named *Chakra*. The wooden bowsprit extending from its prow was so long and pointy, the vessel looked ready to lead an armada into battle. The next video showed *Chakra*'s owner climbing over the top deck's railing, smiling and jumping down into the ocean, thirty or forty feet below. On his right shoulder, I saw a scorpion tattoo. It was Pierce.

I hadn't known he was at the conference, but that night I texted one of Pierce's assistants and asked if I could visit the yacht. He told me to go to a particular dock and he'd send a speedboat to pick me up. As I waited, I could just make out the yacht's lights on the horizon. I stepped aboard the speedboat, and soon we were racing out to sea. Pierce's videographer was on board, too, shooting the yacht for social media. My anticipation built as we approached and the honeycomb of lights came into focus.

. But once the crew helped me on board and led me to the lowest deck, the scene was a bit disappointing. I was expecting a party, but I only found about two dozen people quietly sipping drinks around a bar.

None of the guests seemed to know one another. A crypto venture capital fund manager—wearing a mock souvenir T-shirt from convicted pedophile Jeffrey Epstein's private island—joked about a scam that another yacht guest was running. A crypto public relations man offered what he called "Colombian marching powder" to a young woman. A small group of people dancing told me they were philosophy students who'd come to the Bahamas to intern for FTX's Bankman-Fried.

One of the crew offered us a tour of the maze-like 282-foot, 21-bedroom behemoth. Upstairs, in one of many sitting rooms, we happened upon Pierce, standing and holding court in front of four or five guests, who looked bemused.

He was a small man—maybe about five-foot-five—with a nonchalant grin that recalled the look that had made him a child star. But his hair, once blond with a neat Richie Rich part, was now wavy and grown to shoulder length. His outfit was full-on Captain Jack Sparrow cosplay. He was wearing an ankle-length black vest over his bare chest, a fedora with two brown feathers pinned to it, an array of bangles, and diamond-shaped sunglasses.

"Ultimately humanity has never had sovereignty, unless you're the sovereign," Pierce was telling his audience as I approached. "We're going to claim our sovereignty by declaring our independence."

I introduced myself and blurted out nervously that it was a funny coincidence we both found ourselves in the Bahamas.

"I don't know if it's a coincidence," he said. "I prefer synchronicity."

PIERCE TOLD ME that *Chakra* was not his personal ship. Like-minded crypto fans could buy an NFT (non-fungible token, a kind of one-off crypto asset), then stay on the yacht when they pleased as it traveled from the Caribbean to Art Basel in Miami, the Monaco Grand Prix, and the Cannes Film Festival. He described it as "the first mega yacht club for the crypto community" and a floating home for crypto superheroes.

"We're the Avengers," he said. "It's the Avengers ship."

I realized I had walked in on a presentation for a timeshare that I would pay money not to join. It was also not the best setting for a long conversation. My tour guide soon sent me back downstairs. When Pierce and I did catch up, by phone, he told me he'd dreamed up the idea for a stablecoin back in 2013. He said he knew from the start it would change the course of history.

"I'm not an amateur entrepreneur throwing darts in the dark," he told me. "I'm a doula for creation. I only take on missions impossible."

At the time, Pierce was one of the only Bitcoiners with real money to invest, earned in an almost impossibly picaresque career. After *The Mighty Ducks,* he appeared in a commercial for Gushers—he transformed into a banana after eating one of the fruit snacks—and starred as a mischievous presidential son in *First Kid*. But soon afterward, he lost interest in Hollywood.

When he was sixteen, in 1996 or 1997, an actor friend introduced him to the founder of a dot-com start-up called Digital Entertainment Network, or DEN. The company had raised tens of millions of dollars with a plan to make TV obsolete by streaming four- to six-minute shows aimed at teens. DEN's founder, Marc Collins-Rector, was in his late thirties. He lived in an over-the-top mansion in Encino, California, once owned by Death Row Records founder Marion "Suge" Knight. He and his much younger boyfriend, Chad—only a teenager when they got together—each drove Ferraris.

There were serious problems with DEN's business plan. For one thing, the dial-up internet connections prevalent at the time weren't fast enough to stream video. But for Collins-Rector, the real appeal of the venture seemed to be surrounding himself with good-looking teenage boys. He took a liking to Pierce right away. Pierce, still a teenager himself, was made executive vice president of DEN at the ridiculous salary of $250,000 a year. He was tasked with producing a web show called *Chad's World*. The show, which featured the future *American Pie* actor Seann William Scott, was about a rich, older gay man who takes in a young boy named Chad. It was like a "gay pedophile version of *Silver Spoons*," the 1980s sitcom, a viewer told *Radar* magazine.

This is where the story gets dark. According to a series of lawsuits, news reports, and documents filed in a federal criminal investigation, Collins-Rector threw parties at the mansion where teenagers were plied with drugs and alcohol, pressured to have sex with older men, and, in some cases, raped. "I was passed around like a party favor," one seventeen-year-old later recalled.

One of the first of those lawsuits was filed in 1999, and the next year, on the advice of a private detective, Collins-Rector fled Los Angeles in a private jet, loaded with enough Louis Vuitton luggage to fill two Lincoln Town Cars. His boyfriend and Pierce came along. They only decided the destination once they were airborne, choosing Spain, and eventually settled in the seaside resort town of Marbella.

The authorities caught up with them two years later. Collins-Rector was eventually extradited to the United States, where he pleaded guilty to transporting minors across state lines for the purposes of sex. Pierce was released without charges after spending a month in a Spanish prison.

Pierce told me that while Collins-Rector may have been "creepy," some of the supposed victims made up the stories of abuse as part of an extortion scheme. He said the only parties he saw at the mansion were staid. "None of it is true, at least as far as it relates to me. I'm not even gay," Pierce once said.

Holed up in Marbella, Pierce had been playing a lot of a computer game called *EverQuest*. This was a new kind of online Dungeons & Dragons, where instead of going on a scripted solo mission, players dropped into a virtual world where wizards, druids, and thieves could team up to explore dungeons and battle monsters. Each victory yielded virtual gold, or rare items like swords or battle axes.

The game consumed Pierce, who would play for as long as twenty-four hours at a time as the dark-elf wizard Athrex, using six computers at once to earn more loot. And he wasn't the only one addicted to the endless quests. Players were so eager to win that a real-world market for in-game items sprung up. Someone who wanted the best gear could buy it on eBay and have it delivered by an in-game courier instead of spending hours killing monsters to earn virtual gold.

For some players, particularly in poorer countries, this was a job opportunity: They could battle all day, earn virtual gold, and sell it for real money to better-off players seeking a shortcut. Video-game sweatshops sprung up, where workers clicked around the clock. These virtual serfs came to be known as "gold farmers." One reporter who visited a gold farm in Nanjing, China, back then met a chain-smoking shirtless thirty-year-old Chinese man, working a twelve-hour overnight shift in a small, fluorescent-lit office space. He was playing as a staff-wielding monk, killing wizards for thirty cents an hour.

In 2001, Pierce started a virtual-item brokerage called IGE, or Internet Gaming Entertainment. Other players viewed buying rare items as cheating, and game makers made some attempts to shut down this gray-market economy. But they were ineffective. The market grew and grew. Within a few years, 450,000 people were playing *EverQuest,* millions more had joined a similar game called *World of Warcraft,* and virtual items were, by one estimate, a $2 billion a year business.

Pierce's IGE opened an office in Shanghai to get closer to Chinese gold farmers. Pierce has said he had as many as 400,000 farmers in his supply chain. By 2005, IGE was taking in more than $5 million a month. That year, former Goldman Sachs banker—and future Donald Trump consigliere—Steve Bannon was hired to help take Pierce's virtual-gold company public. Bannon secured a $60 million investment in the company from Goldman Sachs and a group of investment funds. Pierce netted $20 million and stepped down. Bannon took over the company, which soon failed due to a more effective crackdown on virtual-item sales by game makers.

Bannon became fascinated by how the gamers who opposed his company had been able to gather online and pressure big businesses to do their bidding—an insight he'd later share with Trump.

"These guys, these rootless white males, had monster power," Bannon said.

Pierce learned a different lesson: The world of virtual money was a great way to make lots of real money. And it wasn't a big leap from *EverQuest* gold to Bitcoin.

BY 2013, PIERCE was running one of the first Bitcoin venture capital funds. There still wasn't much you could do with Bitcoins, and crypto remained largely the domain of geeks and hobbyists. But around that time, a man going by "dacoinminster" had posted a proposal on the popular message board Bitcointalk that would lead to the creation of Tether and make the entire $3 trillion cryptocurrency bubble possible. He called his idea "MasterCoin."

Dacoinminster's real name was J. R. Willett, and he was a thirty-three-year-old software developer at a calendar-app company in a suburb of Seattle, Washington. When I reached him on the phone a decade after his momentous forum post, he was still working there, and he was happy to recall his moment of glory.

Willett posted the first draft of the paper explaining his idea in January 2012. He called it "The Second Bitcoin Whitepaper." Back then, Bitcoin was just a hobby for Willett, one his wife found annoying. But he was obsessed with the idea of creating a more advanced version of the digital currency—one that could do more than just move coins back and forth. His MasterCoin idea is hard to explain. But basically, it involved encoding secret messages in Bitcoin transaction data, which would represent new coins. If you think back to that two-column Bitcoin spreadsheet, MasterCoin essentially was a way to add more columns, each tracking ownership of a different coin.

Willett imagined that once he created the MasterCoin system, other people would come up with all sorts of ways to use it: coins that tracked property titles, shares of stock, financial derivatives, and even real money. None of the ideas were completely original—he told me he'd read many discussions of them on message boards—but he was the first to put them into practice.

Willett's MasterCoin white paper proposed that his system could be used to create coins that were backed by U.S. dollars. He laid out pretty much the whole plan that Tether would later use. He even anticipated—correctly—that stablecoins would be attractive to criminals.

"If you think Bitcoin has a reputation problem for money laundering now, just wait until you can store 'USDCoins' in the block chain!" Willett wrote in 2012. "I think criminals (like the rest of us) will prefer to deal with stable currencies rather than unstable ones."

Willett raised money for the project in a revolutionary way too. Even though MasterCoin wasn't functional yet, he raised about $500,000 by selling MasterCoins. Users would buy them hoping they'd become valuable once Willett completed development. Willett had essentially invented an easy way to create new cryptocurrencies and pioneered a new way to use them to raise millions of dollars. This was what later came to be known as an "initial coin offering," and it would be the way the entire cryptocurrency industry funded itself.

Willett's plan was innovative. It was also illegal. What Willett did was a textbook example of what the U.S. Securities and Exchange Commission calls an "unregistered securities offering," meaning that Willett was selling an investment opportunity without any of the usual safeguards. Willett told me that the agency probably would have fined him hundreds of thousands of dollars if it had noticed what he was up to. But luckily, the regulators weren't reading Bitcoin message boards.

"They would have made a terrible example out of me if they'd known what was coming," Willett said, laughing. "Never heard anything from them."

FLUSH WITH THE millions he had earned from the sale of IGE, Pierce invested in MasterCoin. He started promoting MasterCoin and announced he would fund programmers who came up with new uses for it. Pierce told me it was his idea to use it to create a stablecoin.

"I came up with the idea for Tether on my own," Pierce said. "Well, I mean, God's will, I guess."

Pierce got in touch with a programmer named Craig Sellars, who'd worked on MasterCoin. A friend named Reeve Collins agreed to serve as CEO. He held the dubious distinction of inventing pop-under internet ads—the annoying boxes you would see only after closing your browser window. They initially called the project Realcoin. Phil Potter, an executive at an offshore Bitcoin exchange, Bitfinex, was developing a similar idea. They teamed up and adopted Potter's name for it: Tether. (Potter told me he was actually the one to first approach Sellars with the idea. "I'm sure Brock will tell you he came down from Mount Sinai with it all written on stone tablets," he said.)

Working from a bungalow in Santa Monica, California, Sellars wrote the code needed to keep track of the accounts and process transactions. The program was simple. Send $1,000 via wire transfer to Tether's bank, and the company will update the blockchain to reflect that your line in the spreadsheet has 1,000 Tethers. Then Tethers could be transferred anonymously, like any other cryptocurrency. Using Willett's MasterCoin protocol, they were able to encode the data into the Bitcoin blockchain.

They pitched the stablecoin business to the venture capital firm Sequoia Capital and some crypto investors. No one was interested.

"You can't even imagine how stupid of an idea everyone thought it was," Collins told me.

The problem was that Tether, like other cryptocurrencies, broke just about every rule in banking. Banks keep track of everyone who has an account and where they send their money, allowing law enforcement agencies to track transactions by criminals. Tether would check the identity of people who bought coins directly from the company, but once the currency was out in the world, it could be transferred anonymously, just by sending a code. A drug lord could hold millions of Tethers in a digital wallet and send it to a terrorist without anyone knowing.

Other people who'd come up with similar ideas had gotten arrested. A Hawaiian marijuana activist who made coins with Ron Paul's face on them was arrested for fraud. The creator of an online currency called e-gold was charged with money laundering.

And in May 2013, just as Pierce and his compatriots were trying to pitch Tether, the creator of a proto-stablecoin, Liberty Reserve, was arrested. Liberty Reserve allowed users to send and receive money using only an email address. Prosecutors said the anonymous online currency appealed to scammers, credit card thieves, hackers, and other criminals. The creator, a Brooklyn man named Arthur Budovsky, had renounced his citizenship and moved to Costa Rica to try to avoid U.S. jurisdiction, but even that didn't work.

Liberty Reserve wasn't a cryptocurrency—the database tracking how much money each user had was kept on Budovsky's servers. But functionally, it worked a lot like Tether. Like Tether's users, most of Liberty Reserve's users actually bought the currency from third parties, which Budovsky argued meant he wasn't responsible for what they did with it. But he eventually pleaded guilty to a money-laundering conspiracy charge and was sentenced to twenty years.

"The U.S. will come after Tether in due time," Budovsky wrote me in an email from a Florida prison. "Almost feel sorry for them."

WHEN I SPOKE with Pierce on the phone, I asked him the central question: Was Tether actually backed up by real money? He assured me it was. He said Tether was preserving the dollar's status as a global reserve currency. "If it were not for Tether, America would likely fall," he said. "Tether in many ways is the hope of America."

But as he droned on, I realized Pierce had little information to offer about the location of Tether's funds. My mind started to wander. In *The Mighty Ducks,* the young Pierce misses a crucial penalty shot in a pee-wee hockey game, and that failure haunts the adult version of his character decades later. Even though I was the one asking questions about whether he was involved in what might be a giant Ponzi scheme, and, as far as I knew, Pierce knew nothing about my work, he started addressing me as if I were a washed-up journalist, and this Tether investigation was my final chance to save my career, or maybe my soul.

"If you get this one wrong, this is your last shot," Pierce told me. "This is for all the marbles. This is your final shot at redemption, for all of eternity."

But Pierce wasn't going to help me find salvation. He told me that he'd actually given up on Tether in 2015, about a year after he started it. The currency had gotten almost no users, and it seemed likely it would be frowned upon by authorities. An SEC lawsuit, or a trip to prison, would prevent him from reaching his own destiny.

"My view was if I made money from this thing it would prevent me from doing the work that I have to do for this nation," Pierce said.

Pierce's joint-venture partner, Bitfinex, was interested in carrying on with the Tether project. Potter and his colleagues at Bitfinex were less worried about Tether's legality, because the exchange was already operating in a gray area. Back then, it wasn't clear whether it was legal to facilitate cryptocurrency trading at all. And because of that, the exchange had difficulty opening bank accounts. But if the exchange used Tethers instead of dollars, it wouldn't need them.

Potter pitched this idea to his boss at the exchange: Giancarlo Devasini, the Italian former plastic surgeon. He went for it. Devasini and his partners already owned 40 percent of Tether, and they bought the rest from Pierce's crew for a few hundred thousand dollars. Pierce told me he handed over his shares for free.

AFTER INTERVIEWING MOST of the people involved with Tether's creation, I realized that they didn't have the answers I was looking for. All of them said something similar: They definitely deserved credit for coming up with one of the most successful companies in the history of cryptocurrency, but they bore no responsibility for whatever the company was doing now. More importantly, they had no idea whether or not it had all the money it claimed.

Devasini seemed like a better target. On paper, he was Tether's chief financial officer. But everyone I talked to who'd done business with the company told me that he was the man in charge. Tether had so few employees that buying or selling coins often involved a text message to Devasini himself. But that was about all they could tell me about the Italian.

"He's a great man—a pioneer," Pierce had said. "A person who took great personal and financial risk to develop this industry."

The life of this "great man" was cloaked in mystery. He was fifty-seven, ancient by crypto bro standards. What little I could find about his past set off mental alarm bells for me: the abortive plastic-surgery career, the software-counterfeiting allegations. Over years of investigating sketchy people in the world of finance, I'd developed a rule of thumb: Scammers rarely changed their ways. If I could find evidence that someone had been dishonest in the past, there were good odds that their current venture would turn out to be fraudulent too. It was time to start digging into Devasini.

CHAPTER FOUR

The Plastic Surgeon

When I started looking for clues about the life of Giancarlo Devasini, I found little online. But what I did see made it clear that Devasini, like Brock Pierce, had taken a circuitous route to the top of the crypto world.

I saw one video that he'd made in 2009 to promote a food delivery service called Delitzia. It showed him on his balcony in a loose-fitting white shirt, making nettle risotto. A large garden gnome sat next to him, for reasons that weren't explained.

One photo of the Tether boss that I found online intrigued me. It was shot for an exhibition at an art gallery in Milan in 2014. In it, Devasini stood in front of a mirror, his face half covered with shaving cream, looking into his own eyes with an expression that suggested he didn't recognize himself.

The show was about turning points, and in an accompanying interview Devasini said that his came in 1992, when he walked away from his career as a plastic surgeon. He spoke of his dismay at being unable to talk a young girl out of reducing her breasts ("that suited her so beautifully," he said) and how the other doctors saw the patients' bodies as "the mortgage of a beautiful house on the seaside, or the first payment for a new Porsche."

"All my work seemed like a scam, the exploitation of a whim," he said.

Devasini said in the interview that he did not inform anyone at the plastic-surgery clinic that he was quitting. Instead, he simply stopped going to work, ignored his supervisor's calls, and moved to China. This seemed odd, to say the least. I tracked down the doctor who I suspected had been Devasini's supervisor when he pulled this disappearing act, but he didn't return my calls or messages.

So I decided to try and pick up the trail in Italy. With the help of an Italian researcher, I came up with a plan to shake something loose about Devasini, and eventually booked a flight to Milan.

His former clinic, Villa Letizia, was in a neoclassical building on a narrow street, around the corner from a five-hundred-year-old Catholic basilica. On its website, the clinic listed an impressive range of offerings, from rhinoplasty to scrotoplasty, which it helpfully defined as "scrotum lift."

In the lobby, two assistants in short black leather shorts and heels walked between waiting women whose faces were so smooth their ages were impossible to estimate. When I asked the receptionist if there was anyone I could speak to who had worked there in the early '90s, a man with an oddly youthful bowl cut emerged from a back office. He seemed angry that a journalist was visiting. "We don't have time now," he told me. I left a note and never received a response.

The clinic was a dead end. But my researcher, and a second Italian reporter I later hired, eventually filled in some of the details of Devasini's biography, with school yearbooks, university records, and calls to classmates and former colleagues. Here's what we found:

Devasini was born in Turin in 1964 and grew up in Casale Monferrato, a town about forty miles to the east of the city, on the banks of the Po River. His father was also a doctor. A classmate remembered that he was "daring, and unafraid to take a leap into the dark." He studied to be a doctor at the University of Milan, where in 1989 he wrote a thesis on skin transplant techniques. After his short stint as a plastic surgeon, and unexplained exit to China, Devasini returned to Milan and got into the low end of the electronics business, importing parts from Asia and selling laptops in Italy.

"He was a guy who *voleva arrivare*—who wanted to make it in life," said Vittorio Bianchi, who partnered with Devasini to import laptops.

The counterfeiting imbroglio came in 1995. Acting on a tip from someone who suspected he'd been sold bogus Microsoft products, police across Italy raided small computer shops and the offices of several software and hardware distributors. Police said they'd uncovered a ring that had distributed 152,000 counterfeit floppy disks—mostly copies of MS-DOS 6.2, Windows 3.11, and Excel. The leader was a twenty-six-year-old with a record of dealing in stolen car parts.

Devasini was accused of selling the bogus products to other companies. Facing criminal charges, he ended up paying 100 million lira—about $65,000—to Microsoft as a settlement. (He also agreed to cooperate with the investigation, and Tether has said Devasini was unaware the software was unlicensed.) After that setback, Devasini kept looking for new ways to eke out a profit from cheap electronics. He started a company that imported low-grade memory modules from RAM manufacturers, then sorted and tested them before sale. It proved to be his biggest success in the industry. He built a factory on the outskirts of Milan, where, in the 2000s, he also produced CDs and DVDs. Workers there recall Devasini as a nice boss.

Devasini's hometown of Casale Monferrato was known for its cement factories, and at some point Devasini married a woman from the family that owns Buzzi Unicem, one of Italy's largest cement manufacturers. She was an architect, and she designed a modern villa for herself and Devasini in the French Riviera, just outside Monaco, close to the Italian border. Photos show a rooftop infinity pool and views of the Mediterranean. It seemed like a place for a man who'd reached his destination.

But in the late '00s, the RAM business declined due to consolidation in computer manufacturing, according to Marco Fuxa, a business partner of Devasini's at the time. And around that time, Chinese companies also started undercutting Devasini's prices for CDs and DVDs, making his small-scale manufacturing facility unprofitable.

This didn't exactly match what I'd read on Bitfinex's website. There, it said that Devasini's group of companies brought in more than 100 million euros a year in revenue, and that he sold them shortly before the 2008 financial crisis. But Italian corporate records showed that the companies had revenue of just 12 million euros in 2007. Some of them even filed for bankruptcy. And none of the former employees I spoke to remembered Devasini selling them.

What they did tell me was that in 2008, Devasini's production facility was destroyed in a fire. Fuxa said it was caused by diesel generators that Devasini had set up because the local utility hadn't provided enough power. "He basically built a power plant in the back and it went up in smoke," Fuxa told me. But a newly unprofitable factory burning down in a mysterious fire struck me as a potential red flag, waving in the distance.

Devasini tried out some other business pursuits around that time, but it was hard to tell if they'd gotten any traction. He started an on-line shopping site in Italy, and licensed a copy protection technology for adult DVDs, according to a press release announcing a special bonus scene in the 2008 film *Young Harlots: In Detention*. In 2007, Toshiba sued another company owned by Devasini for patent infringement on DVD format specifications. Tether called the lawsuit "merit-less" and said it went nowhere.

A detail about one of Devasini's companies called Perpetual Action Group was particularly evocative. In 2010, Perpetual Action Group was banned from an online marketplace called Tradeloop after a buyer complained they'd ordered $2,000 worth of memory chips, then received a box that contained only a large block of wood. "I look forward to see you in court as you wish," Devasini wrote to the buyer, when they threatened to sue. "My lawyers will laugh all the way to the bank, wishing the world was more prolific of idiots like you." Reading about the incident, I couldn't help but imagine Tether's customers asking to redeem their coins, and what Tether would send in return.

As I made more inquiries into Perpetual Action Group, I received a message from a private investigator who said he was looking into it too. He gave me Spanish court documents that showed the company had done business with someone involved with tax fraud. I was intrigued and agreed to meet him in London. "Take the Piccadilly line to Cockfosters and meet me at the Lord John Russell in Bloomsbury," he told me. But once we got together, I realized the investigator had failed to turn up any evidence that Devasini was involved in tax fraud himself. He was hoping I'd be the one who could provide his big break. "It's really a kind of an ouroboros," he said. Perpetual Action Group, like the plastic-surgery clinic, was a dead end.

The most intriguing window into Devasini's past and worldview originated from a clue I found while I was in Milan. Out of leads to fol-low, I spent a morning at a coffee shop scouring the internet for Deva-sini's name, something I'd already spent hours doing. But this time, perhaps because I was on an Italian network, I found something new.

Devasini's name turned up in the comments section of an Italian political website called *Il Blog delle Stelle*. It was the official site of the

Five Star Movement, an anti-establishment party founded in 2009 by internet guru Gianroberto Casaleggio and comedian Beppe Grillo. On a post from January 2012, a commenter who gave his name as "Giancarlo Devasini" wrote in Italian, "If we all pull together, things can really change. Come on Beppe, never give up!" The commenter also posted a link to his personal blog.

I clicked the link. The page that appeared didn't have Devasini's name on it, but within a few minutes of scrolling through, it was clear to me that it was his. Among other clues: The author posted about his birthday, which I knew to be Devasini's.

The blog was illustrated with a suggestive photo of a woman's legs sticking out of the window of a van, her panties around one of her ankles. It was called "Etsi Omnes Ego Non," which loosely translates from Latin as *Even if all others, I will not*. The motto was used most famously by a Nazi officer who participated in a conspiracy to assassinate Hitler. Devasini, it seemed, saw himself as a lone hero in a world gone mad, who also might be down for a van quickie.

He seemed to have started the blog soon after the factory fire. Around that time, he and his wife had divorced. He was forty-four. Judging from his writing, he was bored, lonely, bitter—and horny. From the first post, titled "Addicted to Myself," Devasini describes himself as a rare genius. The writer can barely bring himself to spend time with other people, whom he compares to goldfish, their minds addled by TV, Facebook, and selfies. The writer particularly looks down on women, whom he refers to as "fauna." He depicts them as shallow, manipulative sex objects, who are drawn to him because of his deep insights into their souls. It's as if the whole world is a con that only he can see.

"Intelligence is a rarer virtue than honesty," Devasini writes. In another place he asks, "Is it possible that no one can do this simple calculation? Either I am a genius or everyone else, indiscriminately, is insulting your intelligence."

Devasini describes taking long, hard bike rides through Milan, thinking of what might have been. He also talks, somewhat incongruously, of his hatred of inflation and banks.

"Banks nowadays are worthless," Devasini writes. "They are without money and a bank without money is like a car without gasoline, like a woman without tits. Completely useless and even a little annoying."

Another theme is Devasini's disdain for nine-to-fivers and admiration of men of action, who aren't afraid to take risks—like himself. It seemed a normal attitude for an entrepreneur. But I was taken aback when I came across a post that seemed to extend that respect to Bernie Madoff.

In a 2008 post, a week after Madoff's arrest for running a decades-long Ponzi scheme, Devasini wrote almost admiringly of the man who had just been caught orchestrating a scam so large it amounted to 2.5 percent of Italy's national debt. The post was titled "So What." I read it with disbelief. It sounded like he was having an epiphany. The post read almost like a poem:

> *How is it possible—I ask myself—that one single person could orga-*
>   *nize such a huge scam?*
> *Did he open all the letters himself?*
> *Was he the only guy who had access to the positions in his company?*
> *Was he the one that did reconciliations, that wrote documents and*
>   *reports and then gave them to clients and analysts? And the em-*
>   *ployees didn't notice anything?*
> *What were they doing all day?*
> *Were they chatting on Facebook?*

And then I read what Devasini wrote about regulators:

> *And the controllers of the Security Exchange Commission, what were*
>   *they doing, instead of controlling a Hedge Fund so huge?*
> *Were they playing Tetris?*
> *Were they sleeping with their feet on the table like Homer Simpson*
>   *as the reactor was catching fire?*

What was Devasini getting at? It seemed to me that he had been wondering how Madoff got away with it for so long, and had come up with his own answer. It wasn't that hard. No one noticed. They are all dumb.

Devasini was fascinated with finance. In a December 2011 post titled "The Shell Game," he explained how Italian banks could avail themselves of billions of dollars of low-interest-rate funding. They could use it to gamble on anything, or to buy higher-yielding government bonds to make risk-free profits.

When I grow up, I don't want to be an astronaut or a football player.
When I grow up I want to be a bank!
Yesterday Italian banks got the European Central Bank to lend them
*   116 billion . . .*
They will be able to use that money to do what they want . . .
Take, take all this money, buy scratch cards, tickets of the Italian lot-
*   tery, or just play them in the slot machines in your neighbor-*
*   hood.*
Don't worry, kids, if you come back I can give you more money. . . .

This was almost too on the nose. With Tether, Devasini had more or less created the central bank of crypto. And now Tether's users had supposedly handed him tens of billions of dollars, and I couldn't figure out what the company was doing with the money.

In other posts, Devasini described himself as someone waiting for the right moment to spring into action. "I sensed the possibility of going further, that this could not be all there was to it," he wrote. "We can spend our whole existence doing the same things, living the same day a thousand, ten thousand times, without realizing that life is slipping away from us. Then one day everything changes."

For Devasini, that moment arrived in 2012. It was when he read about Bitcoin.

CHAPTER FIVE

Getting Hilariously Rich

"It's enough to put the word 'bitcoin' on Google to discover an amazing world," Giancarlo Devasini wrote in December 2012. "I stumbled into this thing a few months ago and it changed my life."

Devasini, the future Tether boss, was so fired up about Bitcoin that he was waxing effusive in the comments section of an Italian political blog. He wrote that Bitcoin would eliminate the banks he hated, and that its value would rise because its supply was capped.

He'd been left with a stockpile of 20 million unsold CDs and DVDs from his defunct manufacturing business. Now he decided to sell them for Bitcoin. He posted an ad on the Bitcointalk forum offering them for 0.01 Bitcoin each—about ten cents at the time. Marco Fuxa, his former business partner, told me that Devasini sold them all. If that's true, and he kept the Bitcoins, their value would have later soared to more than $3 billion.

"That's how he got his money," Fuxa said.

Around the same time, Devasini invested in Bitfinex, then one of many websites where people could trade regular money for Bitcoin. The crypto exchange's creator was a young Frenchman who had copied the code from an exchange called Bitcoinica, which itself had been programmed by a sixteen- or seventeen-year-old. Devasini soon took over as the de facto head of the company. On Bitcointalk, he insulted customers who posted any complaints about the exchange. "Are [you] just blowing hot air out of your mouth or you forgot to switch your brain on?" he asked one in February 2014. "Transparency doesn't mean to spend time in justifying ourselves against allegations that don't make sense," he wrote to another.

Compared with other exchanges, Bitfinex was reliable. That's not saying much. Bitcoin exchanges basically have one job: Keep the cash and crypto sent by users safe. Since the beginning of the industry, they've failed at it.

The first big exchange, Mt. Gox, repurposed a website created as a place to trade virtual Magic: The Gathering cards. ("Mt. Gox" stands for Magic: The Gathering Online eXchange.) Unsurprisingly, a former trading card website proved to be a bad custodian for billions of dollars. Its security and record keeping were so poor that hackers would steal Bitcoins as soon as users deposited them. Mt. Gox filed for bankruptcy in 2014, and owned up to the fact that it had lost 7 percent of all Bitcoins in existence. Another early exchange, BTC-e, failed when the government charged its founder with laundering money for drug traffickers and other criminals. And then there's QuadrigaCX, revealed to be a scam after its founder's mysterious death. By one tally, more than four hundred exchanges have failed. Almost half gave no reason for closing—they just disappeared.

With competition like this, Bitfinex won by simply surviving. By 2016, it had become one of the largest exchanges in the world. That year, uncoincidentally, hackers came for the company. Unknown attackers broke into its servers and stole 119,754 Bitcoins—more than half of what the exchange was holding for its customers.

No one knew who was to blame. And the losses left the exchange insolvent—if everyone had asked for their Bitcoins back at once, it wouldn't have had enough. By the traditional rules of finance, Bitfinex should have declared bankruptcy.

But instead, the exchange reduced the balances of all customers by 36 percent (even those who hadn't lost any Bitcoins) and issued IOUs to cover the losses. Then Bitfinex caught an extremely lucky break: Crypto boomed. Trading increased so much that within eight months the exchange had earned enough to pay back its customers, either in cash or in Bitfinex stock. With this gambit, Bitfinex earned customers' loyalty. And judging from what he'd do in the next few years, Devasini had learned a lesson: He could get away with bending the rules.

BITFINEX WAS ABLE to earn the money back so quickly because crypto was in the middle of its first bubble, which lasted from 2017 to 2018. Hundreds of new cryptocurrencies were launched, spurring huge amounts of trading on Bitfinex and other exchanges, which in turn increased the demand for Tether.

These new tokens were sold by start-ups to fund the development of apps, just like Willett did with MasterCoin. Their founders promised the coins would be useful once the apps were created. It was as if the Wright Brothers sold air miles to finance inventing the airplane, in the words of *Money Stuff* columnist Matt Levine. A new programmable blockchain called Ethereum made the process easy. The token sales were called "initial coin offerings," or ICOs. In 2017, start-ups raised a total of $6.5 billion with them. Everyone wanted a piece of the next Bitcoin.

The hype was so powerful, it seemed like anyone could post a white paper explaining their plans for a new coin and raise millions. Brock Pierce, the Tether co-founder, promoted a coin called EOS, which was pitched as "the first blockchain operating system designed to support commercial decentralized applications." It raised $4 billion. Yes, really.

"I don't care about money," Pierce said in an interview around that time. "If I need money, I just make a token."

Newspapers were filled with stories about people getting rich off crypto. On Instagram, crypto bros showed off the Rolexes and Lamborghinis they'd bought with their profits. As one *New York Times* headline put it in January 2018, "Everyone Is Getting Hilariously Rich and You're Not."

These ICO-funded start-ups promised that blockchain would revolutionize commerce by enabling provenance to be tracked and verified. Even big companies like IBM and Microsoft started saying that they would put practically everything on the blockchain: diamonds, heads of lettuce, shipping containers, personal identification, and even all the real estate in the world. It seemed like blockchain-powered ICOs were the practical use that crypto had been waiting for. But there was one problem. None of this stuff ever advanced beyond the testing phases, if anyone bothered to even do that. Most ICOs were scams. And they weren't actually an innovative form of fraud. ICOs made it easier to run a scam that's about as old as the stock market. It's called a "pump-and-dump" scheme.

HERE'S HOW IT works: A pump-and-dump promoter creates a company that's at least nominally involved in some kind of hot business—whether that's railroads and bicycles in the 1800s or dot-com companies a century later. The business plan doesn't matter, as long as there's a mishmash of buzzwords in the mix. As the organizer of the South Sea Company, one of history's first stock scams, told his associates around 1720: "The more confusion the better; People must not know what they do, which will make them the more eager to come into our measures."

Shares—or in the case of crypto, coins—are distributed at low prices to insiders, who trade them back and forth at higher and higher prices to create the appearance of demand. An aggressive sales pitch coupled with the rising share price brings in new investors. Some of the people who buy in are gullible. But most think they understand the game: Buy early, ride the wave, and sell before the inevitable crash.

As the poet Alexander Pope, a South Sea investor, explained to his stockbroker in a letter in 1720: "Let but Fortune favor us, & the World will be sure to admire our Prudence. If we fail, let's e'en keep the mishap to ourselves: But tis Ignominious (in this Age of Hope and Golden Mountains) not to Venture."

Or, put more simply by Mike Novogratz, an ex–Wall Street fund manager turned crypto investor: "This is going to be the largest bubble of our lifetimes. You can make a whole lot of money on the way up, and we plan on it."

Pump-and-dump scams were particularly popular in the 1980s and '90s when discount brokers brought a new group of unsophisticated investors to the stock market. In that era, depicted in the movie *The Wolf of Wall Street,* annual losses to the schemes were as high as $2 billion a year.

Of course, that's $2 billion in gains, if you were the one doing the scamming. The money was so good that the Mafia even muscled in on the action. Gangsters would hand brokers paper bags of cash as bribes for pushing shares of their worthless companies to retirees. New York's tony Financial District became a place for settling scores: In one especially violent incident, some mob-connected brokers beat another broker up and dangled him from a ninth-floor window across from the New York Stock Exchange.

But running a stock scam is a lot of work. It requires crooked lawyers, brokers, and bankers to draft reams of securities paperwork, even if all the information in them is false. And that leaves a paper trail that pretty much inevitably leads to the scammers getting busted.

Crypto didn't require any of that. All it takes is some rudimentary programming, which can be done by freelancers hired online, and some posts by a social media influencer.

IN SEPTEMBER 2017, near the peak of the ICO boom, the boxer Floyd Mayweather Jr. wrote a message on Twitter that would have been indecipherable for anyone not schooled in the jargon of crypto hype. Above a photo of him with twenty-three glittering championship belts, he wrote: "Centra's (CTR) ICO starts in a few hours. Get yours before they sell out, I got mine."

What Mayweather was saying was that he had purchased a new cryptocurrency called "Centra" and that his 7.7 million Twitter followers should too. Centra was supposedly related to some kind of crypto debit card, but Mayweather didn't bother trying to explain that.

With help from Mayweather, Centra raised about $25 million. But like most of the companies that raised money with ICOs, it was a total scam. It never issued its crypto debit card, or anything else at all. Even the CEO listed on its website didn't exist—his picture was a stock photo. It would later be revealed that its founders, including a pot-smoking, opioid-addled twenty-six-year-old who ran a Miami exotic car rental business, had paid Mayweather $100,000 for his endorsement.

This kind of scheme was definitely not legal. But promoters figured—in most cases, correctly—it would take the authorities years to uncover what was going on. One group of researchers would later estimate that 80 percent of ICOs were fraudulent.

ALL THOSE ICOS and new coins meant a lot more trading—at least until the boom died down in 2018. The frenzy seeded many of what would become the biggest companies in crypto: Sam Bankman-Fried made his first big score as a trader exploiting Bitcoin price discrepancies around this time.

For Giancarlo Devasini, the ICO craze was good for both of his companies: his exchange Bitfinex, and his stablecoin Tether, which by then he'd taken over.

For Bitfinex, more trading meant more fees. And those fees added up to $326 million in profits for Bitfinex in 2017. Giancarlo Devasini's share alone would have been more than $100 million.

Tether was at first only available on Bitfinex, which limited its utility. But another growing exchange called Poloniex started accepting Tether. Traders started using Tether to send money back and forth between the two exchanges to take advantage of price differences. That meant Tether had to issue more coins. By March 2017, more than $50 million in Tether was in circulation. By the end of the year, it would hit $1 billion.

But it was hard for Bitfinex and Tether to handle the influx of money. The problem was that banks didn't want crypto companies as customers. It wasn't that it was illegal. It was just viewed as risky. If a crypto exchange was caught laundering money, its bankers could get in trouble too.

Tether was supposed to be a solution to this problem. Back when Bitfinex first acquired Tether, Phil Potter, Bitfinex's chief strategy officer, had pitched his boss Devasini on the idea that banks would be more willing to work with a stablecoin company. That idea convinced Bitfinex to buy out Brock Pierce and carry on with the project. But Potter turned out to be wrong: Most banks didn't want anything to do with Tether either.

By early 2017, Bitfinex was keeping its money in several banks in Taiwan. But the way the international financial system works, running an exchange required the cooperation of other banks too. Bitfinex's Taiwanese bankers relied on other banks—known as correspondents—who acted as middlemen to pass money from Taiwan to customers in other countries.

But the correspondent banks frowned on crypto. One by one, they stopped processing transactions for Bitfinex and Tether. The last one, Wells Fargo, cut them off in 2017. Then the Taiwanese banks closed their accounts.

This meant that Bitfinex's money was stuck in Taiwan. It literally couldn't be transferred overseas. Devasini and his colleagues got so desperate to get the money out that they considered chartering a jet and flying pallets of cash out of the country. They tried suing Wells Fargo but quickly dropped the case.

But somewhere in the United States, an I.T. worker in his early thirties spotted the filing for the abortive lawsuit after it hit the court docket. He couldn't believe what he was reading. Tether was supposed to be backed by real U.S. dollars in a bank. But in the lawsuit, the company itself admitted it had no access to the banking system. What was especially odd was that even after filing the case, Tether kept issuing coins. It created 200 million new ones that summer. But was anyone even sending in the corresponding $200 million, if the company didn't have a functional bank account?

The man signed up for Twitter, Medium, and other social media platforms under the pseudonym "Bitfinex'ed." And what he started posting would create big problems for Devasini. Tether had spawned a powerful troll.

CHAPTER SIX

Cat and Mouse Tricks

Tether's new anonymous critic, Bitfinex'ed, combed through the lawsuit that the company had filed against Wells Fargo. To him, it strongly suggested that Tethers were not really backed by cash. He began posting a litany of damning questions: Where was Tether keeping its money? Why hadn't it produced audited financial statements? He compared Tether to Liberty Reserve, the proto-cryptocurrency whose founder had gotten arrested for money laundering.

"NO BANKING . . . so how are they getting money? It's bullshit," he tweeted in May 2017.

Four years later, when I started looking into Tether on my *Businessweek* assignment, Bitfinex'ed was still posting multiple times a day. His writing was conspiratorial, but it had struck a chord. Everyone in crypto would bring his posts up in conversation with me. Tether defenders tended to blame him for any negative news about the company. I'd seen things he wrote echoed in lawsuits and in mainstream reports. He seemed to know so much about Tether that I wondered if he worked for the company, or if he was a disgruntled government investigator. I arranged a meeting with him, on the condition I wouldn't reveal his identity.

He told me to meet him outside an apartment complex on Biscayne Bay in Miami Beach. As I waited at a table outside and idly scrolled Twitter, a post that seemed to be referring to the person I was about to meet caught my eye. "Imagine waking up, brushing your teeth, drinking some coffee, then spending 16 hours getting mad at stablecoins online," a crypto influencer wrote. I laughed to myself. Then I realized I could just as easily be the butt of the joke.

A man with a maniacal smile approached me, wearing a bright blue polo smudged with grease from the tacos he'd eaten earlier. He had a buzz cut and a scraggly goatee from which stray long hairs emerged at odd angles. In red-and-black sneakers and baggy Levi's, he looked less like a shadowy spy and more like someone who'd recently emerged from a few weeks gaming in his parents' basement. He told me to call him Andrew, and we walked over to the apartment complex's pool, where we sat on beach chairs overlooking the bay.

"I truly believe it's the largest financial fraud in history," he said. "Treat me as if I'm full of shit. Do your research. But there's no way they're not lying now."

"Andrew" seemed a bit too thrilled to be meeting someone he viewed as a kindred spirit, and it added to my discomfort when he presented me with a lapel pin that depicted the Bitfinex logo engulfed in flames. He told me that he didn't want to reveal his real identity because he'd gotten death threats from Tether defenders. As he worked himself up, the pitch of his voice rose higher.

"If I was completely wrong, why don't they prove me wrong? Everyone's calling me crazy. You get self-doubt. But there's no way this makes sense," he said, his voice crescendoing in a squeak.

Andrew gazed out at speedboats crossing the bay. He said he could tell Tether was a fraud because he'd once done something similar himself. In a multiplayer computer game, he'd figured out a way to print unlimited money, so that he could buy the weapons and other items he wanted. He said he didn't earn any real money from the scam, and that he'd gone on to work for the game company as a kind of "white hat" hacker.

"I saw how printing money would affect asset prices," he said. "When I saw the same thing happening with cryptocurrencies, I felt like I understood what was going on."

Andrew told me that a 1989 episode of the cartoon *DuckTales* explained the Tether scam. In it, a chicken invents a device that can duplicate any item in the world. The duck kids start duplicating coins so they can buy whatever they want, eventually setting off hyperinflation in Duckberg so extreme that a lollipop costs $5,000. "Oh no, don't tell me you boys have been spending duplicated money," Scrooge McDuck says in his Scottish accent when he finds out what's happened.

Like the duck kids, Andrew argued, Tether had been printing more and more money, unbacked by anything at all, and using it to buy Bitcoins, pushing up their price. The company could lend money to practically anyone by issuing them Tethers and calling it "accounts receivable," he said, making air quotes. Or Giancarlo Devasini could print new Tethers for himself, send them to an exchange, and use this ersatz money to buy Bitcoins, effectively balancing his books.

"You print a billion Tethers, you buy a billion dollars of Bitcoin," he said. "Now you're backed."

By then, Andrew had lost me. I had been hoping to get new leads at this meeting, not an analogy drawn from a cartoon about anthropomorphic ducks. Andrew told me his mission to expose Bitfinex wasn't personal. It seemed like it was. He said he imagined Kevin Smith—who played a slovenly hacker named Warlock who works out of his mother's basement in a *Die Hard* sequel—portraying him in a movie. "I think it's more humiliating for Bitfinex that way," he said.

When I asked for his sources or evidence, Andrew didn't have anything new to provide. That was where I was supposed to come in.

IF ANYONE WOULD know whether Tether had the money it claimed, it would be its bankers. I tried contacting the Taiwanese banks that Bitfinex had used, but got no response.

I'd read that after those banks cut them off, Devasini and his colleagues had scoured the world for a more agreeable bank for the exchange, and for Tether. Eventually they found one: a start-up in Puerto Rico called Noble Bank International.

I contacted its founder, John Betts, and in June 2021, we met in Manhattan. A tall South African, he carried himself with the self-assurance of the Goldman Sachs banker he once had been. By then, Noble had failed, and he was angry. He puffed on a vape pen as we walked in laps around Washington Square Park. Bitfinex and Tether had been his biggest customers. But he warned me not to trust them.

"You should be suspicious of any financial business that declines to be transparent with its holdings, and refuses regulation and transparency," he said.

Betts explained that Noble wasn't exactly a bank—it was an "international finance entity," organized under looser Puerto Rican laws.

His plan was to open accounts for all the major cryptocurrency hedge funds and companies. That way, they could easily transfer money between themselves without ever sending it out of Noble.

BETTS TOLD ME that when Tether banked with him, it really did have one U.S. dollar to back each coin. But the relationship had ended acrimoniously in 2018, after just one year, and he suspected Devasini had subsequently put the reserves at risk.

The problem, Betts said, was that Devasini wanted to use Tether's reserves to make money. At the time, Tether had about $1 billion parked at Noble. All that money was sitting there, earning nothing. Devasini proposed that he could use the money to buy bonds that paid interest. If he invested the money in corporate debt at, say, 3 percent a year, that would be $30 million a year in profit.

But Betts objected. Tether's website had long pledged that every Tether was fully backed by traditional currency. Investing the money wouldn't be consistent with that. And even relatively safe investments went sour sometimes, which could have left Tether with less than complete backing, and vulnerable to a bank run.

When Betts refused, Devasini accused him of stealing. Betts urged Devasini to hire an accounting firm to produce a full audit to reassure the public, but Devasini said Tether didn't need to go that far to respond to critics.

"Giancarlo wanted a higher rate of return," Betts said. "I repeatedly implored him to be patient and do the work with auditors."

The dispute got so heated that Devasini wanted to pull the company's cash from Noble. Devasini's deputy, Phil Potter, wanted to keep their money in the "international finance entity," so Devasini and his other partners bought him out for $300 million. Potter took the payment in U.S. dollars, not Tethers.

In June 2018, Betts stepped down from his position at Noble for what he said were health and family reasons. Devasini got his way and withdrew his deposits, and the bank failed soon after. Betts told me that after Tether moved its money out of Noble, Devasini would have been able to invest it however he wanted. He said he wasn't sure exactly what Devasini had done, but he was sure it was a lot riskier than keeping the money in cash. Tether could be investing in anything at all.

"It's not a stablecoin, it's a high-risk offshore hedge fund," Betts said. "Even their own banking partners don't know the extent of their holdings, or if they exist."

I KNEW BETTS had his own motivations to criticize Tether. He blamed Devasini for the failure of his business, which had derailed the South African's career. But what Betts was saying made intuitive sense. There was a conflict of interest at the center of Tether's business model: Any gains from its investments would go to Devasini and the company's other owners, but losses would fall on the holders of Tether coins. And if Tether did lose money on a bad investment, it would make sense for the company to try to cover it up rather than disclose it and risk a run.

Banks face the same conflict. They profit by investing customers' deposits. But their deposits are insured; they have regulators to keep them in check. As far as I could tell, there were only one or two people in the government who had been paying attention to Tether. They were lawyers who worked in the investment-protection bureau of the New York attorney general's office. One was named John Castiglione.

CHAPTER SEVEN

"A Thin Crust of Ice"

The investor-protection bureau operated out of an office tower in New York's Financial District. Under former attorney general Elliot Spitzer, it was feared by Wall Street investment banks, but in the years since, its resources had dwindled. It employed few of the data scientists and economists needed to analyze financial markets, and certainly no cryptocurrency specialists.

In 2017, John Castiglione, then thirty-eight, and a colleague named Brian Whitehurst were assigned to investigate the cryptocurrency market. It was a huge assignment for such a small team, especially given that neither of them had specialized knowledge of the industry.

Castiglione had joined the attorney general's office in 2014 from Latham & Watkins, a giant 2,100-lawyer firm where he had generally defended big corporations. The switch came with a big pay cut. At the attorney general's office, he was paid about $80,000, less than half what a first-year associate made at Latham. But he'd always wanted to work in government.

One of his first tasks at the attorney general's office was an investigation of dark pools—private stock-trading pools run by big Wall Street investment banks. Dark pools were marketed as a way for institutional investors like mutual funds to keep their large orders secret, so that sharp players didn't figure out that, say, Fidelity needed to buy $1 billion of Apple stock, then cut ahead of them and drive the price up. But Castiglione and his colleagues found that many dark-pool operators instead gave special privileges to predatory traders. The cases resulted in about $200 million in fines.

Castiglione and his colleagues realized that if the highly regulated

Wall Street banks were this bad, whatever was going on in crypto markets was likely worse. In April 2018, the attorney general's office sent a simple thirty-four-question survey to thirteen of the largest crypto exchanges, seeking relatively basic information, like who owned them, how they handled orders, how they monitored trading, and how they protected customers' funds.

"As with other emerging sectors, the challenge with virtual currency is to prevent fraud and other abuses, safeguard market integrity, and protect individual investors—without stifling legitimate market activity or innovation," Castiglione wrote in a letter to the exchanges.

The crypto industry responded with outrage. Four exchanges didn't respond at all. Some of the others said they had no responsibility to police suspicious activity. Castiglione and Whitehurst decided to focus on Bitfinex, the crypto exchange owned by the same group that owned Tether. It had the most red flags. The company said it didn't do business in New York, but one of its top executives—the chief strategy officer, Phil Potter—lived there. Castiglione sent a subpoena to some New York trading firms, and they informed him that they did use Bitfinex.

It seemed especially odd to Castiglione that the owner of an exchange would also control a currency—Tether—that traded on that exchange. He wondered: Could Tether be used to manipulate prices on the exchange, or even the price of Bitcoin? (That June, finance professor John Griffin had published a paper, called "Is Bitcoin Really Un-Tethered?," arguing that someone had been printing unbacked Tethers to prop up the price of Bitcoin.) Castiglione and Whitehurst sent subpoenas for records to Tether and Bitfinex. He didn't know it yet, but the companies were in the middle of an existential crisis.

FROM THE EARLY days of the companies, Bitfinex and Tether had trouble with banks. Bitfinex had, at times, resorted to shaky workarounds to move money. Potter admitted as much in an online chat with traders in 2017.

"We've had banking hiccups in the past," Potter said. "We've always been able to route around it or deal with it. Open up new accounts or what have you. Shift to a different entity. There have been lots of sort of cat and mouse tricks that everybody in the Bitcoin industry has to avail themselves of."

The crisis sprang from one of these cat and mouse tricks. Bitfinex had been using a Panamanian money-transfer service called Crypto Capital to move funds and hold some of its cash. This was, amazingly, even sketchier than it sounds. Crypto Capital advertised on its website that it enabled users to "deposit and withdraw fiat funds instantly to any crypto exchange around the world." But it didn't have any special technology. Instead, it was essentially a money-laundering service.

Crypto Capital would simply open bank accounts using made-up company names. They'd tell banks they'd use the accounts for normal things, like real-estate investing. Then they'd let companies like Bitfinex use them for customer transfers. (Bitfinex would later claim that it believed Crypto Capital's assurances that everything was on the up-and-up.) The service was used by other crypto exchanges, including Kraken, QuadrigaCX, and Binance. By 2017, it was processing over $100 million a month.

By the summer of 2018, Bitfinex had almost $1 billion parked in Crypto Capital's accounts. But then the money launderer stopped processing withdrawals for Bitfinex customers. Bitfinex and Tether boss Giancarlo Devasini wrote a series of increasingly desperate messages to the head of Crypto Capital, an Israeli man named Oz Yosef.

"We are seeing massive withdrawals and we are not able to face them anymore unless we can transfer some money," Devasini wrote to Yosef in August 2018. "Under normal circumstances I wouldn't bother you (I never did so far) but this is quite a special situation and I need your help."

Yosef made a bunch of excuses to Devasini: corruption, bank compliance, tax issues, typos, bankers on vacation. It was a dangerous situation—if the public found out the withdrawal delay was more than a temporary glitch, it could set off a bank run.

But the situation only worsened. In October, with many customers waiting on withdrawals for weeks, rumors began to circulate that Bitfinex itself was insolvent. The company had never officially acknowledged its relationship with Noble Bank, but that month, it was reported that the companies had cut ties. On October 7, Bitfinex posted a statement on its website suggesting, with misleading wording, that the exchange had barely heard of Noble Bank: "Stories and allegations currently circulating mentioning an entity called Noble Bank have no impact on our operations, survivability, or solvency." Then, a week later, it denied that there were any problems with withdrawals: "All cryptocurrency and fiat withdrawals are, and have been, processing as usual without the slightest interference."

This was not true. The same day, Devasini wrote to Yosef: "I have been telling you since a while. too many withdrawals waiting for a long time. Is there any way we can get money from you? . . . Please help."

Yosef wrote back blaming banks for closing their accounts for no reason. Devasini said that excuse wasn't good enough.

"I need to provide customers with precise answers at this point. can't just kick the can a little more," Devasini wrote. "Please understand all this could be extremely dangerous for everybody, the entire crypto community. BTC [Bitcoin] could tank to below 1k if we don't act quickly."

What Devasini seemed to be short-handing was that if Crypto Capital didn't allow his customers to make withdrawals, there could be a run on Bitfinex and Tether. And if there was a run on those companies, it could cause the entire crypto market to crash.

Three days later, Devasini added: "Too much money is trapped with you and we are currently walking on a very thin crust of ice." And in November, after Crypto Capital still hadn't sent any money, he showed his frustration. "I think you should stop playing and tell me the truth about what is going on," Devasini wrote. "I am not your enemy. I am here to help you and have been very patient so far, but you need to cut the crap and tell me what is going on."

The truth was that Polish authorities had caught on to their scheme and seized their bank accounts in the country, where they were keeping most of the cash. Yosef would later be charged with fraud by U.S. authorities, though he fled to Israel. Another man involved with Crypto Capital was arrested in Poland in 2019. Prosecutors there alleged that Crypto Capital also laundered money for drug cartels.

IN FEBRUARY 2019, Tether's lawyers came to the attorney general's offices for a meeting, a standard part of an investigation like this. Castiglione, Whitehurst, and another colleague sat in a conference room with two lawyers for Bitfinex and Tether. Another defense lawyer joined on speakerphone.

Castiglione and his colleagues asked for proof that all Tethers were paid for with actual dollars by real customers. The defense lawyers acted affronted. But after some back-and-forth, one of the defense lawyers acknowledged that there had been what he called a "development." They didn't exactly come clean. Bitfinex had placed more than $850 million with a payment processor—Crypto Capital—and it appeared to be "impaired," he said. Bitfinex had filled the hole by borrowing from Tether's reserves.

"I'm sorry, can you say that again?" Castiglione asked.

Castiglione couldn't believe it. Impaired seemed to be a euphemism for "gone," and gone meant the exchange was insolvent and on the brink of collapse. On Wall Street, a trading venue in this situation would have to tell the world and shut down. It seemed like Bitfinex didn't even plan on informing its customers. Castiglione asked the defense lawyers to leave so he and his colleagues could confer in private.

"I can't fucking believe what I just heard," he said to his colleagues. "Did they really just say $850 million of investor money has walked out the door? And they're going to patch the hole with Tether's reserves?" Then he heard a voice from the conference room's speakerphone. One of the defense lawyers informed Castiglione he had forgotten to put the phone on mute.

The meeting ended inconclusively. Over the next few weeks, Castiglione continued digging into Tether. He didn't like to think of himself as a conspiracy theorist, but Bitfinex and Tether's lawyers were being so evasive it seemed like anything was possible. Tether's website assured users: "Every Tether is always backed 1-to-1, by traditional currency held in our reserves. So 1 USDT is always equal to one USD." But after the meeting, the site's wording was changed to read: "Every Tether is always 100% backed by our reserves, which include traditional currency and cash equivalents and, from time to time, may include other assets and receivables from loans made by Tether to third parties, which may include affiliated entities." In other words, Tether's reserves could be anything it wanted.

At first, Bitfinex's lawyers said the deal to lend themselves Tether's money was only pending. But after weeks of exchanging letters, they informed Castiglione that it had been completed, though they assured him it was a fair transaction negotiated without conflict of interest. They sent over papers documenting a $900 million line of credit from Tether to Bitfinex. Signing on behalf of Tether was Giancarlo Devasini. And on behalf of Bitfinex: Giancarlo Devasini.

In April 2019, the attorney general went to a state court in Manhattan with its findings, seeking an injunction barring more transfers between the companies. "Executives at Bitfinex, who also own and operate Tether, took hundreds of millions of dollars from Tether's cash reserves, and used those reserves to prop up the Bitfinex trading platform," a lawyer for the attorney general's office wrote.

The accusation was damning. But then something surprising happened: Nothing. The revelation did not set off a run on Tether. The price of a Tether briefly dipped to 97 cents before bouncing back. "The market just doesn't care," one crypto trader told a reporter at the time. "This community has an immense tolerance for pain."

Instead of a bank run, there was a bailout. To pay back the loan, Bitfinex raised $1 billion by selling crypto tokens it called "Unus Sed Leo"—Latin for *one, but a lion*. It promised that it would use future trading revenue to buy them back. Among the buyers were EOS, the ICO promoted by Tether co-founder Brock Pierce; and Sam Bankman-Fried's hedge fund Alameda Research. Devasini had essentially printed his own money to replace what was lost by Crypto Capital and sold it to the biggest players in the crypto industry.

In February 2021, Tether agreed to pay $18.5 million to settle the New York suit without admitting wrongdoing. "Bitfinex and Tether recklessly and unlawfully covered-up massive financial losses to keep their scheme going and protect their bottom lines," Attorney General Letitia James said in a statement at the time. "Tether's claims that its virtual currency was fully backed by U.S. dollars at all times was a lie." Supporters spun this as an endorsement of Tether—would the state attorney general settle if Tether were a massive fraud?—but behind the scenes, the attorney general's office was worn out. It was unclear whether the companies were really subject to New York's jurisdiction, as they said that they no longer did business with U.S. customers.

Castiglione and Whitehurst tried to warn other regulators about Tether and Bitfinex. Devasini had already shown he'd use Tether's reserves as a corporate slush fund. But the SEC didn't seem interested—the agency was still busy sorting out the pump-and-dump scams of the ICO boom. Castiglione had only a short phone call with prosecutors from the Department of Justice. (The Commodity Futures Trading Commission fined Tether $42.5 million in October 2021 in a case that piggybacked on the New York attorney general's.)

The settlement with New York required Tether to publish quarterly reports detailing its holdings, and to send even more detailed information to the attorney general. Castiglione hoped they would inspire someone to look more closely. But no regulators asked to see them.

It had been more than a decade since Bitcoin was invented. Crypto had become practically ubiquitous. In 2020, as crypto trading took off during the pandemic, Tether grew exponentially, selling 17 billion Tethers. The next year, it sold 57 billion. But regulators still weren't sure what to do about it, or the rest of the industry. Crypto was growing wildly, and no one was enforcing any of the usual safeguards.

CHAPTER EIGHT

The Name's Chalopin.
Jean Chalopin.

By the summer of 2021, the only financial institution I could find that was willing to say it was working with Tether was Deltec Bank & Trust in the Bahamas. That was where Giancarlo Devasini had sent the company's money from Noble Bank in Puerto Rico after his dispute with its founder, John Betts. I emailed Deltec's chairman, a man named Jean Chalopin, and he agreed to speak with me. I told him I preferred to meet in person and booked a flight to Nassau.

We met in July at Deltec's office, on the top floor of a six-story building ringed with palm trees in a nice part of the capital. In a previous life, Chalopin had co-created the animated TV series *Inspector Gadget,* and a painting of the 1980s trench coat–wearing cyborg policeman hung on his office door. Magazine covers featuring Chalopin's wife, a former model, and his daughter, a composer, were displayed on a shelf. Chalopin, seventy-one, had a mop of red hair and wore rimless round glasses. As we sat down, he pulled a book about financial fraud, *Misplaced Trust,* off the shelf. "People do funny things for money," he said, cryptically.

He made himself a cup of tea and told me he'd come to the Bahamas in 1987 after selling his first animation studio, DIC Entertainment. The sale had made him rich—he bought a castle outside Paris and a pink Colonial in the Bahámas. That mansion later served as the villain's home in the 2006 film *Casino Royale,* and Chalopin seemed like he could be a character in a James Bond movie himself.

He told me he spoke four languages badly and two well, and that he used to pilot his own jet. Among his past ventures were a failed futuristic amusement center in Paris and a Ming Dynasty theme park near China's Great Wall. He became a Deltec client in the early 1980s, then befriended its aging founder, Clarence Dauphinot, Jr.

Bahamian banks are often depicted in movies as a haven for money launderers. "It's always the guy flying on the plane, big bags of cash," Chalopin complained. But he told me that was an outdated stereotype. He said Deltec's edge was customer service, not secrecy.

After Dauphinot died in 1995, the bank, which once conducted investment banking throughout Latin America, shrunk to a small money-management operation. Chalopin invested, eventually becoming the biggest shareholder. He decided to seek out clients in new lines of business—such as biotech, gene editing, and artificial intelligence—that were too small to get personal attention from bigger banks. Another area was cryptocurrencies, which he said other banks were wrong to avoid.

"Crypto was like, 'Don't touch, it's very dangerous,'" he said. "Well, if you dig a little bit deeper, you realize it's not, actually."

Chalopin told me that he was introduced to Tether and Devasini in 2017 by a customer who'd gotten rich from Bitcoin. Devasini cooked Chalopin a risotto lunch and impressed him with his forthrightness. When they discovered that Devasini had grown up in the same Italian village as Chalopin's mother, they began calling each other *cugino* (Italian for cousin). Devasini bought a house next to Chalopin's in the Bahamas, and together they purchased and divided the waterfront lot between the two properties. Chalopin told me Tether had been unfairly maligned. "There's no agenda or plot," he said. "They are not Enron or Madoff. When there's a problem, they fix it honorably."

Chalopin said he investigated Tether for months before taking the company on as a client in November 2018. He signed a letter vouching for its assets. He was surprised that critics still insisted Tether's currency was not backed by cash. "Frankly, the biggest thing at the time was 'the money doesn't exist,'" he said. "We knew the money exists! It was sitting here."

But when I asked Chalopin if he knew for sure that Tether's assets were fully secure now, he laughed. It was a difficult question, he said. He only held cash and extremely low-risk bonds for Tether. But recently the company had started using other banks to handle its money. Only a quarter of it—$15 billion or so—was still with Deltec. "I cannot speak about what I cannot know," he said. "I can only control what's with us."

A MONTH AFTER my meeting with Chalopin, in August 2021, I finally caught a break in my search. After much cajoling, a source sent me a document showing a detailed account of most of Tether's reserves. My source made me promise not to reveal where I got it, nor publish details that might give them away. The document listed hundreds of investments made by Tether. Most were pretty standard: short-term bonds. But there were also strange things, like investments in hedge funds and small bets on the prices of copper, corn, and wheat.

The part of the holdings that seemed riskiest to me was billions of dollars of short-term loans to large Chinese companies. United States money-market funds avoided buying Chinese debt, because they viewed the country's opaque financial system as risky, and, at the time, investors were speculating that the Chinese property market was in a dangerous bubble. Tether's portfolio appeared to have debt issued by government-linked companies like Shanghai Pudong Development Bank, and real-estate developers like Shimao Group.

The document wasn't comprehensive, so it didn't answer the question of whether any of Tether's money was missing, but what I could see of Tether's portfolio was certainly a lot weirder than the company had suggested publicly.

By then, I'd also learned that Tether was under federal investigation. It didn't relate to any missing money; U.S. prosecutors were looking into its relationship with Crypto Capital and whether Tether executives had lied to banks to get them to open accounts in the early days. I'd heard that prosecutors were looking to speak with Devasini. This wasn't necessarily as dire as it sounded. I knew from experience that many investigations never went anywhere, and that if there were charges, companies often settled them by paying a fine. But I wondered if the crypto world would stick by Tether if the United States filed charges, or if that would set off a run.

As I got closer to publishing my piece about the Tether money trail in *Businessweek*, I sent questions to the company. Devasini blew up. He had recently created an account on Twitter using his old screen name "urwhatuknow," and there, he blasted my pending article. He used the crypto industry's go-to insult for news it didn't like: "FUD," short for "fear, uncertainty, and doubt."

"Another financial enslaved dying magazine trying to come up with some Tether FUD in order to bring in some bucks and delay its extinction for a few more days," he wrote.

Tether's lawyer, Stuart Hoegner, had a little bit more to say to me. In a video chat, he called Tether's critics "jihadists" set on the company's destruction and said their market-manipulation claims didn't make sense. And, in an email, he said my reporting was "nothing more than a compilation of innuendo and misinformation shared by disgruntled individuals with no involvement with or direct knowledge of the business's operations."

"We maintain a clear, comprehensive, and sophisticated risk management framework for safeguarding and investing the reserves," he said, adding that no customer had ever asked for money back and been refused.

Hoegner pointed me to financial statements, prepared by an accounting firm in the Cayman Islands, as evidence that Tether was fully backed. But when I asked Hoegner where Tether was keeping its money, he declined to say. Nor was I reassured when he told me the company had more than enough cash to cover the most money it had ever had to pay out in a single day. Bank runs can last longer than twenty-four hours.

That October, *Businessweek* published my account of what I found, with the headline "The $69 Billion Crypto Mystery." (By then, Tether had issued 69 billion coins.) In the story, I explained the outlandish backgrounds of the Tether founders, and their history of misleading disclosures about their funds. But I didn't actually solve the mystery.

People read into the story whatever they wanted to believe. To crypto fans, it showed that Tether did in fact have at least some money, which was a positive. To those who were skeptical, the information about Chinese commercial paper was damning. I wasn't sure what to make of the financial records myself. I tried digging into the details of their holdings. Many of the loans appeared to be legitimate loans to real companies. Others I couldn't verify at all. But that was unsurprising given the low quality of data on Chinese corporate loans. Rather than a smoking gun, the records felt like another inconclusive clue.

. . .

ON WALL STREET, my report caught the attention of hedge funds. In particular, short sellers. These are funds that make money by betting against shaky companies, then waiting for them to fail. Some of them try to hurry the process along by publishing reports exposing frauds.

Several analysts at large funds that specialized in short selling told me that they had placed bets against Tether, or were considering doing so. For them, it was an appealing bet. There was no risk that Tether would ever rise above $1.00, so they wouldn't lose money. But there was clearly at least a possibility that its price would crash.

"I'm betting a shit-ton of money on them being a crook," Fraser Perring, co-founder of Viceroy Research, told me. "Worst case is, I can't lose hardly anything. I'm already rich, but I'm going to be fucking rich when Tether collapses."

TETHER WOULDN'T HAVE to be a complete fraud for it to fail. If it was revealed that Tether had, say, $60 billion of assets to back 70 billion coins, it could set off a rush of redemptions. Once 60 billion coins were cashed in, the remaining ones would be worthless. That would make the short sellers' bets pay off. Before the creation of deposit insurance, bank runs like that were common. Some of the critics compared Tether to the banks that sprung up in the 1800s on the American frontier, which failed all the time.

The U.S. government didn't issue paper money back then, only gold and silver coins, because its early leaders were fearful of inflation—"an infinity of successive felonious larcenies," according to President John Adams. This led to a currency shortage. But there was a workaround: States allowed banks to print their own notes, redeemable for U.S. coins on demand.

Few banks kept enough hard currency on hand to redeem all the banknotes. Instead, they simply printed as much paper money as they wanted, and used it to buy real assets, like property. As long as the notes stayed in circulation instead of being redeemed, the scheme could continue. These institutions came to be called "wildcats," supposedly because they discouraged anyone from bringing paper money in to exchange for coins by locating their branches in remote areas where wild animals roamed.

These wildcatters would borrow reserves for the day when examiners were coming to visit. Carriages bearing gold would literally rush to beat examiners to branches, or piles of coins would be handed in through the back door during an inspection. One bank in Michigan filled boxes with nails and glass, then covered them with a thin layer of silver coins to fool examiners, who weren't fooled.

"What a temptation was this for the unscrupulous speculator, the adventurer, dreaming only of wealth, and ready to hazard all in pursuit of it," wrote Alpheus Felch, a Michigan bank commissioner at the time.

The wildcat-banking era came to an end when, in the early days of the Civil War, President Abraham Lincoln started printing federal paper money and instituted a prohibitively high tax on other currency. The wildcat notes, which once fueled frontier cities' economies, fell into disuse. Some gave them to children to play with. In rural areas, they were used for wallpaper.

It was easy to see the parallels between the wildcats and crypto companies like Tether. Imagine controlling a machine that could print free money. Who would have the self-control not to run off a few extra million dollars? Tether's bosses had that power.

And rumors alone can be enough to set off a fatal bank run. In 1973, a casual comment from a Japanese high school student about a local credit union started a rumor that led to a damaging panic. More recently, in March 2023, California's Silicon Valley Bank collapsed after worry about its investment portfolio, amplified by a prominent podcaster, caused its customers, mostly start-up executives, to freak out. Many of the short sellers said it was surprising that Tether hadn't suffered a run already.

But none of the analysts seemed much better informed than "Andrew," the conspiracy theorist I'd met who posted as "Bitfinex'ed." One hedge fund trader told me he'd hired ex-CIA analysts to decode the body language of Tether executives during a TV interview, a technique whose value seemed dubious to me. A second was driven for three hours in a black SUV to meet me in upstate New York, where I was on vacation, only to tell me stories from Devasini's past that didn't have much to do with the current state of Tether.

. . .

ONE SHORT SELLER tried a more direct way of digging up dirt. In October 2021, Hindenburg Research announced that it would pay $1 million for details on Tether's backing. "We feel strongly that Tether should fully and thoroughly disclose its holdings to the public," Hindenburg's founder, Nate Anderson, wrote. "In the absence of that disclosure, we are offering a $1,000,000 bounty to anyone who can provide us exclusive detail on Tether's supposed reserves."

I'd known Anderson for almost a decade. When we met, he was working as a low-level analyst at a research firm. At a coffee shop, he gave me a dossier on a hedge fund called Platinum Partners. I wrote an exposé, he filed a report to the SEC, and the fund later collapsed. Since then, Anderson had started Hindenburg and become one of Wall Street's most prominent short sellers. He had taken down, among others, a $20 billion electric truck company called Nikola that faked a test-drive video by rolling a non-working truck down a hill. He was thirty-seven, just a few months older than me. I was jealous. Anderson didn't tease me with selfies like my friend Jay after his Dogecoin score. He didn't need to. I saw glamour shots of him in *The New York Times* and *The Wall Street Journal*.

At first I felt annoyed that Anderson was throwing his money around. I'd been working for months to solve the mystery, trying to talk people into helping me. Like other mainstream reporters, I never pay for information. Who would give me the goods for free now, when they could sell them to Anderson for $1 million? Then it occurred to me that I kind of had the goods Anderson was looking for myself. I arranged a meeting.

In November, we met in front of a hot dog cart by an entrance to Central Park. Anderson showed up wearing a hoodie. As we strolled down a path past children playing baseball, tourists taking photos, and a steel-drum band, he talked about what he could do with detailed documents on Tether's holdings. Anderson said the bounty announcement hadn't produced any great tips so far. I told him I might be able to help. Without revealing any details, I described the documents that I'd received.

"Based on what I've described to you, you would give me a million dollars?" I asked.

"Yes," Anderson said.

"Do you have a million dollars?"

"Not on me," he said, but he assured me that he had a lot more than that in the bank.

He was serious. I couldn't help being excited by the idea that he would pay me several times my annual salary for a few files I had on the iPhone in my pocket. But I'd promised my source that I wouldn't share the documents. I told Anderson it would be unethical for me to trade them for a bounty.

"It's not unethical," Anderson said.

"It's only unethical for me, not for you," I said. "The source gave it to me, not for me to then resell it."

When I told Anderson I'd get fired, he offered me a job. When I said the documents were hard to interpret, he said his team of experts could decode them. And when I asked why he was willing to pay so much for the information, he said the potential reward was many times bigger than $1 million.

He wasn't planning to place a bet against Tether. Instead, he wanted to file a whistleblower report to the government, taking advantage of a program that offered informants a reward of as much as 30 percent of any fine collected. Nikola had paid $125 million, meaning Anderson potentially stood to get a $37.5 million reward for his electric-truck exposé. If the government fined Tether for lying about its reserves, the payout could easily be at least that much. Anderson said he'd share his cut. Doing some quick math in my head, I realized it could mean $10 million or more for me.

I'd been reading about effective altruism, the philanthropic movement that Sam Bankman-Fried belonged to, and I found myself turning to its logic. Even if I didn't want the money for myself, I could donate it to charity. Given to the right causes, $10 million could potentially save thousands of lives. Wouldn't it be even more unethical for me to refuse the reward?

But biking to the meeting with Anderson, I'd seen a NO PARKING flyer put up ahead of a shoot for the show *Billions*. On the show, Bobby Axelrod, an unethical hedge fund manager, declares, "What's the point of having fuck-you money if you never say, 'Fuck you'?" I agreed with the sentiment. But maybe you didn't even need to have fuck-you money to say fuck you. You could just say fuck you if you felt like it was right. You didn't have to take $10 million just because someone offered it, just like you didn't have to buy Dogecoin if you thought it was dumb. Spite won out over greed. I told Anderson that some things are more important than money.

"This book is going to be called *Jay Is Wrong and Zeke Is Right: The Cryptocurrency Story*," I said. "As a writer, you don't want to be compromising in any way, you know? You don't want to have ulterior motives."

WHEN I GOT back home, Anderson texted me. "Our conversation today was a potential systemic risk to the global financial system." And while he was being a bit dramatic, he wasn't exactly wrong. A few days after our meeting, on November 8, 2021, the price of Bitcoin touched an all-time high of $68,000 and the collective value of all cryptocurrencies topped $3 trillion. Could an industry this large really rest on a foundation of Tethers?

What I'd learned so far about Tether was inconclusive, but completely sketchy. I couldn't believe that every day, people sent millions of perfectly good U.S. dollars to the *Inspector Gadget* creator's Bahamian bank in exchange for digital tokens conjured by the *Mighty Ducks* guy and run by executives who were targets of a U.S. criminal investigation. But I didn't think the answers lay in the documents I'd obtained. All my best stories were built on information from people with firsthand knowledge of how schemes really worked.

Of all the people I met researching Tether, one stood out as both a source of information about Tether and a potential story subject for Bloomberg: Sam Bankman-Fried. In the months since we'd met briefly in Miami, he'd become the most prominent crypto booster of all. And on November 10, I read in the crypto publication *Protos* that Bankman-Fried's hedge fund, Alameda Research, had received 31.7 billion Tethers in 2021. That meant that Bankman-Fried had supposedly sent $31.7 billion in real U.S. dollars to Tether, somehow. Bankman-Fried had already assured me in Miami that his dealings with Tether were on the up-and-up. But I figured that as one of Tether's biggest customers, he had to know more. I decided to pitch my editors at Bloomberg on a profile of him, to give me a reason to get to know him better.

The story was irresistible. He was twenty-nine years old, and venture capitalists had just invested in his two-and-a-half-year-old exchange FTX at a $25 billion valuation. *Forbes* estimated his personal net worth at $22.5 billion. People were calling him a financial version of Facebook founder Mark Zuckerberg.

I didn't think FTX was an innovation on par with social media. It seemed like a casino for gambling on random coins, just like all the other crypto exchanges. To me, the most interesting part of Bankman-Fried's story was his motivation.

Bankman-Fried said he'd decided when he was young to dedicate his life to doing the most good he could for the world. As a teenager, he'd tried out animal-rights activism. Then, when he was in college, he'd decided that, for him, the best way to do good would be to make as much money as possible and give it all away. Here he was, less than a decade later, one of the richest and most powerful people in the world.

But so far, he'd donated less to charity than he'd spent on celebrity endorsements, marketing, and lobbying in Washington, D.C. He seemed like a thought experiment from a college philosophy seminar come to life. Should someone who wants to save the world first amass as much money and power as possible, or will the pursuit corrupt him along the way?

My editors approved the pitch. And, conveniently for me, Bankman-Fried had recently moved from Hong Kong to the Bahamas, only a three-hour flight from New York. One of his public relations representatives readily agreed to an interview at FTX's new office in Nassau.

CHAPTER NINE

Crypto Pirates

Long before Sam Bankman-Fried relocated his crypto exchange to the Bahamas, the island territory had been a haven for schemers, smugglers, and pirates. In 1696, the buccaneer Henry Avery sailed into Nassau Harbor in a stolen warship, wanted by the British king. Within two decades, the island was an outlaw state ruled by pirates, among them Edward Thatch, better known as Blackbeard, who used it as a base to target nearby shipping lanes. The pirates pulled down the Union Jack from a fort by the main square and hoisted a black flag with a white skull on it—"death's head," as they called it.

The Bahamas is an archipelago of seven hundred islands that stretches from the western edge of Haiti to within 110 miles of Miami, which made it a convenient base for British loyalists fleeing the American Revolution, Confederate arms runners during the Civil War, and bootleggers during Prohibition. White men who made their fortunes in this era took over the islands, enforcing segregation and ruling like feudal lords. They came to be known as the Bay Street Boys.

When Prohibition ended, the Bay Street Boys started helping Americans avoid another law: income taxes. Island lawyers set up so many sham "personal holding corporations" for American tax dodgers that some office buildings were covered with nameplates from foundation to roof. When the Mafia abandoned Cuba after Fidel Castro's revolution, the Bay Street Boys helped gangster Meyer Lansky develop casinos in the Bahamas. Lansky paid the island's finance minister to adopt new rules restricting local firms from sharing financial information, even with criminal investigators, making it a more attractive destination for money launderers.

By the 1960s, banks seemingly outnumbered bars and restaurants on Bay Street, and they served loan sharks, drug traffickers, and tax evaders, according to a *Life* magazine investigation, which called the island "a lucrative center of international crime." Some Bay Street scammers sold bogus insurance or shares of phony companies to Americans by mail. Others used fake Bahamian certificates of deposit as collateral to borrow real money from U.S. banks. The territory, a British colonial official wrote, "attracts all sorts of financial wizards, some of whose activities we can well believe should be controlled in the public interest."

One Bahamian bank was run by a notorious Wall Street swindler who'd fled to the Caribbean to avoid a U.S. fraud investigation. Another served as a conduit for the Central Intelligence Agency to fund clandestine operations against Cuba. One cocaine smuggler, a megalomaniacal neo-Nazi working with Pablo Escobar, bought his own island and deposited so much dirty cash that some Bahamian banks started charging him a 1 percent counting fee.

In 1967, a new Black prime minister, Lynden Pindling, evicted the Bay Street Boys from power. The corruption continued under his watch. A study in 1979 estimated that the "flow of criminal and tax evasion money" in the Bahamas was as much as $20 billion annually. But over the last twenty years, under pressure from the U.S. and Europe, the Bahamas has reluctantly signed information-sharing treaties and increased money-laundering enforcement. That wasn't good for business. Bank deposits started dropping. Then a new opportunity arrived in the form of crypto. In 2020, the country's legislature passed the "Digital Assets and Registered Exchanges Bill," one of the first laws in any country to move crypto out of a legal gray area and put it on equal footing with traditional finance. The Bahamas was ready for a new generation of "financial wizards."

Among the first to come was Sam Bankman-Fried, who relocated his crypto exchange from Hong Kong to the Bahamas in the fall of 2021. FTX made plans to build a $60 million headquarters, with space for a thousand employees and a boutique hotel for visitors. The location: an oceanside plot on West Bay Street.

"The Bahamas is now recognized internationally as having one of the strongest digital asset legislative frameworks in the world," Philip Davis, the current prime minister of the Bahamas, said in October

2021 at an event celebrating FTX's move. "The arrival of FTX is proof positive that we are headed in the right direction."

I ARRIVED IN February 2022, four months after the prime minister's speech. When I got into a taxi at the Nassau airport carrying an L.L.Bean backpack, the driver immediately pegged me as a crypto bro. "FTX, right?" he said, and he took me to the office park where FTX was based while the new headquarters were being built.

Bankman-Fried worked in one of a series of squat, one-story buildings with red roofs, built in a parking lot not far from the airport. Propeller planes periodically roared overhead. Inside, a few dozen coders and salespeople were crammed together at long desks, in front of banks of monitors. The workspaces were still marked with names on sticky notes, as if everyone was too busy making money to unpack. The walls were bare, other than a tacked-up skull-and-crossbones pirate flag.

I was chatting with Bankman-Fried's assistant in the kitchen when the billionaire shuffled in, shoeless, wearing white crew socks, blue shorts, and a gray FTX T-shirt. He grabbed a packet of microwavable chickpea korma, ripped it open, and started spooning it into his mouth, cold. The assistant reminded Bankman-Fried that I was a journalist who'd come to interview him. "Oh, hey," he said to me. He seemed so uninterested that I wasn't sure he'd even known I was coming. His assistant told him I'd be shadowing him the following day.

The next morning, I returned to the office in time to watch Bankman-Fried give a virtual talk at the Economic Club of New York. The 115-year-old organization had hosted kings, prime ministers, and presidents, as well as Amazon's Jeff Bezos and J.P. Morgan's Jamie Dimon. Central bankers' comments there moved markets. Now it was the twenty-nine-year-old boy king of crypto's turn.

Bankman-Fried spoke via Zoom, reclining on a gaming chair. I pulled up a chair and watched over his shoulder. If he was impressed to be joining such august company, he didn't show it. As he fielded questions from club members about how the United States should regulate his industry, he pulled up a fantasy game called *Storybook Brawl,* chose to play as "Peter Pants," and prepared for battle with someone who went by "Funky Kangaroo."

"We're anticipating a lot of growth in the United States," Bankman-Fried said as he cast a spell on one of the knights in his fairy-tale army.

The novelty of appearances like this had long since worn off for Bankman-Fried, who had testified before Congress twice since December. Earlier that morning he'd appeared on National Public Radio. As he ran through familiar talking points, my attention drifted over to his workspace, which was covered with the detritus of someone who more or less lived at the office. Littering his desk, I observed crumpled bills from the United States and Hong Kong, nine tubes of lip balm, a stick of deodorant, a 1.5-pound canister of sea salt labeled SBF'S SALT SHAKER, and the empty packet of chickpea korma he'd eaten in front of me the day before. The bean-bag chair where he famously slept sat so close to his desk he could practically roll onto it.

As I shadowed him that day, Bankman-Fried was so blasé about my presence that he let me read the kinds of messages that most executives protect like state secrets. His top Washington strategist wrote to say that Senator Cory Booker would sign on to his preferred approach to regulation. Billionaires and reporters for *The New York Times* and *Puck* sent messages asking for Bankman-Fried's time. That evening, his schedule showed, he was flying to Munich for a meeting with the prime minister of Georgia. At one point, Bankman-Fried fielded a message saying the money-transfer service MoneyGram was for sale for about $1 billion, and he spent a few seconds considering whether the company could be a good bet. His assistant informed him that the head of an investment bank was in the Bahamas and wanted to visit him for five minutes. "Meh," Bankman-Fried wrote back.

WHEN HE WAS finished with his talk to the Economic Club, Bankman-Fried pulled up an Excel spreadsheet that tracked his exchange's revenue. FTX, like its competitors, was simply a place where people could go to bet on the prices of cryptocurrencies. Each time someone bought a Dogecoin or sold a Cardano token on FTX's website, Bankman-Fried collected a tiny cut.

Bankman-Fried proudly showed me that the year before, those fees had added up to $1 billion. He showed me a graph indicating that his exchange was growing faster than its biggest rival, Binance. And he told me that taking over crypto was just the start.

"We're sort of playing in the kiddie pool," Bankman-Fried said. "Ideally, I would want FTX to become the biggest source of financial transactions in the world."

His friends had told me that for all his bluster, Bankman-Fried showed little interest in the trappings of his newfound wealth. One said he worked so hard that he rarely showered. When he wasn't sleeping at the office, he crashed at an apartment with ten or so colleagues. When I asked, Bankman-Fried told me that he didn't see much value in buying things.

"You pretty quickly run out of really effective ways to make yourself happier by spending money," he said. "I don't want a yacht."

But from what I was hearing, the word "yacht" was doing a lot of work in that sentence. The apartment he shared with his roommates was a penthouse at the island's most exclusive resort. And the weekend before my visit, he'd flown to Los Angeles on a private jet to attend the Super Bowl. Bankman-Fried told me that given how fast FTX was making money, the convenience was worth the cost.

Super Bowl weekend had been full of parties. Bankman-Fried said he didn't even know how or why he got invited to them. There was lunch with basketball legend Shaquille O'Neal and a party DJ'd by the head of Goldman Sachs. The singer Sia—whom he'd never met—invited him to a dinner at a Beverly Hills mansion, where he chatted about crypto with pop star Katy Perry. Amazon's Bezos and Leonardo DiCaprio were there too. Bizarrely, the actor Kate Hudson sang the national anthem before the meal. I asked if he'd had fun.

"I don't know if 'fun' is exactly the word I would use to describe it," Bankman-Fried said. "Parties are not my scene."

Perhaps Bankman-Fried's difficulty in having a good time was related to another one of the billionaire's traits that his friends had mentioned. They told me that no matter what Bankman-Fried was doing, he was constantly assessing the odds, costs, and benefits. Any decision could be boiled down to an "expected value," a term in probability that means the weighted average result, whether that was a move in a board-game marathon, a billion-dollar trade, or whether to chat with Bezos at a party. Bankman-Fried's goal was always to make as much money as possible, so that he could give it to charity. By this metric, even sleep was an unjustifiable luxury. The expected value of staying awake to trade was too high.

"Every minute you spend sleeping is costing you x-thousand dol-lars, and that directly means you can save this many less lives," Matt Nass, a childhood friend, told me.

LATER IN THE day, Bankman-Fried led me to a conference room where he tried to sit cross-legged on a couch, then stuck out his right leg and started tapping it aggressively. He'd blocked out time to speak with me, but he seemed uncomfortable without any screens to look at. As we talked, I noticed Bankman-Fried scratching a medicinal-looking patch on his arm. I thought it would be impolite to ask what it was. But he relaxed as we started talking about how he'd decided to become a hyperaggressive capitalist. His inspiration was an Australian moral philosopher named Peter Singer.

In 1971, Singer, then a student at the University of Oxford, began posing a deceptively simple ethical question: If you walked by a child drowning in a shallow pond, would you stop to pull her out, even if it would muddy your clothes? If you'd rescue the kid—and who wouldn't?—Singer would argue that you have no less of a duty to save any other child, if you have the means to. A donation to an interna-tional aid group could save a child from starvation, at little cost to yourself. Not making that donation is as bad as letting the child drown.

Singer's thought experiment, which he called "the Drowning Child," became influential within the school of philosophy known as utilitarian-ism. Utilitarians argue that the proper action is the one that maximizes the world's collective well-being. Bankman-Fried was practically raised to be one. His parents were both Stanford law professors, and dinners at their house in Palo Alto, California, often featured philosophical debate.

Choosing the proper action is not always as clear as it is in the Drowning Child. Should we kill one person if doing so would save the lives of five others? Is it justified to break the law if it's likely to help people? At one extreme, some utilitarians argue that a world with more humans is always better than one with fewer, even if overpopu-lation leads to unhappiness. The argument, called "the repugnant conclusion" by its detractors, is that all human lives are worth living, so more is better.

"When Sam was about fourteen, he emerged from his bedroom one evening and said to me, seemingly out of the blue, 'What kind of person dismisses an argument they disagree with by labeling it the Repugnant Conclusion?,'" his mother, Barbara Fried, wrote in the acknowledgments of her 2020 book, *Facing Up to Scarcity: The Logic and Limits of Nonconsequentialist Thought.*

Coming from a household like this, it's not surprising that Bankman-Fried was bored by his schoolwork. In high school, he competed in tournaments for the fantasy trading card game Magic: The Gathering, and organized math puzzle contests in which teams would race to solve a series of connected brain teasers. For the senior class prank, students reportedly made $100 bills with his face on them.

He did well enough in school to be admitted to MIT, where he had vague plans to study to be a physics professor. But he said he quickly realized he wasn't cut out for academic research. He joined a coed fraternity called Epsilon Theta, and moved into its yellow mansion in Brookline. There, instead of throwing keggers, members stayed up all night playing board games and slept in an attic full of bunk beds. "Think of a fraternity but replace all the alcohol with the nerdiest stuff you can imagine," one of Bankman-Fried's friends from the time told a reporter.

By then, Bankman-Fried had fully embraced utilitarianism. "I am a utilitarian," he wrote on his blog when he was twenty. "Basically, this means that I believe the right action is the one that maximizes total 'utility' in the world (you can think of that as total happiness minus total pain)." At MIT, he started thinking more about what that meant for how he should lead his life. He became a vegan and for a time he recruited other "Thetans" to hand out pamphlets for an anti-factory-farm group. Then, in 2012, Bankman-Fried went to a talk by Will MacAskill, a twenty-five-year-old doctoral student at Oxford who was trying to turn Singer's ideas into a movement. MacAskill and his collaborators aimed to use mathematical calculations to figure out how individuals could do the most good with their money and time. They dubbed their movement "effective altruism."

Over lunch at Au Bon Pain, MacAskill told Bankman-Fried about one of his ideas: "earning to give." He said that for someone of Bankman-Fried's mathematical talents, it might make sense to pursue a high-paying job on Wall Street, then donate his earnings to charity. Effective altruists calculated that a few thousand dollars spent on insecticide-treated bed nets in Africa could prevent one death from malaria. MacAskill estimated at the time that a successful banker who donated half their income could save ten thousand lives over the course of a career.

It was a controversial theory. Some argued that working as a banker would perpetuate inequality and undermine whatever good might be done by donations. The movement had also been criticized for painting the rich as heroes and failing to address the root causes of poverty. But MacAskill's pitch seemed like common sense to Bankman-Fried. When I spoke with MacAskill, he laughed when he remembered Bankman-Fried's matter-of-fact response: "He basically said, 'Yep, that makes sense.'"

Another young MacAskill acolyte had gone to work for Jane Street Capital, a stock trading firm. It was one of a handful of companies that had used mathematical models and computer programs to take over the business of making markets on Wall Street. Anytime someone bought or sold a share of a stock or exchange-traded fund, there was a decent chance Jane Street was on the other side. Entry-level jobs there paid around $200,000 annually.

Bankman-Fried secured an internship at the trading firm. And after graduation, he moved to New York to work there. He was a trader on the international ETF desk, which meant he spent his time developing and supervising computer algorithms that bought and sold stocks, trying to profit by predicting price movements or by earning the tiny spreads of a hundredth of a percentage point between buyers and sellers. He enjoyed the work and felt comfortable with his colleagues, who were mostly math nerds like him. They even competed in puzzle contests too.

Bankman-Fried said he gave away about half of his salary to animal-welfare groups and other effective-altruism-approved charities. He could see a future at the firm where his salary would rise into the millions and he'd become a big supporter of the movement. But after a few years, he started to think that career path was too conservative. His logic here is hard to follow for a non-utilitarian. Here he was, already on a glide path into the 1 percent, and he was thinking he should find something riskier to do. But, like he always did, Bankman-Fried evaluated the decision by expected value.

Expected value is a weighted average of potential outcomes. Let's posit that his Jane Street career was 100 percent sure to generate $10 million in lifetime earnings. That would be its expected value. Another option he considered was founding a start-up. That had, say, a

95 percent chance of failing and generating nothing. But if Bankman-Fried thought that it had even a 5 percent chance of turning into a billion-dollar unicorn, that would give it a much higher expected value: $50 million.

Bankman-Fried thought that it would be selfish for him to choose the less risky path, even if the alternative one was overwhelmingly likely to leave him with nothing. As a true utilitarian, he had to maximize the expected value.

"You should be willing to accept a substantial chance of failure," he told me. "Even once you are doing pretty well, often the best thing to do in terms of maximizing impact is not to settle for that."

Bankman-Fried considered working in politics, where he might create policies that would impact millions of people, or becoming a journalist, where a well-written story could influence the world's thinking on the most important issues. Then, in late 2017, he quit Jane Street, moved back to California, and took a job as director of business development for MacAskill's Centre for Effective Altruism. He said that his idea was that he could play an important role in getting the movement off the ground. But another possibility also caught his eye—one that would pull him right back into trading within a few weeks.

By then, crypto was in the middle of its first boom: the scammy initial coin offering craze. The prices of Bitcoin and hundreds of other recently created coins were spiking wildly. The CEO of the Centre for Effective Altruism, Tara Mac Aulay, had been playing around with trading strategies in her spare time. She showed Bankman-Fried some promising results. He didn't know much about crypto. What caught his attention was a page on CoinMarketCap.com that quoted prices from exchanges around the world.

Bankman-Fried saw that certain coins were selling for way more on some exchanges than others. This was the kind of buy-low, sell-high arbitrage opportunity he'd learned to exploit at Jane Street. At the firm, he'd built complex mathematical models for trades that aimed to make money off tiny price differences. On crypto exchanges, the discrepancies were hundreds of times bigger. It looked like free money, and it didn't require any special blockchain knowledge—click BUY on one website, hit SELL on another, and earn guaranteed returns.

"That's too easy," Bankman-Fried recalled thinking. "Something's wrong."

Bankman-Fried opened accounts at several exchanges and started trading with Mac Aulay. Many of the apparent arbitrages were in fact too good to be true. Some of the prices he'd seen were false, and others would disappear quickly. But enough trades did work that Bankman-Fried knew he was on to something. He rented a three-bedroom house in Berkeley, and started recruiting more friends to help.

They needed a coder to create the kind of trading systems they had at Jane Street. Bankman-Fried wasn't much of a programmer himself, but he knew a prodigy named Gary Wang. The two had met at a sleep-away math program in Oregon when they were teenagers. A year younger than Bankman-Fried, Wang had emigrated from China when he was eight. He grew up in Cherry Hill, New Jersey, a suburb of Philadelphia, where he taught himself to code and ranked among the top students in the United States in math contests. The duo reconnected at MIT, where Wang joined Bankman-Fried's frat. Wang was quiet and shy, happy to let Bankman-Fried take the lead on projects, like their team, *The Vegan Police,* in the annual Battlecode competition.

Wang, too, had become an effective altruist. After college, he had gone to work for Google as a software engineer, focused on flight data. In November 2017, Bankman-Fried told him that if they worked together on crypto, they could make and give away much more money. He became Bankman-Fried's trusted deputy and, later, FTX's chief technology officer.

Then there was Nishad Singh, a friend of Bankman-Fried's younger brother who'd been a regular guest at family dinners in Palo Alto. He was sincere, diligent, friendly, and a committed effective altruist. Singh was just a few months out of the University of California, Berkeley, and had just started a job at Facebook, but he bought into Bankman-Fried's pitch too. He started as a lower-level developer, but as the firm grew, his personality made him a natural fit to manage the other programmers.

A few months later, Bankman-Fried recruited another young mathlete whom he'd worked with at Jane Street. Her name was Caroline Ellison, and she was a soft-spoken redhead and a Harry Potter superfan. The daughter of MIT professors, she'd grown up in Newton, a suburb of Boston, where she was captain of the math team. Her effective-altruism awakening came at Stanford. Like Bankman-Fried, she liked to post online about weird utilitarian thought experiments, like whether a doctor should harvest a healthy patient's organs to save five sick ones. As an arbitrage trader, she caught on right away when Bankman-Fried explained the opportunities in crypto.

FOR THE NAME of their new company, Bankman-Fried and his friends wanted something innocuous to avoid setting off alarms at banks, many of which still preferred not to do business with cryptocurrency traders. They picked Alameda Research. "Especially in 2017, if you named your company like We Do Cryptocurrency Bitcoin Arbitrage Multinational Stuff, no one's going to give you a bank account," Bankman-Fried later told a reporter.

Everyone at Alameda pooled their savings to fund the firm and agreed to give the profits to charity. They were able to raise more funding from wealthy effective altruists. Alameda started making real money: about $500,000 in profits in November, then $4 million the next month. By the start of 2018, Bankman-Fried had about fifteen people trading out of his place at all hours. The kitchen was filled with standing desks, and a closet was reserved for naps.

There was one arbitrage in particular that Bankman-Fried wanted to take advantage of. On exchanges in Japan, Bitcoin generally traded at higher prices than on U.S. exchanges. If one Bitcoin cost $6,000 in the United States, it would go for the equivalent of $6,600 in yen in Japan. In theory, someone could earn a 10 percent return by buying a Bitcoin on a U.S. exchange, sending it to a Japanese one, selling it, and converting the yen back to dollars. That's an unheard-of return. At that rate, in a little more than four months, $10,000 would turn into $1 billion.

The main obstacles to the Japan arbitrage were practical. Sending that much money back and forth rapid-fire looked like money laundering to banks, and telling them it was actually cryptocurrency trading was hardly reassuring. It would only lead to Alameda getting its bank accounts closed, just like Giancarlo Devasini and Bitfinex. Bankman-Fried had so much trouble sending the money that he started calculating whether it made sense to charter a plane, fly to Japan, and have a planeload of people withdraw cash and bring it home. (It didn't.)

A Japanese grad student volunteered to help open accounts there. By January 2018, Alameda had managed to work out a janky combination of banks and wire transfers that worked. Each day became a race. If they didn't wire the money out of Japan before the branch closed, they'd miss out on that day's 10 percent return. Completing the cycle required the precision logistics of a heist movie. A team of people spent three hours a day camped out in a U.S. bank to ensure money transfers went through, and another team in Japan waited for hours to make sure they'd be at the front of the teller line when it was time to wire the money back. At the peak of the arbitrage, Alameda was generating a $1.5 million profit each day. The price difference only lasted for a few weeks. But before it disappeared, Alameda had earned about $15 million.

But in February, Alameda erased nearly all those gains. The firm lost millions of dollars on a few poorly designed trades. And it was sending so many transfers from exchange to exchange that $3 million of coins were simply misplaced. Its biggest backer asked for his money back. Mac Aulay and about half of Alameda's employees quit, blaming Bankman-Fried for the mistakes. Among their complaints were that he was a bad manager, failed to keep track of important details, and was so aggressive about trying to make a giant score that he overlooked what could have been consistent profits.

Later in 2018, Bankman-Fried went to a Bitcoin conference in Macau where he met some of the other big players in the market. Most of them were located in Asia. He realized he'd be able to make more connections and boost his trading if he moved there too. He told his colleagues on Slack that he wouldn't be returning to Berkeley. Eventually, many of them joined him in Hong Kong.

There was another benefit of moving to Hong Kong: It had more permissive crypto regulations than the United States. Most of the largest crypto exchanges, like Bitfinex and Binance, were based outside the United States. Once Bankman-Fried and his colleagues left California, they decided to build their own. They called it FTX.

It took Bankman-Fried's team four months to write the code for a new exchange. It opened for business in May 2019. By then, the ICO boom had turned into a bust, but there was still plenty of crypto trading going on. The marketplaces that people used to buy and sell tokens were in a sorry state. They were buggy, frequently crashing when prices plummeted or spiked. Bitfinex, of course, had lost half its Bitcoins in a hack only a few years earlier. And another one of the largest exchanges, BitMEX, was under U.S. investigation.

Word quickly spread among professional crypto traders about the new exchange. FTX was a hit. It had complex derivatives, like tokens with built-in leverage or index futures, and even bets on elections and stock prices. It offered margin loans, so traders could ramp up their returns. By the time of my visit, the exchange was generating about a million dollars a day in profit, Bankman-Fried told me. And Alameda hadn't stopped trading. He said that his crypto hedge fund made an additional $1 billion in profit in 2021.

Owning an exchange (FTX) and a firm that trades on it (Alameda) was an obvious conflict of interest. On Wall Street it wouldn't have been allowed, due to the risk that the trading firm would be given preferential treatment or access to confidential information. But Bankman-Fried assured me, and others who asked, that Alameda played by the same rules as other traders. Caroline Ellison and another young trader had been appointed co-CEOs of Alameda, and Bankman-Fried told me he now worked solely on FTX.

In September 2021, Bankman-Fried relocated to the Bahamas. He uprooted the company again partly because Hong Kong required a lengthy quarantine for anyone who left the territory. While Ellison and some traders stayed behind, most of his crew of crypto pirates followed him to the Caribbean.

CHAPTER TEN

Imagine a
Robin Hood Thing

By the time I arrived in Nassau, in February 2022, Sam Bankman-Fried was swimming in money. He was just four years removed from his days of trading in his Berkeley crash pad. But the previous month, FTX had raised $800 million from venture capitalists, at a new $32 billion valuation, just three months after raising $420.69 million. The weed-sex number was picked on purpose, to turn an investment round into a juvenile joke.

He was developing a public profile as the boy genius of crypto, the man who was going to take the industry mainstream. Compared to the self-styled crypto prophets like Tether co-founder Brock Pierce, or the hucksters like Celsius's Alex Mashinsky, Bankman-Fried seemed grounded in reality when he went on TV to talk about the boom. He was comfortable discussing numbers with Wall Street traders or public policy with congressional staffers. And his style gave him an air of authenticity. When a colleague suggested he cut his hair, Bankman-Fried refused.

"I honestly think it's negative EV for me to cut my hair," Bankman-Fried said, citing expected value as always, according to the colleague's memory of the conversation. "I think it's important for people to think I look crazy."

Bankman-Fried seemed to be spending the money as fast as it came in, mostly on marketing. FTX signed a $135 million contract to name the Miami Heat's arena after his crypto exchange and a $210 million deal to sponsor a professional video-gaming team, and signed up a slew of professional athletes as endorsers, including Shaquille O'Neal and Tom Brady. Just a few days before my visit, the exchange had aired an ad during the Super Bowl, at an estimated cost of about

$20 million. It featured *Curb Your Enthusiasm*'s Larry David as a time-traveling Luddite who scoffs at major inventions in human history—from the wheel, to toilets, to the Walkman. When he's presented with FTX's cryptocurrency trading app, he says, "Ehh, I don't think so." The text reads, "Don't be like Larry. Don't miss out on the next big thing."

Sitting across from Bankman-Fried and listening to him talk about effective altruism, I couldn't help thinking that pushing people to gamble seemed at odds with his pledge to have a positive impact on the world. Bankman-Fried was a sophisticated trader, and he acknowledged to me that many cryptocurrencies had unsustainably high prices, and that some were scams. But here he was, telling regular people to drop what they were doing, open an FTX account, and start clicking BUY.

"Aren't you leading people to probably not do that well financially?" I asked.

Bankman-Fried, unconvincingly, tried to argue the ad was only intended to raise FTX's profile, not to get people to sign up and trade. And even if some people did, he said, they could pick the best cryptocurrencies by doing their own online research. This sounded like a cop-out to me.

"But can the average person really even do this research?" I asked.

"Well, who do you think *is* doing their research?" he said.

"I don't know," I said.

"Is anyone?" he said.

"You tell me," I said.

THERE WAS ONE other thing that was incongruous with Bankman-Fried's public image: the itty-bitty matter of U.S. law. If Bankman-Fried had stayed in Berkeley, many of the bets FTX offered would've been not quite legal. Or entirely, deeply illegal. Nearly all the coins it listed would have been deemed unregistered securities offerings, like MasterCoin. The exchange itself didn't comply with SEC trading rules either.

FTX opened a U.S. exchange with a limited menu of tokens to trade. And Bankman-Fried set his sights on molding U.S. regulations to his liking. He told me he wanted the United States to adopt rules that would effectively legalize all the coins traded on FTX but also require crypto companies to disclose some financial information, like public companies do on the stock market. He said it was in the best interests of the crypto industry and the public to allow for innovation while reining in the worst of the scams.

In the previous two years, Bankman-Fried had become one of Washington's biggest political donors. He gave $5 million to a committee supporting Joe Biden in the 2020 presidential election, and FTX and its executives spread around at least $90 million in campaign contributions, making them one of the biggest donors for the 2022 midterm elections. Most went to Democrats, but FTX executives also gave at least $20 million to Republicans. One in three members of Congress received donations.

If Bankman-Fried was trying to buy his way to a new version of U.S. regulations that favored him and boxed out his competitors, it seemed to be working. In Washington, he was treated like a financial innovator, not a crypto pirate. A week before our meeting in Nassau, he'd testified at a congressional hearing, offering advice about how the industry should be regulated. Senator Cory Booker, who'd received a $5,700 donation, fawned over him, even joking: "I'm offended you have a much more glorious Afro than I once had."

WHEN I ASKED about his philanthropy, Bankman-Fried told me he gave away $50 million in 2021, including money directed to pandemic relief in India and anti-global-warming initiatives. It didn't seem like a lot to me for one of the richest people in the world, even if most of his net worth was tied up in the valuation of FTX and not easily accessible.

It made me think of something he'd said on a podcast two months earlier. In that interview, Bankman-Fried had criticized the way many rich people give money away, calling it "doing things which seem kind of good-ish and also are sort of like weird brand-building exercises." I figured he'd gotten at least $50 million worth of good press for his donations.

When I put that to Bankman-Fried, he said that only time would demonstrate the sincerity of his intentions. He said that in the coming year he planned to donate at least a few hundred million and up to $1 billion, as much as the largest foundations.

"I think that hopefully puts it at a stage where it would be like an insane thing to do for PR," he said.

As had happened with some other effective altruists, Bankman-Fried's attention had drifted from the movement's initial focus on charities with easily measurable impact, like malaria-prevention groups. Instead, he told me, he was most interested in combating threats that could lead to humanity's extinction, like terrorist-engineered bioweapons and artificial intelligence gone rogue. They sounded like science-fiction plotlines. But in his view, something that had even a tiny chance of saving the lives of the trillions of people who might live in future generations could be more valuable than alleviating suffering today. His top priority was pandemic preparedness.

"We should expect that pandemics will get worse over time and more frequent, just because of the possibility of lab leaks," he said. "This has a nontrivial chance of destabilizing the world if we don't get prepared for it."

BANKMAN-FRIED SPOKE LIKE he really believed he could save the world. But it seemed like his philosophy would justify doing almost anything to make money. I wondered where he would draw the line. Why not run a scam, and spread the proceeds around to epidemiologists and A.I. safety researchers? The biggest of the ICOs raised $4 billion, enough to fund work that could save millions of lives. Looking at it from a utilitarian perspective, the gain in total happiness from preventing those deaths would clearly outweigh the pain for the people who lost money.

"You've built up a good reputation," I said, needling him a bit. "You could probably run some crypto scam and make a few billion dollars right now. By your logic, wouldn't that make sense?"

"Charities don't want that money," he said. "Reputation is so important for everything you do. And as soon as you start to think about the second-order effects, it starts to look worse and worse."

When I thought about it more, his answer did make sense. Getting caught running a scam would sink FTX, which was valued at $32 billion already. Setting the law aside, an honest business was the better play. But there was a flaw in my logic that I didn't spot at the time. Scammers don't plan on getting caught.

·　·　·

MOST EXECUTIVES WOULDN'T have entertained questions about running a hypothetical fraud. But even the bluntest queries seemed to simply set the gears in Bankman-Fried's mind spinning. He generated analytical, even clinical responses to almost anything. He seemed like he was observing his own life from afar, weighing the expected value of each of his decisions. It seemed like he gave his own happiness little weight in those equations.

In fact, one of his friends had told me that Bankman-Fried was unhappy, despite all his success. He said Bankman-Fried had broken up with a girlfriend to have more time for work. When I asked him about this, Bankman-Fried told me it was true.

"I can't promise to be there for someone in the way that I think most people would want me to be able to," he said. "There's always things I need to be doing in the background and responding to and mulling over in my head."

I asked Bankman-Fried whether he'd ever consider leading his life a different way. He pressed his face in his hands for a few seconds before answering. "It's not a decision that I constantly reevaluate, because I think it just doesn't do me any good to be ·constantly reevaluating anything," he said. "It doesn't, minute to minute, feel to me like a decision anymore."

I WANTED TO interview Bankman-Fried's inner circle, to gain more insight into his trustworthiness. But I didn't see Gary Wang, the coder, at his desk. I heard he liked to arrive at work in the evening and work through the night. And Caroline Ellison was in Hong Kong, like usual, running the hedge fund Alameda.

The only one I spotted was Nishad Singh, who'd taken the title of FTX's head of engineering. He sat at the desk to the right of Bankman-Fried. I pulled him aside for an interview. He was twenty-six years old, only a few years removed from University of California, Berkeley. He looked chubby compared to photos I'd seen of him as a teenager, when he set an ultramarathon running record. When I asked if he still ran, he patted his belly. "Do I look like I do?" he joked, adding that he didn't have time for anything other than work.

Singh seemed grounded and humble for someone I figured was likely a billionaire. And he really won me over when, after I asked him about his favorite crypto stories, he pulled out his phone and read out loud from something I'd written. After an hour of chatting, I decided to level with Singh. I told him that it seemed clear that people would lose money gambling in his crypto casino. But I could see how the harm to investors—likely first-world gamblers who could afford it—might be outweighed by the donations FTX made to, say, anti-malaria charities.

Singh nodded along.

"Oh sure," he said. "You could imagine a Robin Hood thing."

But I wasn't sure that Bankman-Fried really would give his money away. In my experience, philanthropy held little appeal for shady financiers. I told Singh I'd gotten to know many scammers through my reporting. I'd even suggested to some of them that they might be happier if they gave the proceeds to charity. None of them had.

"The mean people that do the scams, they don't want to give it away," I said. "They just buy some house or something, and then they sit there, and they're sad."

"Yeah, I agree," he said. "I mean, frankly, this was like a worry of mine. Like I only know my internal world and my internal head and heart."

Singh said he trusted that Bankman-Fried was serious about effective altruism. Both of them had been giving away much of their money since their first jobs. And, he argued, it wouldn't make sense for Bankman-Fried to make such a big deal about his plan if he didn't intend to follow through.

"That'd be like a really weird way to sort of like wreck your reputation," he said.

AROUND 5:00 P.M. on the day of his talk to the Economic Club, Bankman-Fried crashed, passing out first in his gaming chair, then curling up on the blue beanbag next to his desk, his elbow cradling his curly hair. The office was quiet, other than the clicking of employees chatting on Slack. Behind him, a programmer examined some code, his feet up on his desk and his shorts stained with soy sauce from lunch. During Bankman-Fried's catnap, traders swapped about $500 million of Bitcoin, Dogecoin, Tether, and other cryptocurrencies on his exchange, and FTX skimmed off $100,000 in fees. After about an hour, Bankman-Fried stirred, ate a package of Nutter Butters, then closed his eyes again. I saw myself out.

DURING ONE OF my conversations with Bankman-Fried, I had managed to work in some questions about Tether. Some people had speculated that Tether's reserves might include IOUs from FTX or Alameda, but he assured me again that wasn't the case. He said Alameda had sent the company billions of dollars, so he knew at least some of the reserves were real.

"The people saying that it's like not backed or fraudulent or is a Ponzi scheme, I think they're basically wrong," he said. "It is backed. It is almost certainly backed."

He told me that Tether was basically bad at public relations, but that the guys behind it were perfectly trustworthy. I wondered if he knew anything about their backgrounds. Had he read the New York attorney general's lawsuit, and seen the texts between Giancarlo Devasini and his Israeli money launderer at Crypto Capital? I asked him why we should believe them, when they'd lied in the past.

"I think that's fair," he said. "There is no transparency or oversight or system or even long track record to feel confident that, like, it will not become a big problem in the future."

Bankman-Fried tried to assure me that Tether's portfolio was pretty solid. He said that in a worst-case scenario, Tether's assets might still be worth 90 cents on the dollar. This actually seemed like cause for concern to me—Who would want to buy Tethers for a dollar if they weren't worth that much?—but he acted nonchalant.

"There's a lot of weird stuff in there," he said. "If they had to market-sell all of it into cash tomorrow, it's not the most liquid shit in the world."

I FELT LIKE I wasn't getting anywhere. I already knew Tether had a lot of weird stuff in its portfolio, and so did the rest of the crypto world. As risky as that seemed, it hadn't set off a run on the stablecoin. In fact, by then, Tether had grown to 79 billion coins. And it was becoming clear that Bankman-Fried was a big enough user of Tether that he wasn't likely to tell me if something worse was going on. The short

sellers and conspiracy theorists kept promising to reveal some big secret, but it hadn't happened. As far as I knew, the federal bank-fraud
investigation hadn't advanced at all. And though I kept researching
Tether's holdings from the document I'd obtained, that hadn't turned
up any leads either.

But while I was in the Bahamas interviewing Bankman-Fried, a bizarre story was unfolding back in the United States that promised to
reveal new information about the people behind Tether. Prosecutors
in Washington, D.C., said they'd tracked down the people who'd gotten their hands on the Bitcoins that were stolen from Devasini's exchange, Bitfinex, back in 2016. Because the price of Bitcoin had
climbed so much since the hack, the stolen coins were now worth $4.5
billion, making the heist the largest of any kind in history.

The funds were not in the possession of shadowy North Koreans or
some other group of cyberterrorists. The stolen billions were traced to
a couple in their early thirties who lived in downtown Manhattan, not
far from my place in Brooklyn. Their names were Ilya Lichtenstein and
Heather Morgan. Judging from social media, the two didn't exactly
appear to be criminal geniuses.

Lichtenstein, who went by "Dutch," had curly hair and an impish
grin, like a baby-faced Elijah Wood. He seemed very fond of the couple's Bengal cat, Clarissa. Morgan's thing was music—extravagantly
bad music that she wrote, performed, and released in videos on You-
Tube and TikTok. In one, she danced and pretended a toy reptile was
her penis. In another, she gyrated down the streets of the Financial
District wearing a gold track jacket, a fanny pack, and a flat-brimmed
hat reading OFCKS. She called herself the "motherfucking crocodile of
Wall Street." In one song, she even bragged about her hacking skills:
"Spearphish your password / All your funds transferred." Her rap
name was "Razzlekhan."

If these two were able to get ahold of Devasini's money, why should
Tether customers trust him with $79 billion? I decided to dig in.

CHAPTER ELEVEN

"Let's Get Weird"

The hackers had been inside the Bitfinex servers for weeks before attempting the heist. Throughout the summer of 2016, they'd watched users on the cryptocurrency exchange buy and sell Bitcoins. They'd studied the commands that controlled the security system. It was as if they were hiding in an air duct above a bank's vault, watching as tellers meticulously moved cash in and out, looking for vulnerabilities.

They weren't after Bitcoins, exactly. You can't really steal a line in a spreadsheet. What they needed were the private keys: cryptographic passwords that would allow them to unlock the coins. With the keys, they could lower the number on Bitfinex's line in the giant Bitcoin spreadsheet to zero, and write a very big number on their own line.

Once they found the keys, they struck. At 10:26 A.M. on August 2, 2016, the hackers raised the exchange's daily withdrawal limit from 2,500 Bitcoins to 1 million, more than enough to empty out the whole vault. Then, using the private keys, they started broadcasting instructions to transfer Bitfinex's Bitcoins to addresses they controlled on the blockchain. Over the next three hours and fifty-one minutes, the hackers stole 119,754 coins—more than half of the exchange's Bitcoins.

When Bitfinex executives realized what had happened, they hired a security team to search the servers' memory for clues. The hack was ambitious and sophisticated, and some users suspected an inside job. Others suggested the culprits were part of North Korea's elite hacking corps, which, six months earlier, had stolen $81 million from Bangladesh's central bank. But the researchers had little to go on. Before logging off, the hackers had effectively wiped their digital fingerprints.

The only information Bitfinex had was the 34-character addresses on the blockchain where the hackers sent the money. In an attempt to get help from the public, the company put those addresses on the internet for all to see. But for years, most of the funds stayed in those digital wallets, more or less untouched, even as Bitcoin went from being a nerdy curiosity to fueling a global mania. The money was sitting right there, but there was no obvious way to figure out who'd taken it. And without the hackers' private keys, there was no way for police to get it back.

AROUND 2020, AN Internal Revenue Service agent working from his basement in Grand Rapids, Michigan, found a clue. People had once assumed that cryptocurrencies were untraceable, because the blockchain doesn't record users' names. But the way the blockchain database works, transaction records are never erased. And while it doesn't record names, it does assign a unique address to each wallet. If any wallet can be tied to a specific individual, then an investigator can easily see every transaction that person has ever made.

Investigators could tie a person to an address by making a purchase from them, just as they might buy drugs from a dealer before arresting them; or they could watch for transfers to exchanges, like Bankman-Fried's FTX, then send subpoenas to the exchange for user records. Once the FBI busted Silk Road, the dark-web drug market, it was able to track down many of the dealers on the site. As the writer Andy Greenberg explained, "Bitcoin had turned out to be practically the *opposite* of untraceable: a kind of honeypot for crypto criminals that had, for years, dutifully and unerasably recorded evidence of their dirty deals."

It wasn't easy, but the IRS agent followed pieces of the Bitfinex money through a convoluted trail of addresses and exchanges. That's what led him to the New York City couple, Ilya Lichtenstein and Heather Morgan.

MORGAN, THEN THIRTY-ONE, was the founder of a small copywriting business called SalesFolk. She was living with Lichtenstein in a $6,500-per-month high-rise apartment at 75 Wall Street, in New York's Financial District. In her TikTok posts, the apartment was stuffed with knickknacks, including a crocodile skull, a camel figurine, and an item she described only as "Ukrainian sewer rocks." A zebra pelt hung on the wall near a zebra-striped elliptical trainer. Two long-horned antelope skulls were mounted there too, along with a framed X-ray of Morgan's lungs from when she contracted MERS in Egypt.

She portrayed herself as an always hustling, rule-breaking tech disrupter. She wrote a regular column for *Forbes;* her author bio read: "When she's not reverse-engineering black markets to think of better ways to combat fraud and cybercrime, she enjoys rapping and designing streetwear fashion." Or, as she put it in her song "Versace Bedouin": "I'm many things. / A rapper, an economist, a journalist, / a writer, a CEO, / and a dirty, dirty, dirty, dirty ho."

As a performer, Razzlekhan was both hypersexual and aggressively unappealing. She alternated jokes about diarrhea and sex with boasts about her edgy business practices. Her signature move, if you can call it that, was to throw up her hand with her fingers split into a "V," stick out her tongue, and say, "Razzle Dazzle!" Then she would make a loud phlegmy cough.

Her songs, from "Pho King Badd Bhech" to "Gilfalicious," were full of painfully forced rhymes, with a delivery so stilted she made Chet Hanks sound like Kendrick Lamar. Her lyrics were nonsensical. In "High in the Cemetery," she describes a hallucination in which she's given a magic lamp and meets a genie who offers to fulfill her wishes in exchange for "a handie." Only later does she learn the genie's true identity: "This was no ordinary perv / It was Mark Zuckerberg."

In her *Forbes* columns and self-help YouTube videos, Morgan explained that she created her rap persona as a way to embrace the weirdness that used to make her a target of ridicule. She'd grown up in a small town of about four hundred people outside Chico, California, where she was "bullied mercilessly" about her lisp and braces. While at the University of California at Davis, she studied abroad in South Korea and Turkey. After graduating, she found a home among the backpacker set, first in Hong Kong, then Cairo. Friends remembered her being a fan of the satirical rappers Lil Dicky and the Lonely Island and spontaneously breaking into freestyles.

"When she meets someone, it's like they're forever her friend," said Amina Amoniak, who stayed in touch with Morgan after meeting her through the website Couchsurfing.com.

. . .

MORGAN MET LICHTENSTEIN around 2013 in San Francisco. She'd moved there to work at a start-up that was going through an accelerator, and he was serving as a mentor for the program. I found traces of their early flirting on LinkedIn, where Lichtenstein left Morgan a recommendation. "Heather crafts precisely targeted messaging that sticks in customers' brains like a finely sharpened meat hook," he wrote. One friend told a reporter he remembered Lichtenstein trying to lure a drunken Morgan out of a bar around that time. Another recalled Morgan saying something unusual when she introduced her to Lichtenstein.

"This is Ilya," the friend remembered Morgan saying. "He's a black-hat hacker."

Lichtenstein was born in Russia and grew up in Chicago, where his parents had moved to avoid religious persecution. He was about five-foot-eight and had thick, wavy black hair. Friends described him as weird and nerdy. "Nice kid. Smart. Would be like if McLovin from *Superbad* ended up pulling off the heist," a high school classmate told a reporter.

While at the University of Wisconsin–Madison, he discovered a shady business known as "affiliate marketing," where people buy ad space in bulk on Facebook or Google and craft ads for diet pills, brain boosters, and offshore gambling sites. Lichtenstein claimed in forum posts that he made more than $100,000 a year from affiliate marketing while he was still a student.

I'd written an exposé about affiliate marketing a few years earlier, and it turned out that one of my sources had done business with Lichtenstein. The source, Ryan Eagle, had been a teenager at the time. He was also from suburban Chicago. He'd made a fortune with online ads like Lichtenstein's and had acquired a chrome-covered Bentley, iced-out watches, a diamond-encrusted chain-mail mask—and a nasty drug habit. He told me that even in an industry full of obnoxious bros, Lichtenstein's intelligence and arrogance stood out.

"He was one of these fucking nerds that tries to get under your skin," Eagle, who's now sober, said.

After graduation, Lichtenstein co-founded an advertising technology company, then left it in 2016, around the time of the hack, for reasons he never explained. On social media, he and Morgan posted photos from business class flights to Hong Kong and Mexico. In Morgan's TikTok videos, he often seems like a grudging participant. "You keep filming me, expecting something to happen, what do you want me to do? You want me to shove something up my ass and do a little dance?" he says in one video, after Morgan asks him about his habit of tasting Clarissa's cat chow. ("It needs salt, it needs pepper, but other than that it's pretty good," he says.)

And in what was either an unfortunate coincidence or another stunning act of hubris, on the day before the hack Morgan posted a photo on Instagram of her and Lichtenstein sitting on a blue plush couch, with the caption "I will always love getting into trouble with this crazy guy."

IT SEEMED UNLIKELY that someone who tried to rhyme "Razzlekhan's the name" with "that hot grandma you really wanna bang" could in fact be a master thief. Then again, this was the crypto world, where a lack of experience or competence has never been a barrier to fame and fortune, and where large-scale hacks are a regular occurrence.

Asked why he robbed banks, the famed bank robber Willie Sutton supposedly said, "Because that's where the money is." But these days, with the rise in electronic payments, the average branch might hold as little as $50,000. And bulletproof barriers, dye packs, timer locks, and high-resolution security cameras have largely made bank robberies a relic of the past.

Meanwhile, crypto has created whole new categories of crime. Take ransomware, in which hackers break into a corporate or government computer system, lock it, and demand payment to restore access. The idea has been around since at least the 1990s. But paying with wire transfers or credit card made it relatively easy to catch the perpetrators. Crypto solved that problem. By 2020, hackers were taking in more than $600 million worth of crypto a year in ransom payments.

Another is hacking exchanges. An exchange like Bitfinex or FTX is like a bank for cryptocurrencies. Each one holds huge sums of coins. And to steal them, a thief doesn't need to risk a trigger-happy security guard or hide their face from cameras. All that's needed is to break into a computer system, many of which are apparently not very well guarded.

Mt. Gox, the first big crypto exchange, was hacked, of course. And the hacks didn't stop after Bitfinex was robbed. Among the biggest: Coincheck was taken for $530 million in 2018 and KuCoin for about $250 million in 2020. In 2021, a total of $3.2 billion in cryptocurrency was stolen from exchanges and decentralized finance (or DeFi) apps, in which crypto traders make deals directly with one another. That's a hundred times more than the total stolen in all bank robberies in an average year in the United States. Much of the money was taken by North Korea's Lazarus hacker group.

BACK IN 2015, Bitfinex had set up a new security system after it lost about $400,000 of cryptocurrencies in a hack. Other exchanges generally mixed users' coins together and stored the private keys on computers that weren't connected to the internet, a practice known as "cold storage." Bitfinex's new system kept each user's balance in a separate address on the blockchain, allowing customers to see for themselves where their money was. It used software from the crypto-security company BitGo.

"This new level of transparency and security makes breaches such as those of Mt. Gox impossible," Mike Belshe, BitGo's CEO, said in a press release announcing the deal.

The BitGo software was programmed to automatically approve transfers under a certain limit, so small withdrawals wouldn't be delayed, but it required a Bitfinex executive to manually sign off on large ones. This was supposed to mean that if Bitfinex got hacked, only a small number of Bitcoins would be stolen at most. But the system configuration was flawed. The limit could be changed with a computer command sent by someone with a Bitfinex executive's electronic credentials.

That's what the hackers did after first using a "remote-access Trojan" to infiltrate the exchange. Such malware lets attackers gain full control of a target's computer, as if they were sitting at the keyboard. The hackers were only stopped when someone at Bitfinex happened to check account balances and noticed something was off.

Bitfinex reported the hack to authorities, but there were no leads. The hackers erased the servers' memory on their way out, wiping any pointers to their location. Ledger Labs, which investigated the breach on behalf of Bitfinex, was unable to determine how exactly the hackers got into the exchange's servers. BitGo has maintained that its software functioned properly, though it changed its rules so that withdrawal limits could only be raised after a video call with a BitGo employee.

Michael Shaulov, a former coder for the Israeli Intelligence Corps and co-founder of the crypto-security firm Fireblocks, told me hacks like these generally don't require a high level of technical expertise. Often, he said, the hardest part is crafting an email that tricks an insider into opening a malicious attachment. "The social-engineering vector is key," he said.

THAT SEEMED LIKE a clue. In 2019, Heather Morgan had given a talk titled "How to Social Engineer Your Way Into Anything" at an event called NYC Salon. In a promotional flyer for the speech, she posed in a tight, snakeskin-print metallic dress while holding a large pipe wrench. "I hate the term 'manipulating,'" she said in the talk, after attempting to warm up the bemused crowd by rapping a few lines from "Versace Bedouin." Social engineering, she said, involves "getting someone to share information or take an action that they otherwise would not."

On the day of the hack, a Bitfinex employee logged in to the main Bitcoin forum on Reddit and posted all the addresses where the hackers had sent stolen Bitcoins. It didn't look like much—it was just a list of thousands of 34-character codes. But it was like setting off a dye pack to mark the money in a bank robber's bag of loot.

All transactions on the Bitcoin blockchain are public, so anyone can look up an address and see all the other addresses it sent coins to or received coins from. Few people would accept Bitcoins from the addresses Bitfinex had disclosed on Reddit. Even if they had no qualms with stolen money, they'd be concerned about whether they could spend it themselves—or if they'd become suspects.

For five months the stolen Bitcoins didn't move. It seemed the hackers had forgotten a crucial part of their plan: To actually use the Bitcoins they'd stolen, they'd have to find a way to erase their connection to the hack. One place where stolen Bitcoins were welcome was AlphaBay. It was a dark-web marketplace, one of many successors to Silk Road, where users posted classified ads offering opioids, guns, and stolen credit cards in exchange for crypto. On its website, Alpha-

Bay said it wanted to be "the largest eBay-style underworld market-place." In case anyone missed the point, its FAQ had the question "Is AlphaBay Market legal?" Answer: "Of course not."

In January 2017, about $22,000 worth of the hacked Bitcoins were moved to AlphaBay in a series of small transactions. All Bitcoins sent to AlphaBay were mixed together, making them harder to connect to wherever they'd come from on the blockchain. Once a user withdrew their funds to a new address, their Bitcoins could be traced back only as far as AlphaBay. Although all the major exchanges were unwilling to accept Bitcoins that had come from addresses associated with the hack, some smaller exchanges were willing to take coins that came from a dark-web drug bazaar.

From AlphaBay, those hacked Bitcoins were sent to one crypto exchange, then another. The second exchange account was opened by Lichtenstein, using his real name. He'd even sent in a selfie to verify his identity. The only person who'd know the connection between Lichtenstein and the hacked funds would be the person running AlphaBay, who went only by "Alpha02."

Unfortunately for the thieves, AlphaBay was already the target of a separate investigation. Police from several countries thought they'd figured out that Alpha02 was a twenty-five-year-old Canadian named Alexandre Cazes, who'd moved to Thailand and bought three properties, a Lamborghini, and a Porsche with his profits. Among his mistakes: On some early messages he used an address, Pimp_Alex_91@ hotmail.com, that was connected to his real name.

On July 5, 2017, the investigators put in motion what they called Operation Bayonet. Royal Thai Police rammed a car into the front gate of a compound in Bangkok where they and U.S. authorities suspected Cazes was living. The commotion lured him out, and, while police detained him, other agents rushed inside. Cazes was arrested and died in prison a week later in an apparent suicide. But he left behind lots of evidence. Inside his compound, police found his laptop, open and logged in to AlphaBay.

Among the U.S. federal agents who'd traveled to Bangkok for the AlphaBay bust was Chris Janczewski, then thirty-three and a special agent with the IRS. Strange as it sounds, Janczewski had wanted to work for the IRS ever since a special agent had visited his accounting fraternity at Central Michigan University. The speaker had regaled Janczewski and his fellow aspiring accountants with stories of high-speed chases and kicking in doors. But at his first job there were no chases and no doors to kick in—just audits of a bunch of plumbers and car dealers in and around Charlotte, North Carolina. "As you can imagine, people aren't super excited that you're there," Janczewski told me.

In 2015 he was recruited to a new cybercrime unit in Washington. The team of about a dozen agents first focused on hacked data used to commit tax fraud. Then they shifted to cryptocurrency cases. The agents realized that while the blockchain was anonymous and criminals often shuffled their coins from wallet to wallet, the trail of transactions almost always led to an exchange, which would ask for identification before allowing someone to sell their Bitcoins for cash. Even if the crooks used an intermediary or a fake ID, they would leave clues. All the agents had to do was follow the transactions long enough. "Eventually everybody screws up," Tigran Gambaryan, another former member of the IRS cybercrime unit, told me.

Crypto tracing led Janczewski and his colleagues to drug dealers, money-laundering services, and even a site that had been selling child abuse videos. With each bust, they gathered data that allowed them to link more crimes to more Bitcoin addresses, and more Bitcoin addresses to more people.

Janczewski wouldn't tell me when he and his colleagues made the connection between the stolen Bitcoins and Lichtenstein and Morgan, nor discuss other details of the hack investigation. But by 2020, legal filings show, they had started the painstaking process of turning leads into evidence usable in court. They sent legal requests to exchanges that touched the stolen funds and to the internet service providers that the couple used. It took more than a year to gather enough evidence to justify a search warrant.

FEDERAL AGENTS FIRST arrived at 75 Wall Street at 3:00 A.M. one morning in 2021. "We're picking up signals that someone in this building is trafficking child pornography," one said to the startled doorman, according to *Vanity Fair*. "We need to go up to the roof to see if we can track where the signal is coming from."

They returned after a few weeks and then a third time a few weeks after that. "You sure you're in the right building?" the doorman asked. (At the time, police were investigating the death of a prostitute in the tower across the street—surveillance video had shown men rolling a 55-gallon drum that concealed her dead body out of the building.) The agents assured him they were.

On January 5, 2022, Janczewski and other federal agents returned. It was a cold and wet morning. This time, they took the freight elevator to the thirty-third floor and knocked on Morgan's door. Her parents were visiting and had brought a batch of her favorite persimmon cookies, baked by her grandmother. As the agents started looking for phones and computers, she and Lichtenstein said they wanted to leave the apartment and take their cat Clarissa with them. Then, Morgan clumsily attempted to create a diversion.

She said the cat was hiding under their bed and crouched down next to a nightstand. While calling for Clarissa, she grabbed a phone off the nightstand and started frantically hitting the lock button. Janczewski pulled it from her hands.

Under the bed, the agents found a bin full of electronics, including a ziplock bag labeled BURNER PHONE and a red-and-white-striped toiletries bag holding nine more phones. They seized at least four hardware wallets—thumb drives that hold the cryptographic passwords to a user's Bitcoins—and a pocketbook stuffed with $40,000 in cash. In Lichtenstein's office, they found two books that had been hollowed out to create hidden cavities. The couple had a brief conversation in Russian, which Morgan had been studying. None of the agents understood it.

After an initial search of their electronic devices, the agents hadn't found the private keys to the stolen Bitcoins. They didn't have enough evidence to arrest the couple.

Five days after the search, Morgan released a new song, "Moon n Stars." Over a spooky-sounding drum-and-organ beat, Razzlekhan rapped for five and a half minutes about her connection with Lichtenstein—their shared weirdness, his green eyes and "nice bottom," and their inside jokes, such as how he always keeps snacks in his pockets or how they both can't drive. She said she didn't want a regular job and took risks to feel alive. At one point she even said, "Don't forget an exit plan." She and Lichtenstein had married a few months earlier. In the song she says she wants to be with him "until the goddamn end."

Her delivery in the song is as awkward as ever, but with the knowledge that she posted it while likely contemplating a long prison sentence, the lyrics take on a poignant tone. "We're too weird for average Joes / Everyone knows," Razzlekhan raps in the last verse. "You're the best for me / This is how our story goes. / This is the Razzlekhan and Dutchie shows. / Ready to party down and let's get weird!" As the song ends, Razzlekhan says, in Russian with a thick American accent, "I love you."

The agents had also gotten warrants to search Lichtenstein's cloud-storage accounts. In one of them they found a list of fake IDs, both male and female, and notes suggesting the couple had gone to Kyiv in 2019 to buy debit cards under pseudonyms. It looked to the agents as if Lichtenstein and Morgan had been preparing to flee the country. On January 31 they cracked the encryption on one of Lichtenstein's files and found something even more explosive: the private keys to nearly two thousand Bitcoin addresses tied to the Bitfinex hack. The government now had control of $3.6 billion in stolen crypto.

A week later, the agents returned to the couple's apartment and arrested them. Lichtenstein and Morgan weren't charged with committing the actual hack. Instead they were charged for the steps they'd taken to conceal their handling of the stolen money.

THE ARREST WAS national news. It was the largest seizure of stolen funds ever. "Today, the Department of Justice has dealt a major blow to cybercriminals looking to exploit cryptocurrency," Deputy Attorney General Lisa Monaco said at a press conference. The TikTok commentariat tore through Morgan's music videos, and within hours Razzlekhan was already a social media legend, having air-humped her fanny pack into the ranks of famous grifters. "The Bitcoin crimes are nothing compared to calling this shit rap," Trevor Noah said on *The Daily Show.*

True-crime producers saw parallels to fake heiress Anna Delvey or Theranos founder Elizabeth Holmes. Netflix commissioned a Razzlekhan documentary from one of the makers of the salacious private-zoo docuseries *Tiger King* just three days after the arrest. Among the other projects that got announced: a podcast, a fictionalized series from the producer of the heist movie *Den of Thieves,* and a competing documentary from Forbes, the publisher of Morgan's columns.

Both Morgan and Lichtenstein pleaded not guilty. Lichtenstein was held in federal prison in Virginia, and Morgan was released on a

$3 million bond and moved back to 75 Wall Street. She argued that she wasn't a flight risk because she was storing frozen embryos in New York and planned to have a child with Lichtenstein via in vitro fertilization.

Not far from Morgan's apartment, on a traffic pole just across from the entrance through which criminal suspects are led into Manhattan federal court, I saw a sticker with a cartoon that depicted a topless Razzlekhan riding a crocodile, her tongue sticking out, her fingers split into her trademark "V." It looked new. I imagined her slapping it up, defiant, on her way into court.

In May 2022, I saw that Morgan had put many of her belongings up for sale on the 75 Wall Street message board, including three electronic deadbolts and a fake Banksy print. According to copies of the posts given to me by a neighbor, she was moving and needed to downsize.

I'd hoped to ask Morgan for her side of the story. Pretending to come for the tag sale seemed rude. I thought about calling, but in "Versace Bedouin," she'd recommended against it: "Email me, fuck your message at the beep, beep, beep." Then I realized she'd given entire presentations about how to get people to respond to emails. Her first rule was to "e-stalk" your audience to understand them. Having subjected myself to hours of her songs and videos, I figured I had that one covered. Then it said to think about what the competition is doing. "Heather," I wrote, "the documentary people are out to make you the next Tiger King. Your input could help reshape the narrative." She didn't reply.

Years after the Bitfinex heist, a fifth of the missing Bitcoins were still unaccounted for. Roughly $70 million worth had been sent to Hydra Market, a Russian dark-web site. No one knew where the money went from there, but on Hydra, vendors called "treasure men" were known to exchange crypto for shrink-wrapped packets of rubles that they buried in secret locations. It was possible there were underground bundles somewhere in Russia, waiting for Morgan and Lichtenstein to dig them up.

HERE'S WHERE THE story of the heist, as far as the bosses of Bitfinex and Tether are concerned, contained a twist. Even if the missing portion was never recovered, it appeared the hack might eventually turn out to be profitable for them. I couldn't get a straight answer on who would get the Bitcoins the United States seized from Razzlekhan and Dutch, but it seemed likely it would be Giancarlo Devasini and the exchange's other owners. Bitfinex said it had already more or less repaid all the users who lost money in the hack. The Bitcoins had been worth about $70 million when they were stolen. Devasini and his crew stood to recoup billions of dollars. It gave me little confidence in their abilities to safeguard money that their Bitcoins ended up in the hands of a pair of idiots, but having the coins sitting locked up in the couple's wallets was probably a lucky break.

Doing some mental math, I calculated that the former plastic surgeon was probably sitting on quite a slush fund. There was whatever he was going to recover from the Bitfinex hack, plus the profits he was earning from the exchange. And, if he really had bought tons of Bitcoin like his associate had told me, he could have made billions of dollars that way too.

As my estimate of Devasini's potential Bitcoin fortune increased, it seemed increasingly bizarre to me that he was so eager to invest Tether's deposits in potentially risky places. Did he, like Razzlekhan, take risks to feel alive? After reading what he had written about Bernie Madoff, I wouldn't have put it past him. But if some of Tether's investments went bad, it could set off a run.

The riskiest move I'd heard of so far was Tether's 1-billion-coin loan to the quasi-bank Celsius. Its founder, Alex Mashinsky, had told me about it at the Bitcoin 2021 conference in Miami. To me, Mashinsky's company—which promised returns as high as 18 percent a year—sounded like a Ponzi scheme. And in addition to lending Celsius money, Tether had also invested in it.

I quickly found that Mashinsky had an interesting history. I'd found a 1999 article in a defunct tech publication in which he listed a few very different businesses that he'd tried out after moving to the United States: "importing urea from Russia, selling Indonesian gold to Switzerland, and brokering poisonous sodium cyanide excavated in China for use by gold miners in the U.S." He also said in the article that he wanted to get into the business of whole-body transplants. "Give an old person a new body—keep the head, keep the spine, and re-create the rest," he said.

His new pitch was only slightly more reasonable. Mashinsky told users—he called them "Celsians"—that Celsius would let them stick it to greedy banks and help the less fortunate. They praised him for helping them make enough money to pay off their debts or even quit their jobs. One said, in a testimonial posted on Twitter, that he took out home equity and cashed in his work pension in order to put the money into Celsius.

"The beauty of what Celsius managed to do is that we deliver yield, we pay it to the people who would never be able to do it themselves, we take it from the rich, and we beat the index," Mashinsky said during one livestream. "That's like going to the Olympics and getting fifteen medals in fifteen different fields."

Celsius was effectively a bank for cryptocurrencies. Users deposited their Bitcoin, Ethereum, or Tether and received weekly interest payments. But the rates Celsius paid were tens or hundreds of times higher than what conventional banks paid on savings accounts. And Mashinsky never gave a good explanation of what Celsius was doing to earn the money to pay all that interest.

But despite his sketchy background, desperate sales patter, and laughably implausible business plan, Celsius had raised hundreds of millions of dollars from venture capitalists. The company said its assets more than quadrupled in 2021, to $25 billion. Mashinsky's ownership stake made him a billionaire, at least on paper.

I called around to people affiliated with Celsius, looking for more insight into its operations. One name kept popping up: a former trader for the company named Jason Stone. A few contacts recommended I seek him out. They told me that after Mashinsky trusted Stone with huge sums, he'd moved to Puerto Rico and gone on an epic spree of risky bets and partying before leaving the company in a bitter dispute. "He's an absolute psycho," said one source. He meant it as a term of endearment.

Stone, they said, was behind an anonymous Twitter account called "0xb1," which used an image of a demonic mutant ape as its avatar. The ape image was an NFT, or non-fungible token, and it cost the unbelievable sum of $1.1 million. (More on that later.) On Twitter, Stone wrote about all kinds of crazy cryptocurrencies he was investing in, from SushiSwap to FODL Finance to OHM—a "decentralized and censorship-resistant reserve currency" that paid yields as high as 7,000 percent. He called what he was doing "yield farming." Was this what Celsius was doing with the money it borrowed from Tether?

When I called Stone, he was happy to talk. He said he'd left Celsius in 2021 because he discovered shady dealings at the company. He told me if I knew how Celsius really managed its money, I wouldn't believe it.

"I was seduced," he said. "We all fucked up by letting it get so big."

We arranged to meet.

CHAPTER TWELVE

"Click, Click, Click, Make Money, Make Money"

Jason Stone answered the door of his apartment in New York's financial district in a black Hermes T-shirt, tight black joggers, and gray Allbirds sneakers. The thirty-four-year-old crypto trader had curly hair and the stubble of someone who hadn't shaved for a few days. He looked like the actor Jonah Hill recovering from a bender.

Laundry was piled on a coffee table. A *Star Wars* helmet, a replica of bounty hunter Boba Fett's, was on a shelf under the TV. A Polaroid on a table nearby showed a masked woman pulling Stone by a chain tied around his neck. A small bookcase held four pink boxes of Agent Provocateur bondage gear, including a leather harness and a spanking paddle.

"These aren't just for girls that I fuck," Stone said. "It's for my friends who want to bring accessories to sex parties."

STONE WAS IN the middle of a legal dispute with Celsius and, as we spoke, he was texting with three people and preparing for a court hearing. When he got too excited to write, he sent voice memos. At one point, he offered me chocolate laced with hallucinogenic mushrooms. He'd just received a copy of his corporate email archive and he was reviewing messages between him and Alex Mashinsky, the founder of Celsius.

"My god, dude," he yelled to his lawyer on the phone, with a high-pitched trill of a laugh. "They are so good for us, it's crazy! The emails, it's fucking hilarious!"

While Stone went over the emails, I asked him about his relationship with Mashinsky. The two men had met when Mashinsky invested in Stone's crypto start-up, which was called Battlestar. It was 2018, and Stone was thirty. He had grown up in a stately co-op on the Upper West Side and was educated at the elite private school Fieldston, spending weekends at house parties in fancy apartments or friends' houses in the Hamptons. His mother was a banker at Citigroup, and his grandfather was a Lehman Brothers executive. As a teenager, Stone was encouraged to play the stock market by his grandpa. One of his picks was Apple. That trade eventually netted him more than six figures.

It was Ethereum—the blockchain that enabled the ICO boom—that got him interested in crypto. He did some Ethereum mining on his laptop around 2016, abandoned it when it was too hard to sell the tokens for real money, and then kicked himself when a friend told him at a poker game that their price had increased tenfold. Stone took his money out of stocks and went all-in on Ethereum, eventually starting Battlestar, which was supposed to help investors earn a return on their crypto holdings through what it called "institutional grade Staking-as-a-Service." (Don't ask.)

The concept of using your crypto to accrue income was new, and Battlestar didn't take off right away. But around the summer of 2020, Stone noticed a new corner of the cryptocurrency market called DeFi. People were earning ridiculously high interest rates by investing in new kinds of coins, using yield farming. Pretty much no one understood it. It wasn't exactly what Battlestar specialized in. But when Mashinsky asked him about it, Stone had been playing around with it for a few weeks, which made him a relative expert.

By then, Celsius had taken in more than a billion dollars. It was paying as much as 12 percent interest to users who sent in Tether and other stablecoins. That meant Mashinsky needed to find ways to invest the billion dollars that earned at least that much. DeFi seemed like it could work. Mashinsky decided that Stone was the DeFi expert he needed. He hired Stone to invest some of Celsius's money into the new crypto market.

As Stone explained yield farming to me, he ground up some weed, rolled a blunt as fat as a dry-erase marker, grabbed my pen to pack it, and puffed away. The first DeFi investment Stone made at Celsius was in something called C.R.E.A.M. Finance. (The name references "Cash Rules Everything Around Me," the 1993 classic by the Wu-Tang Clan.) According to its creator, a former member of a Taiwanese boy band, it was supposed to be "an open and inclusive financial system built on smart contracts."

By then, the ICO boom was over. It was no longer plausible for someone to announce they were going to create Dentacoin, a cryptocurrency for dentists, and raise millions of dollars —a real thing that happened in 2017. DeFi was different. It was based on "smart contracts." These are, basically, simple programs that run on the blockchain. Remember that the Bitcoin blockchain is a two-column spreadsheet, and MasterCoin, Ethereum, and the like allowed for adding new columns that represented new coins. Now imagine if the spreadsheet added functions. Instead of just allowing users to add Bitcoins to one person's row and subtract them from someone else's, these smart contracts enabled them to swap one kind of coin for another, or make a loan to another user.

DeFi used these smart contracts to create decentralized, anonymous versions of exchanges like Sam Bankman-Fried's FTX. It was a genuinely powerful innovation. But naturally, crypto bros quickly turned DeFi into a series of get-rich-quick schemes, just like they had with the ICOs.

Each new DeFi program came with a new coin. With Cream, anyone who traded or borrowed got paid a reward in Cream tokens. The coins themselves could be deposited on Cream to earn even more coins. Or, as Method Man, a Wu-Tang member, explained in a cringey rap promoting Cream: "Supply crypto, get Cream, or borrow crypto, get more Cream!" (Method Man never confirmed or denied whether it was actually him in the rap.)

It didn't entirely make sense that Cream tokens would have any value, but their price kept rising as long as more people wanted to participate. Stone said he was earning $150,000 of Cream tokens every hour for the first three days.

"I'm just like click, click, click, make money, make money, make money," Stone said. "I'm not fucking like doing research yet, you know?"

"Maaaaaaake money!" he yelled, like he was introducing a rap video.

Reviewing his old emails in front of me as we talked, he came across one from the fall of 2020 in which Mashinsky said he didn't believe in DeFi, even as he was telling Stone to sink more and more customer money into it.

"DeFi may not exist in January," Mashinsky wrote. "What we want is for every DeFi player to have a Celsius account, so when the Ponzi runs exhaust themselves they will all park their coins with Celsius."

The investment strategy may have been ill-advised, but it worked. Stone reported $4 million in profit in October, and by the end of the year Celsius was sending him tens of millions of dollars a week to invest.

All of that money was Celsius's. The company hadn't paid him yet. But under the terms of his agreement with Mashinsky, Stone was supposed to receive 20 percent of whatever he made for the company using DeFi. He figured he was due a few million dollars at least. To avoid paying taxes on it, he decided to move to Puerto Rico.

IN 2012, PUERTO RICO created huge tax breaks to attract wealthy people from the mainland. Move to the island, and pay no federal income tax, no taxes on capital gains, and only a 4 percent tax on Puerto Rican income.

Five years later, after lots of crypto bros got rich on ICOs, some of them decided it would be a good idea to suddenly become Puerto Ricans. Among the first to arrive was Brock Pierce, the co-founder of Tether. He bought a nine-bedroom mansion in Old San Juan, next to the governor's, turned it into a Bitcoin shrine and party venue, and recruited other acolytes to move to the island too. Dozens went for it. They said they were building a community they called Puertopia, Sol, or Puerto Crypto.

"We're here to take our skills—our superpowers—and figure out how to help Puerto Rico, the Earth and the people," Pierce told a reporter in 2018.

Pierce liked to walk the streets of San Juan with a Bluetooth speaker pumping out Charlie Chaplin's speech from *The Great Dictator*. He performed quasi-religious rituals, like blessing crystals, kissing an old man's feet, or praying over a historic tree. For most of his followers, avoiding taxes was the main lure. Reeve Collins, Tether's first CEO, was among those who heeded Pierce's call.

"So, no. No, I don't want to pay taxes," Collins once told a visiting reporter at a poolside bar. "This is the first time in human history anyone other than kings or governments or gods can create their own money."

Some locals resented their rich new neighbors. Flyers went up around San Juan that looked like wanted posters. Under Pierce's face, they denounced him as an *imperialista*. "This is what our colonizers look like," they said. At one point, protesters gathered in Old San Juan to protest the tax breaks, spray-painting graffiti that read: BROCK PIERCE IS A COLONIZER and GRINGO GO HOME.

Stone came around December 2020, moving into the house of a crypto trader friend. Mashinsky was happy with Stone's move to Puerto Rico, seeing as Celsius wasn't licensed to do business in New York. By then, Stone was making so much money for Celsius that he figured he'd be saving tens of millions of dollars in personal income taxes. He brought with him two dogs—a terrier and a pit bull—and he'd take them jogging on the beach.

Stone tried ketamine for the first time on the island—the drug of choice for crypto people, he said—and would smoke weed in the afternoon while he came up with ideas for investments. "I think it actually helped with my work," Stone said.

His description of life in Puerto Rico sounded like a montage from a crypto version of *The Wolf of Wall Street:* "dancing, partying, drugs, beach." Stone set up two big screens at the dining room table. He rarely looked up from them, even when his host threw weekly parties. As people danced around the room, he'd stare at the screens and snort lines of ketamine. Other crypto traders would bring their laptops too. Some preferred Adderall or cocaine. Stone liked to say he was one of the largest players in DeFi, a friend who hung out with him then told me, often yelling about hacks or how much money he was making. "He'd type loud, like he wanted people to know," the friend said.

Mashinsky told Stone to invest as much as he could. More money was coming in than he knew what to do with, lured by those high interest rates. On January 7, 2021, Mashinsky emailed Stone and some other Celsius executives to tell them $46 million had been deposited that day alone. "We need to move faster on all fronts if we have a chance to deploy all this money," Mashinsky wrote. "MAX it out!!! You need to do larger deals faster." Before long, Stone was managing more than $1 billion.

Because it was crypto, all that money was stored on Stone's laptop. It was as if Stone kept a billion dollars in bundles of hundreds, just sitting on his friend's dining room table. The account was protected by a password, but Stone grew paranoid. He couldn't sleep for more than a few hours at a time. He'd stay up until three in the morning trading, then start again at six or seven.

"I wasn't, like, leaving my house. I was scared North Korea was going to come and put a gun to my head," he said. I laughed. "It's not funny," he said.

STONE TOLD ME that one of the other big players in DeFi was Sam Bankman-Fried. Stone could tell from watching Bankman-Fried's crypto wallet addresses that his hedge fund, Alameda Research, was farming giant sums on tokens like SushiSwap. Stone estimated that Alameda earned billions of dollars this way. And Stone became an influential trader himself. Other investors started watching his crypto wallet, buying when he bought and selling when he sold, which helped his returns.

Essentially, Celsius was collecting deposits from investors and promising them gigantic returns, blasting the money over to Stone's computer for him to invest in untested DeFi projects and Ponzi schemes, and hoping for the best. Some of the money Celsius was investing was borrowed from Tether too. Mashinsky was claiming Celsius was safer than banks, but the company didn't even have a system for tracking what Stone and its other traders were doing with the money. As one Celsius executive wrote in an internal email in December 2020: "As things stand currently, Celsius does not have a clear, real-time, and actionable view of our assets and liabilities."

In March 2021, Stone decided to leave Celsius and start his own money management firm. Mashinsky wasn't happy. And it turned out their crypto accounting was so sloppy that they couldn't even agree if Stone had made money. In dollar terms, Stone said, he'd made hundreds of millions of dollars. But the price of Ether had spiked, and Mashinsky said Celsius would have made more money by simply holding onto it, meaning the maniacal trading had been a waste of time. This became part of the dispute that later landed in court.

Stone told me he wanted to quit because he'd discovered shady trading by Mashinsky. But he kept this to himself at the time and offered to keep managing Celsius's money at his own firm.

Publicly, Mashinsky would later insist, "We are probably one of the least risky businesses that regulators worldwide have ever seen." I didn't need Stone to tell me this was not true. But he said that Celsius's continued viability depended on a token called CEL that Mashinsky made up himself. The only thing propping up its value, according to Stone, was Mashinsky's trading.

"I think he's convinced himself he's not running a Ponzi scheme," Stone said. "He's a real sociopath. He's the most dangerous type of person."

EARLIER IN MY research into Celsius, I'd met up with Mashinsky at a smoothie shop in Manhattan to ask him about some of the company's investment activity. I hadn't heard the full extent of it from Stone yet, and I didn't know about their legal dispute, but I knew Celsius had invested in DeFi. Mashinsky insisted it was safe. Celsius took advantage of the high interest rates while they lasted, then shifted to other types of investments, he said.

"DeFi's one of the five legs. Like this stool has three legs," he said, pointing to his seat. "Add two more legs. That's what Celsius is. It's a stool with five legs."

Mashinsky started explaining the other legs to me, but before he got to number three, he grew distracted by his disintegrating paper straw and asked his public relations representative to bring him another one. Had Celsius been a traditional finance company, it would have had to disclose details about its trading to regulators and customers. But as far as I could tell, no one was regulating Celsius. I asked Mashinsky if Celsius should be regulated like a bank, because it took deposits.

"We're not a bank," he said. "We take a loan from you with the promise of repayment, and then we lend it to an institution, charge them interest, give you most of that interest."

"It sounds very similar to a bank," I said.

Mashinsky tried to explain with a metaphor. "Let's say we're neighbors, and I came to you and I borrowed sugar because I'm out of sugar," he said. "And then I came back later, and I gave it back to you. And I said, 'You know, you were so nice to lend me your sugar, here is your original sugar, plus here's a little bucket of sugar that I got you as a present.' Sugar is a commodity. I don't need a regulator."

I asked him what he was doing with Tether then. He continued to belabor his confectionary analogy. Sometimes, customers would all deposit Bitcoin, but he could earn more interest if he had stablecoins instead. When that happened, he said, he would call Tether's Devasini.

"When I don't have enough sugar, I go to Giancarlo and I say, 'Hey, I need more sugar. I'll give you chocolate,'" Mashinsky said to me.

This was confusing. Sticking with the metaphor, I didn't understand how Devasini was able to transmute chocolate into sugar. And even if he did have a foolproof method, Celsius was getting so big, it seemed like it could hide countless risks. Celsius was dealing in billions of dollars, and Mashinsky was talking about it like he was trying to bake a cake.

"But, like, you're just sitting on a mountain of sugar," I said. "You could even imagine that the Building Department would have to come in because there's too much sugar, and it's spilling into the street."

The argument went on, but Mashinsky was distracted by the roar of the smoothie shop's blender.

"Can we get out of here? It's just driving me crazy!" he yelled.

He led me and his public relations assistant around the corner to his apartment, which he and his wife had purchased for $8.7 million in 2018. Upstairs, on a mezzanine overlooking a grand living room, Mashinsky picked at a tray of fruit brought by another assistant.

Mashinsky argued that crypto was better than dollars, because inflation would inevitably erode the value of all government-issued currency. I told Mashinsky I didn't have any savings in cash, so it wasn't like I was sitting on a pile of money that was getting less valuable. And I wasn't worried about the safety of my bank account.

"If I give Bank of America a pile of sugar, I mean, I can be pretty sure I'm going to get that sugar back," I told him.

"As long as the music plays," he said. "When the music stops, everybody loses."

MASHINSKY CUT OFF our debate by saying he had to go to another meeting. As I walked out of his building, I felt frustrated I hadn't been able to win the argument. It seemed so obvious to me that dollars were safer than crypto. The whole industry seemed to be a collection of flimsy schemes. But coin prices were holding strong. How do you argue with "number go up" logic when the number keeps going up?

But around the time of Razzlekhan's arrest, I'd read about a crypto number that had stopped going up. In fact, it had crashed in spectacular fashion. It was a token called Smooth Love Potion. Its value, which topped thirty-six cents in 2021, had dropped below a penny. And it was one of the cryptocurrencies I'd been hearing the most about since I started looking into the industry.

Smooth Love Potions were the official cryptocurrency of a mobile game called *Axie Infinity,* in which players bought teams of cute blob-like creatures for real money and earned tokens by sending them into battle. The game had become incredibly popular in Southeast Asia, especially in the Philippines. The craze had spread throughout the island nation, attracting more than a million players through word of mouth, social media, viral videos, and national news stories. Entire families were spending all day playing *Axie Infinity* instead of working.

In 2021, when I'd ask crypto promoters for examples of crypto being used in the real world, many pointed to the Philippines. They called *Axie Infinity* a new form of employment and a potential panacea for global poverty. It was the most prominent demonstration of what some had taken to calling Web3: an internet in which users own their data and it's tracked on blockchains, rather than controlled by big tech companies like Facebook. Some even told me that one day, we might all own our social media profiles on the blockchain and earn money from them, just like Filipinos did with those little Axie blobs.

But after the price of Smooth Love Potions crashed, I stopped hearing about *Axie Infinity.* I started to wonder what was going on in the Philippines. I felt like whatever happened there would be a message from our crypto future. It was time to find out the truth about *Axie Infinity.*

CHAPTER THIRTEEN

Play to Earn

The *Axie Infinity* craze started with an ad on Facebook, seen by a twenty-eight-year-old in a hot, dusty city about seventy miles north of Manila. His name was Arthur Lapina, but his friends always called him Art Art. He was a chubby man, with a buzz cut and glasses.

It was March 2020. Cabanatuan City, like most of the world, was suddenly on lockdown after the global coronavirus outbreak. The shutdown meant Lapina had just lost his job at the bar where he had been working as an assistant cook, chopping up pig ears and jowls to make *sisig* and preparing other bar snacks.

What caught Lapina's attention about the Facebook ad was *Axie*'s colorful creatures—they're based on the bizarre-looking axolotl, a type of salamander native to Mexico City, which one writer aptly described as a "cheerful tube sock." He'd always played mobile games and now he was looking for a new distraction. He was still single, and the lockdown had left him largely confined to the leaky, rickety wooden house where he lived with his mother and extended family. He clicked.

The mechanics of the game Lapina downloaded would be familiar to anyone who'd played *Pokémon* or Magic: The Gathering. Build a team of three friendly-looking cartoon blobs with interchangeable body parts, then battle other creatures. Lapina had dabbled in crypto before, so he wasn't put off by the requirement to pay in tokens to buy his team. He paid about 150 Philippine pesos ($2.50) and started battling.

The game was no better than many of the free-to-play games Lapina had tried on his mobile phone before, but it helped him pass the time. When he won battles, he would net small amounts of the game's cryptocurrency, which bore the odd name Smooth Love Potions. These could be used to breed more blobs. What made the game different from others was that these potions could also be traded on some crypto exchanges. At the time, each one—represented by a cartoon image of pink liquid sloshing inside a round-bottomed flask—was only worth about one cent. Lapina didn't mind. He enjoyed strategizing to win the battles and seeing his name rise on the app's leaderboard.

But that summer, the price of Smooth Love Potions started to climb, and with it, Lapina's winnings. He started telling his friends that he'd found a way to earn a few dollars a day, just by playing a cellphone game. He found a receptive audience. The city's stores were still shuttered. Its fleet of thousands of tricycle taxis were gathering dust. Most people were unemployed. Families were so short on money that the city issued rations: rice, canned sardines, and tinned beef.

Word spread quickly about Lapina's discovery. Other people from town started asking him for help buying their own Axies. One tricycle driver told me she'd borrowed money from a loan shark before seeking Lapina's advice on which blobs to buy. Another said he'd pawned his trike. "My friend told me it was legit," he said.

The money kept pouring in. It was as if Lapina had cast a magical spell that granted the entire town's wishes. Houses around Cabanatuan started sprouting second floors. The local dealership sold out of powerful Yamaha NMAX scooters. Some grocery stores and gas stations started accepting Smooth Love Potions in lieu of cash.

Townspeople were so grateful to Lapina that they would bring gifts of fast food to the gate of his family home: pizza, burgers, or fried chicken from the local chain Jollibee. Some of them would call him "master."

Lapina started using his earnings to buy more teams of blobs, and he hired other people in town to play with them on their own phones. He let them keep 60 percent of whatever they won in the game. Before long, Lapina had more than a hundred people battling for him, including teachers, his grandmother, and even a police officer, who Lapina had to talk out of quitting the force.

OTHER OWNERS OF Axie blobs were hiring serfs and creating their own little fiefdoms in other towns across the Philippines, and the pattern soon repeated itself in Vietnam, Venezuela, and other countries where hourly wages were low enough to make the potential earnings attractive. It was reminiscent of the Chinese *World of Warcraft* gold farmers that Tether co-founder Brock Pierce profited from a decade earlier, but on a larger scale. The Axie owners invented a euphemism for their Smooth Love Potion farmers: "scholars." By the summer of 2021, they were all over the Philippines.

"A house and a lot and 1 million pesos, all of this you can get through playing the now popular online game *Axie*. But the question is, are you sure about it?" Jessica Soho, the anchor of a popular Filipino TV news show, said in Tagalog during a segment on *Axie* that August.

Sky Mavis, the small company that created *Axie,* was taken by surprise by its growth. It was founded in 2018 in Ho Chi Minh City by a group that included a twenty-five-year-old Vietnamese programmer, a Norwegian competitive gamer, and a twenty-seven-year-old former Yale fraternity president who'd been working as a recruiter for hedge funds. Few players downloaded *Axie* until the end of 2019, when the company started paying them in its Smooth Love Potion cryptocurrency. Even then, growth was slow until the game was discovered by Filipinos.

But once it caught on in the Philippines, *Axie*'s user base increased exponentially—exactly the kind of growth venture capitalists are looking for. The game signed up 61,000 new players in May 2021, 139,000 in June, and 475,000 in July. By that October, about two million people were playing the game every day, most of them in the Philippines. Sky Mavis capitalized by raising $152 million from venture capitalists, including the prominent firm Andreessen Horowitz, at a valuation of around $3 billion.

"It's actually the beginning of the metaverse, in our opinion, just hiding in a very cute little game," Aleksander Larsen, the Norwegian co-founder of Sky Mavis, said on a podcast. "I actually believe that *Axie* has the potential to impact the globe very heavily with letting people interact with the global economy, actually exiting their prisons, where they are born."

Others in the crypto industry took notice of the *Axie* craze. They didn't call it out as unsustainable, or ask where all the money was coming from. Instead, they took it as validation that crypto was the future. They imagined a world in which social media profiles were crypto assets, and everyone earned money online the way *Axie* players in the Philippines did.

"One of the main criticisms of crypto so far is that it has no real-world value or application, but *Axie* makes you reconsider what real-world value is," Packy McCormick, an investor, wrote in his popular newsletter. "Kids in the Philippines, Vietnam, Brazil, and beyond are applying for Axie Scholarships like they would apply for college or a job, hoping to bend their trajectories upwards."

Sam Bankman-Fried's exchange, FTX, paid for in-game naming rights to one group of scholars. Among the game's other backers was Mark Cuban, the *Shark Tank* judge and owner of the NBA's Dallas Mavericks. "Anybody around the world can play and make money playing," Cuban said in a quasi-documentary on *Axie* posted on You-Tube. "And it makes perfect sense once you dig into the numbers."

THE NUMBERS ACTUALLY made no sense. Lapina told me that in the early days of the craze, a player could buy a set of Axies for about 5,000 pesos and earn around 400 pesos' worth of potions a day. In U.S. dollars, that amounts to a $91 investment with a daily return of around $7.25. Most players would send the potions to a more sophisticated intermediary, like Art Art, who would swap them for Tether and then trade that for cash on a crypto exchange, but even with a bite taken out by a middleman, a player would be in the black after just a few weeks—and keep earning.

The returns didn't strike the Filipinos I talked to as unreasonable. But a more sophisticated investor would have realized the daily rate of return was 8 percent—way, way too good to be true. At that rate, with earnings continually reinvested for ten months, Lapina and everyone else who bought a single set of Axies would be trillionaires.

The limits of the global money supply meant that the game's economy was bound to collapse long before Lapina and his Cabanatuan friends turned into history's richest men. The exact mechanics of the quests and the potions were irrelevant. Smooth Love Potions had no use other than to breed more creatures within the game. The only thing that kept the *Axie* economy afloat was new players buying in.

In the summer of 2021, the price of Smooth Love Potions started to drop precipitously. The game allowed for an infinite supply of Smooth Love Potions. Sky Mavis could issue as many as it wanted, at no cost.

By the end of 2021, there were more than three billion potions in circulation. If they were real-world lab flasks, they would have covered every inch of the Manila metroplex with tempered glass.

But the more potions that *Axie Infinity* generated, and that players sold on the open market, the more the price fell. The price dropped below one cent in February 2022. Lapina had to let his scholars go.

LAPINA SAID THAT in his best week in the summer of 2021, he earned about $10,000—more than the average annual salary in the country. He always advised his players that the potion riches might not last forever. But he didn't take his own advice. He bought custom anime-themed watches for himself and his friends, lent money to anyone who asked, and donated thousands of dollars of food and toiletries to the inmates of a local prison. After the crash, he had nothing left.

I later visited him at his house a few miles outside Cabanatuan City, which he'd built with his earnings from the game. By U.S. standards, it was modest—a ranch with bare walls and faux marble-tiled floors—but for Cabanatuan, it was a palace. I could see he'd run out of money before completing construction—there were gaping holes in the ceiling. The leak-proof cement house he built for his grandparents was also unfinished, with rebar for a once-planned second floor sticking out of the roof.

Lapina had been reluctant to meet, because the night before he'd drunk so much gin he'd fallen on his face, and he still had large scrapes on his chin and cheek. But his aunt coaxed him into reliving the glory days for me. We sat together on the lone piece of furniture in his living room, a black-and-white-striped leather couch.

"Those things I was able to do back then like build this house, it was just a dream," he told me in Tagalog. "I can't really believe it."

He told me the people he'd helped were avoiding him. He said that he needed a loan to pay for his father's medical care, but some wouldn't lend to him because they thought he was secretly still rich, while others refused because they doubted his ability to repay. From another room, I could hear the theme music of a different play-to-earn game. But none of the copycat games had been profitable for him. He said he still held onto a few Smooth Love Potions.

"It's just like a token for me to always remember," he said.

. . .

SKY MAVIS HAS denied responsibility for the *Axie Infinity* debacle. "Trading patterns for these blockchain assets generated a speculative bubble unintended by Sky Mavis," a lawyer for the company told me. The company "never promised Axie Infinity players any returns." For some of the potion farmers, the collapse of the scheme just meant the end of a job. But many Filipinos told me they had invested their earnings to buy their own blobs, or even borrowed money to sink into the game. My driver in the Philippines, Patrick Alcantara, told me he contemplated suicide after losing about $2,100 that he'd borrowed from his wife's sisters, more than he'd ever invested in anything before. "It's like I was addicted," he said.

In Manila, I went to visit another one of the game's losers. Her name was Shiela Quigan. Her house was on a narrow alley that ran along a fetid creek filled with floating trash. It was made narrower by the residents who used it as an extension of their small homes. Outside, toddlers chased each other around parked tricycle cabs. A stack of cages held roosters raised for cockfights. A tent made of faded blue tarps hosted a karaoke party. I heard a woman belting out an American country ballad. "How do I live without you—oooo-ooo," she sang loudly.

Quigan, thirty-eight, worked as a community organizer for a women's health organization. She earned about $500 a month, so little that to save money on transportation, she slept at the office during the week. Her husband, Ryan, drove a delivery truck. They lived in one room with their eleven-year-old son and five-year-old daughter. It was a precarious situation: The entire informal settlement where they lived had burned in fast-spreading fires in 1997, 2008, and 2017, and Quigan told me she hoped to move to a better neighborhood before it happened again—or before they were evicted to make way for development.

"Sooner or later the owner of this land, they will kick us out," she said. Outside, I could hear the whir of the neighborhood's peso-a-minute clothes dryer.

When they heard about *Axie Infinity* around the height of the mania, Quigan was skeptical at first. She asked five people for proof they were really earning money from the game, and she saw that they'd been receiving consistent payouts for months. She calculated that within a few months, they might earn enough to renovate their house. They borrowed about $1,500 from her mother to buy a team. It consisted of a furry blob, a plant, and a sea creature with a misshapen tail.

Ryan would play at night for hours after coming home from his job, sitting at one end of the couch while Shiela slept on the other. He didn't let his son control the creatures, telling him that there was a chance he would make a mistake and hurt their earnings. As the price of potions dropped, the couple started to argue about whether to cut their losses and sell the 30,000 potions he'd earned. They never did. Quigan said optimistic statements from Sky Mavis convinced her not to.

"The company said wait for a surprise, and we will rock the world," she said.

Quigan told me she and her husband were considering going abroad to Dubai to seek better-paying jobs. But she still checks the price of potions daily.

"I don't get angry," she said. "I'm still optimistic that sometime, somehow, it will still go up."

QUIGAN MIGHT NOT have been angry, but I was. Crypto bros and Silicon Valley venture capitalists gave Filipinos false hope by promoting an unsustainable bubble based on a *Pokémon* knockoff as the future of work. And making matters worse, in March 2022, North Korean hackers broke into a sort-of crypto exchange affiliated with the game and made off with $600 million worth of stablecoins and Ether. The heist helped Kim Jong Un pay for test launches of ballistic missiles, according to U.S. officials. Instead of providing a new way for poor people to earn cash, *Axie Infinity* funneled their savings to a dictator's weapons program.

In April 2022, two months after my visit to FTX's offices in the Bahamas and Razzlekhan's arrest, Sam Bankman-Fried was hosting a conference in Nassau. Dubbed simply "Crypto Bahamas," it was billed as "an exclusive gathering of the leading investors and builders in the blockchain, digital assets and Web3 space."

These were the type of people who'd been promoting *Axie Infinity* as a vision of the future. I decided to go see if they were chastened by its failure. Maybe there would be fewer get-rich-quick schemes and more about the practical uses of crypto that I sometimes saw cited: allowing for round-the-clock trading, speeding up bank transfers, or enabling migrant workers to send funds home more cheaply. And there was always a chance that I'd meet the elusive Tether boss Giancarlo Devasini, who had property on the island.

CHAPTER FOURTEEN

Ponzinomics

On my first morning in Nassau, a shuttle bus waited outside my hotel to bring me to the Baha Mar, the 2,300-room resort and casino where Sam Bankman-Fried was hosting his Crypto Bahamas conference. Baha Mar had sold out. Katy Perry and her husband, Orlando Bloom, were rumored to be flying in, along with Tom Brady, retired baseball great Derek Jeter, and former president Bill Clinton and prime minister Tony Blair. I was staying on the other side of the island.

As we pulled away from the entrance, I was surprised to see that my ride had a police escort. The officer, on a motorcycle, sped through stoplights, sirens blaring, making martial hand gestures as the bus's engine strained to keep up. A bumper-to-bumper traffic jam parted like a zipper as drivers pulled off the road onto the sidewalk to make way. I turned around to check if Clinton was on the bus. I saw only three other people, none of them ex-presidents. If this was how the Bahamas treated me, I thought, imagine what they did for Bankman-Fried.

Anthony Scaramucci, the bombastic hedge fund manager who'd done an eleven-day stint as Trump's communications director, was co-hosting the event. Never one to miss the chance for a press conference, he had reporters assemble before the program started. Scaramucci, fifty-eight, looked tanned and Botox-smooth. He was wearing a well-fitting suit and his pompadour was freshly dyed jet black. He told us that FTX might one day turn all stocks into crypto tokens, which he said might allow Starbucks to sell us shares with our lattes. But he seemed hung up on the crypto guys' clothing.

"These people are unbelievable the way they dress," he said. "I'm here in a Brioni, these guys are in Lululemon pants. These guys are moving into the future. These are some of the worst-dressed people I ever met in my life."

When the conference started, Philip Davis, the prime minister of the Bahamas, took the stage and invited the crowd to move to the islands, like Bankman-Fried had. "If the world of cryptocurrency is where you see your possibilities, then the Bahamas has a place for you," Davis said. "You are, ladies and gentlemen, most welcome to the Bahamas."

Later in the morning, the writer Michael Lewis took the stage to interview Bankman-Fried and a crypto venture capitalist. I'd grown up reading his books, like *Liar's Poker* and *The Big Short,* and I was excited to hear what the guy who taught me how Wall Street blew up the world economy with collateralized debt obligations thought about crypto. Bankman-Fried was going to be the subject of his next book, I'd heard.

Lewis looked like a prep school headmaster, wearing a blue blazer with peak lapels and a white button-down with blue accents, his floppy hair parted perfectly to the side. And as he started lavishing Bankman-Fried with praise, he sounded as if he was presenting a prize to his star pupil.

"Three years ago, nobody knew who you were. And now you're sitting on the cover of magazines. And you're a gazillionaire. And your business is like one of the fastest growing businesses in the history of the planet," Lewis said, to applause from the crowd and giggles from his subject. "You're breaking land-speed records. And I don't think people are really noticing what's happened, just how dramatic the revolution has become."

As Lewis went on, Bankman-Fried tapped the toes of his silver New Balance sneakers, sometimes pressing his legs with his elbows as if to hold them still. It seemed like Lewis saw him as another one of the truth-telling, system-disrupting outsiders he liked to write about. But the author's questions were so fawning, they seemed inappropriate for a journalist. Listening from the packed auditorium, I started to question whether Lewis was really writing a book, or if FTX had paid him to appear. (Lewis later told me that he had in fact come to report for his book and that he was not compensated.)

Lewis said he knew next to nothing about cryptocurrency. But he seemed quite confident that it was great. The writer said that, contrary to popular opinion, crypto was not well suited for crime. He posited that U.S. regulators were hostile to the industry because they'd been brainwashed or bought off by established Wall Street banks. I wondered if he simply hadn't heard about the countless crypto scams, but the thought seemed preposterous.

"You look at the existing financial system, then you look at what's been built outside the existing financial system by crypto, and the crypto version is better," Lewis said.

Bankman-Fried's other turns on stage at Crypto Bahamas were similarly mindless. He stumbled through an interview with Blair and Clinton, who at one point extended a fatherly hand of support. (Clinton was reportedly paid at least $250,000 to appear.) He exchanged banalities about charity with Gisele Bündchen, the supermodel—the two had posed for an FTX ad campaign that ran in *Vogue* and *GQ*—and platitudes about leadership with her husband, Tom Brady.

"Does it ever get boring to win so much?" the moderator asked.

"I get a little desensitized," Bankman-Fried said.

"I never get tired of winning," Brady said.

It was depressing to see how many people I admired had been co-opted by Bankman-Fried to promote crypto gambling. (I'd later learn Brady and Bündchen were paid about $60 million for their endorsements.) In addition to Lewis, Clinton, and Brady—whom I'd cheered at a Super Bowl parade in high school—there was Larry David, my favorite comedian, who starred in FTX's Super Bowl ad, and David Ortiz, who led my hometown Red Sox to their first World Series championship in eighty-six years. "Oh I'm in, bro," Ortiz said in a TV ad for FTX.

The crowd at Bankman-Fried's conference lacked the quasi-religious fervor I'd seen at the more plebeian Bitcoin gatherings in Miami. Instead, the attendees here fell into three groups. There were the venture capitalists, who'd gotten in early, watched the tokens they bought climb to ludicrous heights, and now believed they could predict the future. There were the founders of crypto start-ups, who'd raised so many millions of dollars that they seemed to believe their own far-fetched pitches about creating the future of finance. Then there were the programmers, who were so caught up with their clever ideas about new things to do inside the crypto world that they never paused to think about whether the technology did anything useful.

At a party for a project called Degenerate Trash Pandas, I asked one coder if crypto would ever be helpful for regular people. "Why is it that you think that is important?" he said to me, in a tone of total sincerity. "I really would like to know."

In the pressroom, I saw Kevin O'Leary—the *Shark Tank* judge who goes by "Mr. Wonderful"—polishing his already shiny dome with an electric razor as he prepared to go on TV. (He was paid $15 million to endorse FTX.) And I spotted a man from New York I'd investigated years earlier. He sometimes went by the alias "Jim Stark," though his real name was Andrew Masanto, and he'd been accused in three lawsuits filed by angry consumers of involvement with a "plant stem cell" miracle hair-loss cure. (He has denied the connection.) After I awkwardly reintroduced myself, he told me he was building a "Web3 social platform" and that he had helped create a popular cryptocurrency. I looked up its market value and saw it was almost $4 billion.

"There's a lot of legitimacy behind the technology," he said.

Through FTX's press representatives, I arranged a string of interviews with attendees. One was with John Wu, the president of Ava Labs, which ran a popular blockchain called Avalanche. If anyone at the conference was going to be sober-minded, I imagined it would be him. Two weeks earlier, the company had raised money at a $5 billion valuation. Wu was fifty-one and his résumé included Cornell University, Harvard Business School, and a stint at the giant hedge fund Tiger Global.

But when we sat down, he and a colleague bragged to me about a *Zelda*-like play-to-earn game on their blockchain that had attracted forty thousand users in less than a month. They said the game was teaching people about DeFi and letting them earn high returns. It sounded a lot like *Axie Infinity*. I couldn't believe they were pitching it with a straight face after *Axie*'s collapse. "Now you can get ten percent in DeFi," Wu said. "You can be a true freelancer. There are literally people who quit their jobs. It's not magic. If you know what you're doing here, you're going to change your life."

Michael Wagner, the founder of a space-themed crypto game called *Star Atlas*, cited *Axie Infinity* as a proof of concept. Instead of colorful blobs and Smooth Love Potions, *Star Atlas* players had to buy spaceship NFTs to earn ATLAS tokens, and he told me he'd already sold nearly $200 million worth of them. But when I asked if I could try out the game, he said it didn't exist yet. Even though he'd already sold the spaceships, he said it would be at least five years before the game was ready. "It's very early stage," he said. "We believe the game could bring in billions of users."

Another crypto executive showed me a digital image of a sneaker that he bought for eight dollars, which he said had grown to be worth more than $1 million. He told me that recently, all owners of these imaginary sneakers had been issued an image of a box, which was itself worth $30,000. When he opened the box, he found another picture of sneakers and another box, each of them valuable in their own right. "It's this never-ending Ponzi scheme," he said, happily. "That's what I call Ponzinomics."

The most popular "real world" use of crypto seemed to be an app called Stepn. It tracked users' movement, paying them in "Green Satoshis" for walking or running. Users had to first buy virtual sneakers, which cost $500 or $1,000. This was definitely *Axie Infinity* all over again, but no one seemed to care. A writer who visited FTX's offices around that time noticed employees walking around the parking lot to earn crypto in Stepn. The company that made the app was earning around $40 million a month.

"What do you say to critics who say that—and they probably say this about a lot of projects—but like . . . this is a Ponzi scheme," I asked Stepn's co-founder, Yawn Rong, over Zoom, trying to be polite.

Rong, a thirty-seven-year-old former tile wholesaler in Australia, was not offended. He acknowledged the similarities right away. "Yes, it is a Ponzi structure. But it is not a Ponzi," he said.

Rong explained that in a true Ponzi scheme, the organizer would have to handle the "fraud money." Instead, he gave the sneakers away and then only took a small cut of each trade. "The users are trading between each other. They are not going through me, right?" Rong said. Essentially, he was arguing that by downloading the Stepn app and walking to earn tokens, crypto bros were Ponzi'ing themselves.

It struck me that almost any of the companies I'd heard about would be good fodder for an investigative story. But the thought of methodically gathering facts to disprove their ridiculous promises was exhausting. It reminded me of a maxim called the "bullshit asymmetry principle," coined by an Italian programmer. He was describing the challenge of debunking falsehoods in the internet age. "The amount of energy needed to refute bullshit is an order of magnitude bigger than to produce it," the programmer, Alberto Brandolini, wrote in 2013.

In between meetings, I kept my eye out for Bankman-Fried's cherubic sidekick Nishad Singh, who had flattered me so effectively when we first met. When I didn't see him, I imagined he'd be annoyed by the poor quality of the business plans too. I had hoped to finally meet Gary Wang, FTX's star coder, or Caroline Ellison, the former Jane Street colleague who was by then the head of Alameda. But I didn't see them anywhere either.

A DAY BEFORE Crypto Bahamas, Sam Bankman-Fried had all but admitted that much of his industry was built on bullshit. Not on stage, of course—it was in an interview on a podcast with Matt Levine, the *Money Stuff* columnist. Levine asked a simple question about "yield farming," the investment technique Jason Stone had used at Celsius. As Bankman-Fried attempted to explain how it worked, he had more or less laid out the how-to of running a crypto pyramid scheme.

"You start with a company that builds a box," Bankman-Fried said. "They probably dress it up to look like a life-changing, you know, world-altering protocol that's gonna replace all the big banks in thirty-eight days or whatever. Maybe for now actually ignore what it does, or pretend it does literally nothing."

Bankman-Fried explained that it would take very little effort for this box to issue a token that would share in the profits from the box. "Of course, so far, we haven't exactly given a compelling reason for why there ever would be any proceeds from this box, but I don't know, you know, maybe there will be," Bankman-Fried said.

Levine said that the box and its "box token" should be worth nothing. Bankman-Fried didn't disagree. But he said, "In the world that we're in, if you do this, everyone's gonna be like, 'Ooh, box token. Maybe it's cool.'" Curious people would start buying box token. And the box could start giving out free box token to anyone who put money inside, just as *Axie* had rewarded players with Smooth Love Potions. Crypto investors would see they could earn a higher yield by putting their money in the box than in a bank. Before long, Bankman-Fried said, the box would be stuffed with hundreds of millions of dollars, and the price of box token would be rising. "This is a pretty cool box, right? Like this is a valuable box, as demonstrated by all the money that people have apparently decided should be in the box. And who are we to say that they're wrong about that?" Sophisticated players would put more and more money in the box, Bankman-Fried said, "and then it goes to infinity. And then everyone makes money."

"I think of myself as like a fairly cynical person," Levine said. "And that was so much more cynical than how I would've described farming. You're just like, well, I'm in the Ponzi business and it's pretty good."

Bankman-Fried said that was a reasonable response. "I think there's like a sort of depressing amount of validity . . ." he said, trailing off.

I was not surprised that Bankman-Fried had been so candid, but it didn't make me feel very good about my profile of him, which had been much less focused on the potentially scammy basis of his entire industry. I'd built the piece around the question of whether he really would give his money away.

I was able to wrangle a quick meeting with Bankman-Fried outside the pressroom.

"Did I go too easy on you?" I asked.

"Maybe," he said. A few minutes later he ran off to meet Tom Brady for lunch.

AS I THOUGHT more about the giant volcano of crypto bullshit erupting at Crypto Bahamas, I realized that Tether was its molten core. Each scheme depended on exchanges like FTX to enable investors to buy and sell their tokens. And those exchanges in turn counted on Tether as a crucial connection to real U.S. dollars. Without Tether, it was possible this entire economy would never have developed.

None of the people I interviewed seemed particularly concerned about where Tether's money was or what was backing Tether tokens. It made sense: If you'd made a fortune from crypto tokens backed by absolutely nothing at all, would you spend your time worrying about whether Tether had all the dollars it claimed, or would you be heading to party with Katy Perry and Orlando Bloom? Still, I thought they were all overlooking a risk to their entire economy.

"The people who are shorting it are morons," Kyle Samani, a crypto venture capitalist whose fund made hundreds of millions of dollars on a token called Solana, told me. "It's real, it's legit. They fail to appreciate the ways in which the system is over-collateralized. I'm not worried."

I had been hoping that I would finally get a chance to lay my eyes on the mysterious boss of Tether, Giancarlo Devasini. The venue for the conference, I noted, was just a few miles from his Bahamas property, and all his biggest customers were there. But I didn't see him or any other Tether employees.

Deltec Bank & Trust, where Tether kept some of its money, was one of the conference's major sponsors, and I was happy to run into its chairman, Jean Chalopin, out on the resort's lawn. We'd stayed in touch after our interview at his office, and we would meet up for drinks or breakfast on his regular trips to New York. I liked talking with the French banker about his *Inspector Gadget* days, and trying to see if he'd let any Tether clues slip, and he seemed to enjoy hearing my stories too, though I did sometimes wonder if he was keeping tabs on me for Devasini.

When I asked why no one from Tether was at the conference, Chalopin informed me that the company had actually sent a representative: Jean-Louis van der Velde, its CEO. Van der Velde was a fifty-nine-year-old Dutchman with a home address in Hong Kong, who'd worked with Devasini since his days in the electronics business. If Devasini was a recluse, Van der Velde was a phantom. He had never given an interview, and was so rarely seen in public that some particularly conspiratorial Tether followers had speculated he might not be a real person at all.

I'd heard that Van der Velde's title carried little weight and that he always deferred to the real boss, Devasini. Still, it seemed likely he would know all about Tether's reserves, or lack thereof. Chalopin told me he might be able to make an introduction, but I'd have to be careful what I said. "Think of them as a wounded animal that has been unfairly beaten. You need to approach it slowly," he texted me.

On the last day of the conference, Chalopin called me to meet him in the hallway right outside one of the conference's auditoriums. As I approached the banker, I spied a tall man with silver hair, brushed to the right, with a wisp hanging down his forehead.

"If you screw this up, I'll kill you," Chalopin said, smiling.

I extended my hand to the other man. "It's a pleasure to finally meet . . ."

"The man who doesn't exist," Van der Velde said.

Chalopin left us to talk, and we arranged to meet the next day. Unlike most of the other executives from large crypto companies, who were treated almost like celebrities, no one approached him as he walked away.

We met again at a bar in Baha Mar, empty except for us. He was wearing a white polo shirt with three X's on the left breast, blue jeans, and blue sneakers. His face was well-lined and he had a bulbous nose with a small indentation near the tip. He looked like the fastidious captain of a perfectly polished charter yacht.

"I hate casinos," he said as we walked in. He folded his glasses, tucked them into a thumb-sized case, sat down on a small sofa, and ordered a seltzer.

Van der Velde told me the reason he'd avoided the press and speaking at conferences was that he was worried about his family's safety, not because he had anything to hide. The way Van der Velde explained it, while his intentions were only good, he was the victim of a plot. He said powerful forces were working together to harm him and Tether. Anonymous posters on Twitter were seeding lies, and the media was spreading them. He suggested that my *Businessweek* story about Tether, which had been published six months earlier, was part of this grand conspiracy.

"You have been manipulated to be here with me today," he said, slowly.

Over the next three hours, Van der Velde talked in circles, hinting that he was telling me something about Tether without saying it directly. He said that without Tether, the cryptocurrency industry as we knew it would not exist. In his telling, Tether provided access to cash at a time when banks didn't want to handle money for exchanges. But the company had paid a price for doing that.

If these lies were so harmful, I asked him, why wouldn't he show me how Tether's business worked and where its money was, and lay the questions to rest? I told him that Bankman-Fried had allowed me to sit with him at work, and seemed to be very open about his business. Van der Velde seemed annoyed. He hinted that there was something in Tether's past that he couldn't reveal.

"It's very easy to invite a journalist into your office when you don't have any battle damage," he said. "Tether saved the whole industry. We had to carry those heavy loads. Sam had the luxury of making a nice clean start. Sam never had to deal with that."

Van der Velde said he was taking a leap of faith by even talking to me. He was upset that the *Financial Times* had written an article critical of his résumé. Among other issues, he ran a Chinese electronics exporter that had made a government list of "seriously untrustworthy and law violating" companies, and worked as a salesman for a Hong Kong company that sold a product it claimed made smoking cigarettes good for you. "If you dip the butt of the cigarette into VitaCool when you smoke a cigarette, surprisingly 80 percent of nicotine will be transformed into vitamins," the company claimed.

But he said he was an honest businessman. He told me that at one point, when he was working for a different electronics company, venture capitalists had asked him to alter his financial projections to make them seem better, to help them raise more money. He was fired after he refused. "Once you start a lie, sooner or later it will come back to bite you," he said.

Van der Velde told me three times that he didn't care about money. He even said he didn't like thinking about money at all, an odd comment for someone who ran a company that issued a new kind of money. "Blockchain is not about money," he said. "It kills me that the kids are only about making that first million and buying a Ferrari."

The critics of Tether, he maintained, were conspiracy theorists, jumping to conclusions based on flimsy connections. But he spun an elaborate conspiracy theory of his own about those critics. He didn't want me to believe what was printed in newspapers, but he wanted me to accept his assurances that Tether was safe, without giving me any additional proof.

"Trust. That is really the biggest problem between humans now," he said, rocking forward toward his toes.

We'd been skirting the real question for hours. Whenever I asked for more specifics about Tether and its backing, he demurred. Over in the casino, I could hear the ringing of the jackpot bell and a waterfall of clinking coins as someone made a winning pull on a slot machine. I told him I needed to speak with Devasini. He said he didn't think the plastic surgeon would be willing to meet.

"Some passions run stronger," he said.

I WASN'T SURE what to make of my first face-to-face meeting with someone from Tether. Van der Velde seemed out of his depth, like someone who never imagined he'd be CEO of a company that, by that point, supposedly controlled more than $80 billion. It was ridiculous to blame conspiracy theorists for skepticism about Tether, when the company had given them so much fodder with its long history of lies. But he didn't seem like a criminal mastermind either.

When I returned to Brooklyn, my mind kept replaying a different conversation I'd had at the conference. I'd somehow heard about a pool party at a villa inside a gated resort related to a project called Solana Monkey Business. When I asked to attend, the host had told me that I didn't understand a huge part of crypto, and I was wondering if he was right.

Solana Monkey Business was a collection of five thousand pixelated images of monkeys wearing hats that looked like the characters from an imaginary Nintendo game from the 1980s. This was what crypto people called NFTs, or non-fungible tokens, and the market for them had taken off with the rest of the everything bubble. In 2021, tens of billions of dollars' worth had changed hands. What connected them to the crypto world was that the ownership of each monkey image was registered on a blockchain. This meant that, for the first time, it was possible to identify an owner of a digital image.

Crypto bros called it "digital art" and said that NFTs would soon be regarded as highly as the finest paintings of the Renaissance. So far, most NFTs were collections of unimaginative and derivative cartoons that a buyer could use as their profile picture on social media. But that wasn't stopping them from selling for absurdly high prices. Even celebrities were snapping them up to use as Twitter avatars.

The party in the Bahamas I was angling to attend was only for owners of Solana Monkey Business NFTs. The cheapest ones were going for $25,000, which seemed a bit steep for a swim, even at an exclusive resort. So I messaged the party's host, Patrick Loney, a forty-year-old former corporate lawyer. I told him I had only $600 worth of crypto—I'd purchased some Solana tokens in a failed attempt to attend a different party—and asked if he would give me a press pass. He refused and accused me of being insufficiently committed to my project.

"How do you expect to write a book about crypto if you have only dedicated $600 to crypto?" Loney said.

I told him it was pretty common for writers to write about, say, presidential politics without serving as president, or baseball without being able to hit a fastball. But he wasn't convinced.

"People spend massive amounts of money to buy monkes because they believe in it," Loney texted me, using a misspelling that had become an inside joke online. "Invest heavily in crypto, lose your ass, come back for more, make insane money, learn about monetary policy and tech in the process, make incredible friends who share these same experiences."

At first I thought Loney had just gone too far embracing his cool-but-rude monkey persona. But then I started to think that maybe he had a point. Maybe there was something I was missing about crypto by being an observer and not a participant. My inquiries into Tether were starting to make me feel like a scold. Maybe it was more fun not to care if Tether was lying, or if the infrastructure underlying this entire industry was fraudulent. I had to see for myself. But if I was going to spend thousands of dollars on a JPEG, I didn't want some monkey I'd never heard of, let alone a "monke." I wanted an A-list monkey, the NFT that rappers and actors and sports stars were buying. It had to be the Bored Ape Yacht Club.

CHAPTER FIFTEEN

All My Apes Gone

In January 2022, three months before Crypto Bahamas, the celebrity heiress Paris Hilton was perched on an armchair in Studio 6B at Rockefeller Center, an image of the Manhattan skyline behind her, for an appearance on *The Tonight Show,* with Jimmy Fallon. Hilton was wearing a sparkling lime green dress, her wavy blond hair in a massive two-part ponytail that emerged from the crown of her head and draped across her chest, down to her belly. After sharing some pictures from her recent wedding, she and Fallon started talking about the NFTs they'd recently purchased from the Bored Ape Yacht Club.

"I jumped in," Fallon said. "You taught me what's up and then I bought an ape."

"I got an ape too," Hilton said. "Because I saw you on the show with Beeple and you said you got it on MoonPay and I went and I copied you and I did the same thing."

"You did?" Fallon said, pretending to be surprised.

"This is your ape," Fallon said, pulling out a framed photo of an ape wearing sunglasses and a hat with a visor. She had paid about $300,000 for it.

"Yeah, it's really cool," Hilton said.

"We're part of the same community," Fallon said. "We're both apes."

"I love it," said Hilton, sounding bored.

"This is my ape," Fallon said. He looked serious, almost grim, as he produced a printout of a cartoon ape wearing red heart sunglasses, a captain's hat, and a Breton-striped sailor shirt. It cost him $220,000.

The segment had the badly disguised bleakness of an infomercial for a multilevel-marketing company. It was hard to imagine that Fal-

lon or Hilton had paid hundreds of thousands of dollars for ape cartoons, or that their endorsement would lead anyone else to buy one.
But within three months of the segment, the price of the cheapest
Bored Apes rose to $410,000. Tons of other celebrities were buying
them. There were pro athletes, like Warriors star Steph Curry, Shaq,
Dez Bryant, Neymar, and Von Miller; rappers Snoop Dogg, Eminem,
and Post Malone; DJs, including Steve Aoki and Diplo; and musicians
like The Chainsmokers. Justin Bieber paid $1.3 million for his.
Gwyneth Paltrow bought one too. On Twitter, many of them made the
apes their profile picture.

For stars, it was a way to show they knew about the latest investing
trend, even if that was a questionable distinction. For crypto bros, it
was a way to join the same club as celebrities, who, even if they weren't
the coolest, definitely had more social cachet than them. And for people from Wall Street, it was a way to do both—though it also gave off
a try-hard vibe. "It's a way to signal you are a Web3 native person. You
are one of the cool kids," one ex–Goldman Sachs banker told a reporter, sounding very much like he wasn't.

A COMMON MISCONCEPTION about NFTs is that the buyer
owns a unique, verifiable digital image. That's not the case. There's
nothing stopping anyone from simply right-clicking Justin Bieber's
ape and downloading the image file to their computer. The replica is
indistinguishable from the $1.3 million original, and perfectly usable
for a profile picture. What a Bored Ape buyer pays hundreds of thousands of dollars for is not a digital ape cartoon—it's the ability to prove
they are the one who paid hundreds of thousands of dollars for a digital ape cartoon.

Think back to that giant Excel spreadsheet in the cloud—the blockchain. What if, in addition to keeping track of how many Bitcoins or
Ethereum tokens each person owns, it could also track who owns
which ape picture? NFTs did that by adding an additional column:

	ETHEREUM COINS	BORED APE
ZEKE	103	#2,735

The blockchain doesn't even hold the actual image file. It just con-
tains a pointer to the image, which is stored elsewhere on the internet.

In this case, my line in the spreadsheet would have a link to Bored Ape #2,735, which has an army helmet and heart-shaped glasses. Anyone could look at that Bored Ape, or even download the image, but only I would be able to use the blockchain to prove that I owned it.

It might not sound like much. But ownership brought bragging rights during the crypto boom, when people judged each other by the size of their wallets, and one of the highest terms of esteem was "degen"—short for *degenerate gambler*. And by the time of Hilton's late-night TV appearance, NFT prices had gone up so much that crypto investors, celebrities, Hollywood talent agencies, and fine-art auction houses were calling NFTs the future of art, culture, and video gaming.

Most NFTs were part of collections of thousands of avatars that could be used as profile pictures. This made them easier to show off, and having so many nearly identical items made it easier for traders to bet on their prices. CryptoPunks—one of the first such collections—traded for less than $1,000 a pop in 2020, then jumped past $40,000 in early 2021.

The NBA had started selling basketball highlight videos as NFTs, which functioned something like digital sports cards. Trading in them was so frenzied that in March 2021, *The Wall Street Journal* featured a photo of a twenty-seven-year-old who'd made $15 million flipping them.

That same month, the auction house Christie's offered a collage of drawings by Beeple, the most popular NFT artist. The drawings were childish and often misogynistic—think Hillary Clinton with a penis, or Trump with boobs in bondage gear—but the reviews in NFT world were rhapsodic. "I look at my life as pre-Beeple and post-Beeple," said Noah Davis, the head of digital at Christie's. "The same way the world thinks about before Jesus Christ and after." The collage went for $69 million.

Many people cranked out their own collections after they saw how much other NFTs were going for. The effort involved was minimal. The buyers didn't care too much what the images looked like—they just wanted to get in early on the next CryptoPunks. One collection, called Pixelmon, raised $70 million before revealing images that looked like melted Lego animals. Another one, called Loot, skipped the art altogether. It sold eight thousand images of black squares printed with white text that listed items someone might use in a Dungeons & Dragons–style adventure—think "wand / chain mail / demon crown." The game itself did not exist, nor did Loot promise to make one, but NFT collectors went wild, praising the open-ended design that would let the community figure out what to build with the named items. The price for each square quickly topped $80,000.

For a few months, it seemed like anyone with a modicum of fame or crypto-savviness could make huge money selling NFTs. It was even easier than creating an ICO back in 2017. Jack Dorsey, the co-founder of Twitter, sold an image of his first tweet for $2.9 million. A woman known online for selling jarred farts started selling NFTs of her flatulence instead. Her slogan was "Imagine the smell."

BORED APES CAME in April 2021. It was a set of ten thousand cartoons of apes, which all looked quite similar to Fallon's or Hilton's. Some smoked pipes and others wore Hawaiian shirts. "Aping in" had become slang for betting big without doing research, and the idea was that the Bored Ape Yacht Club's members were the crypto millionaires of the future, too rich to care about anything but hanging out.

There was no big marketing push for Bored Apes at first, and its four creators weren't well known. In fact, they went by pseudonyms and kept their real names secret. One went by "Gordon Goner," and another by "Gargamel." They commissioned the cartoons from a few previously unknown artists. "Come ape with us," its creators wrote on Twitter to announce the sale, adding a skull-and-crossbones emoji, a monkey emoji, and a sailboat emoji.

But by the low standards of NFT collections at the time, Bored Apes was well designed. The ten thousand apes sold out for $220 each. Within a month, the cheapest went for $1,000. Prices skyrocketed from there. Their success spurred a series of simian imitators. Solana Monkey Business, the collection that turned me away from its Bahamas pool party, was one of those. The creators of Bored Apes started pumping out more NFT collections too. There was the Bored Ape Kennel Club—dogs to keep the apes company—and then the Mutant Ape Yacht Club, gross-looking apes that seemed like they had been melted by nuclear fallout.

By September, five months after their release, Bored Apes were selling at Sotheby's. The auction house sold a lot of 101 Bored Apes for $24.4 million to an anonymous buyer, suspected to be Sam Bankman-Fried. The next month, Sotheby's auctioned a Bored Ape with gold-colored fur. "Less than 1% of all Bored Apes have the gold fur trait, making it an NFT with historical significance," Sotheby's wrote. It went for $3.4 million.

IT WAS ALL so easy to laugh at. But the people who were buying NFTs took it seriously, extolling the benefits of the NFT community. They would post pictures from wild parties, where strangers with nothing more in common than owning similar JPEGs would dance and hug each other. They said it was like owning a piece of the next *Star Wars* or Mickey Mouse, and playing a role in creating an epic narrative. That sounded kind of fun.

Biking to Manhattan one day, I saw the side of a building in Williamsburg spray-painted with a giant orange ape skull. NO SLEEP TIL APEFEST, the ad read. Apparently, the company behind the Bored Ape Yacht Club NFT collection was planning a festival at a pier on the East River. Its website promised "four wild nights of music, merch, and art, plus treats and beats from your fellow apes." It seemed to be aimed at my aging millennial demographic: the previous year's performers included The Strokes and Beck. Like the Solana Monkey Business pool party, it was only open to owners of Bored Ape NFTs. I decided to buy one.

The friends I told about the idea said it was terrible. "Dude, don't buy one," my friend Sam said. "You're not going to buy one, are you? The price could collapse instantly. Won't they just give you a press pass?" Another friend suggested just showing a screenshot of an ape and sneaking in. But I didn't want a free ticket. To me, the foolhardiness of the idea was the point. I wanted to know what it felt like to be a degen.

And so, one night in June, I waited until my kids were asleep before I told my wife, Nikki, that I had to talk with her about something. Not being a natural degen, I wanted her approval before I gambled with our money. By then, she was used to talking with me about my weird crypto investigations. She'd always encouraged me to follow the story wherever it led, even if that meant me leaving her alone in Brooklyn with our one-year-old daughter and four-year-old twins while I jetted to Miami or the Bahamas, or Miami again, or the Bahamas again. (It would ultimately prove necessary to visit the beautiful white-sand beaches of the Bahamas four times.)

I told her there was a big crypto party coming up and that if I wanted to go, I'd have to buy a Bored Ape NFT. She asked how much, and when I asked her to guess, she said that she figured since I was asking, it must be at least a couple thousand dollars. I explained that Bored Apes cost hundreds of thousands of dollars, but that I could attend by purchasing a Mutant Ape. Those went for more like $40,000.

"Zeke, that's like a year of college," she said, her face contorting into a look of horror.

I explained that I planned to sell it after the party, and if all went well we wouldn't lose much. The odds were low, I figured, that the price of Bored Apes would collapse the week I happened to buy one. As far as crypto investments went, I told her, it was pretty much blue chip. "Are you making fun of me?" she said.

As we talked, Nikki came around to the idea. We even daydreamed a bit together about getting lucky like our neighbors who'd invested in crypto. We could upgrade our minivan to a Tesla with gull-wing doors, or even buy a lake house and a boat to go with it. She agreed that going to the party would be worth the risk.

"I feel anxious," she said. "Thank you for telling me, but I wish you hadn't."

I tried not to let on, but I felt anxious too. I'd seen many people become the butt of internet jokes after losing their Bored Apes. One owner made a typo while listing an ape for sale and lost $391,000. "This was my kids college. My mortgage. Just absolute shit that some of you out there think it's okay that I got ripped off," an ape-theft victim tweeted. The actor Seth Green, who was developing a TV show around his Bored Ape, which he named Fred Simian, had it stolen by hackers and appeared to spend $297,000 buying it back. (In the show, a *Who Framed Roger Rabbit* mix of live action and animation called *White Horse Tavern,* Simian was to be a friendly neighborhood bartender.) In December, a Chelsea art-gallery owner named Todd Kramer had lost $2.2 million of apes. "I been hacked," he tweeted plaintively, "all my apes gone."

These events were amusing as long as they were happening to someone else. But then I pictured myself, twenty years in the future, telling my son that we might have had enough money to send him to Wesleyan if I hadn't spent $40,000 on a picture of an ape.

By the time I got around to buying a Mutant Ape, the price had crashed to around $20,000. While I was happy the price had dropped from a brand-new Honda Odyssey to a used Dodge Caravan, it wasn't exactly reassuring that they had lost half their value in two weeks.

The process of buying the ape didn't make me feel any better. It could only be purchased on an NFT marketplace using the cryptocurrency Ether. (That's what the Ethereum blockchain's coins are called.) First, I had to acquire $20,000 of Ether. I decided to use Coinbase, the most popular U.S. exchange. To get my money onto Coinbase, I had to send a wire transfer from my account at Bank of America. A bank wire cost $40 in fees—$30 to Bank of America and $10 for Coinbase. But I'd never sent tens of thousands of dollars electronically before, and I was nervous. I sent two small transfers as tests. Once they went through, I clicked to send $20,000.

Ten minutes later, a Bank of America representative called me. Apparently sending that much to a crypto exchange had raised some alarms. The friendly representative, Oyet, warned me that I might be defrauded. "We're making sure this is your account and you're not a victim of fraud," Oyet said. "Since this transaction was initiated by you, it may be difficult to recover your money. If something happens with that investment, we will not be able to recover the funds. Do you want to continue with this transaction?"

I felt like Oyet was probably right. But I told her to go ahead.

Once my money was on Coinbase, I had to trade it for Ether, which was easy enough. Coinbase works just like E-Trade, except that instead of Apple stock, you're buying and selling cryptocurrencies. It's not exactly what Satoshi Nakamoto had in mind when he invented the first peer-to-peer electronic cash system—Coinbase is simply taking the place of your online trading site. But exchanges like Coinbase are the way nearly everybody buys Bitcoin, Ether, or any other coins.

Buying Ether on Coinbase was just the first step. I learned that to get my Mutant Ape, I'd have to transfer my coins to one of the decentralized services that allows you to hold your own crypto on your computer, with no intermediary. The best place to buy NFTs is an exchange called OpenSea, but as a decentralized exchange it doesn't handle payments itself. Instead, my Ether and my ape would live in a digital wallet app called MetaMask.

MetaMask made me watch a two-minute video before I signed up. On the screen, a pastel-colored animation of a faceless person, a lock, and a key appeared. "On traditional websites, a central database or bank is responsible for controlling and recovering your accounts. But on MetaMask, all of the power belongs to the holder of a master key," the narrator said. "Whoever holds the key controls the accounts."

He explained that the master key was a series of twelve words that I was to keep safe. The narrator said that if someone obtained my key they could easily take all my funds. "If anyone ever asks you for it, they're trying to scam you," he said. He showed examples of a man shoveling dirt over a hole and another user engraving their words on a metal plate, and suggested these might actually be good ideas.

Despite the soothing electronic music that played in the background, all this talk about losing passwords and scams and stealing did not feel good at all. I imagined myself telling Nikki I'd lost my ape, or checking my phone only to see that it had disappeared somehow.

I felt even worse when I realized that MetaMask was a browser extension, one of those little programs inside Google Chrome that do things like block ads or remember passwords. Instead of being safely inside Bank of America, watched over by a massive antifraud department with supercomputers and thousands of friendly representatives like Oyet, my $20,000 would be held inside a tiny cartoon fox icon next to the box where you type URLs.

To send my money from Coinbase, I had to direct a transfer to my MetaMask wallet address, a 42-character string of random letters and numbers. (Mine was 0xfDE68e4ABbE0A25a7a57626956E9A9B844C F4Cd3.) If I mistyped it, the money would be gone forever. I waited for minutes after I entered the address, feeling my heart race. Then it happened: The Ether appeared on the list of my assets in the popup window.

Finally, armed with a fox-head button full of Ether, I went over to the OpenSea website and pulled up the Mutant Ape Yacht Club collection. There were apes with melting faces, apes with burning shirts, apes with teeth in their ears, apes with eyeballs in their necks, and apes with exposed brains. They all looked disgusting. It would have been hard to imagine making any of them my online avatar even if they were free.

When I clicked to make an offer on an ape with a bloody bowler hat, a popup window informed me that I'd need to convert my Ether to "wrapped" Ether. I had no idea what this meant. It felt like one of the scams I'd been warned about. I really didn't want my money to disappear into my browser extension before I even acquired a $20,000

JPEG. But I was sick of researching crypto terms and I'd come too far to back out. I clicked OK.

Each offer charged me a "gas fee" of about three dollars, an annoying sum for a technology advertised as an improvement on credit cards. These are paid to the operators of the Ethereum network—similar to the rewards paid to Bitcoin miners—and vary with demand, sometimes spiking past a hundred dollars per transaction. When my offer for the bloody-hat ape wasn't accepted immediately, I moved on to another one. I ended up with Mutant Ape #8,272. He was an orange ape with orange hair. His stubble-covered face appeared to be melting, and he was wearing a turtleneck sweater made of maggots. He was smoking a pipe, and his eyes were bloodshot, like he was high. The price, at prevailing exchange rates, was $20,680.27. I had to buy more Ether to cover it.

As soon as I bought the Mutant Ape, a thought popped into my mind: *Who else would be dumb enough to buy one of these? What if I'm this industry's final sucker?* Then I checked my fox-head browser extension to see what I'd purchased. My ape was not there. After frantically searching the internet, I learned that MetaMask, despite being the industry standard wallet, didn't automatically display NFTs. Only when I navigated to OpenSea, the NFT marketplace, and then clicked the fox head, could I see evidence the ape was mine.

This was supposed to be the future of the internet and art and commerce. Instead, it had turned online shopping—a process so seamless and fun that some use it for self-soothing—into a terrifying ordeal. I could see how it all might make sense if I was planning to get rich and then hide my winnings from the IRS. The fox icon did not ask for my name or Social Security number. But I couldn't imagine that anyone would be willing to go through this risky and ridiculously complicated process without the hope of generational wealth on the other end. And I definitely didn't believe that Jimmy Fallon or Steph Curry had done it themselves.

I wanted to show off my new Mutant Ape, so I sent a picture to a few friends. Some, upon receiving the message, worriedly asked if I'd been hacked. Others responded only with a polite "haha." My mother sent the ape picture back to me and asked me whether I really owned it. I wanted to prove it to her, but she didn't know enough about the blockchain to understand.

Whatever, I thought. At ApeFest, I was sure to make new ape friends who wouldn't make fun of my Mutant Ape. To prepare, I named him Dr. Scum. I'd seen other Mutant Apes who'd gained followings on Twitter by inventing elaborate backstories. I decided Dr. Scum would be a private detective who gains superintelligence from smoking weed.

It turned out that owning a Mutant Ape was not in fact enough to get into ApeFest. While NFTs were often touted as a potential improvement on online ticketing systems, apparently they didn't work well enough for the Bored Ape Yacht Club. Instead, potential attendees had to sign up early for a separate ape ownership verification process, which I had missed.

Luckily, Jason Stone, the former Celsius trader, was a famous ape collector. He invited me to come as his guest.

CHAPTER SIXTEEN

It's the Community, Bro

I could hear the bass pumping from a block away as I approached the East River pier in downtown Manhattan that was hosting Ape-Fest. Outside, a yacht-sized inflatable ape reclined on the pavement. A sailboat moored next to the pier was rigged with a black ape-skull flag. One food truck sold "Bored Tacos" while another, called "Bored & Hungry," hawked cheeseburgers.

I met Jason Stone at a bar down the street, at a tailgating moment of sorts for the Mutant Cartel, a group of Mutant Ape collectors. He had his Bored Ape Yacht Club ball cap pulled down low. He seemed depressed. When he went to snort a bump of ketamine, he made only a half-hearted attempt to bend down and hide under the table. He told me an Australian billionaire had backed out of a deal to buy one of his rarest apes, a "mega mutant." "Ten million, it's yours. Today only," Stone said.

Lior Messika, the head of the Mutant Cartel, was more enthusiastic. The trim and tan twenty-six-year-old sported neatly gelled hair, a black polo shirt, and a thin gold chain around his neck. "Welcome to the family, bro," he said, pulling me in for a hand clasp and hug. "You bought at a good moment."

Messika, whose family owned the jewelry company of that same name, said he'd bought his first ape early and now had a collection worth about $25 million. We'd spoken a few weeks earlier, via Zoom. He'd been cruising near Greece on his 160-foot yacht. "I've been collecting what we call 'grails'—the Mona Lisas of the Bored Ape Yacht Club collection—for the last year or so," he said. "I have some of the nicest apes in the world."

Messika and the group were gossiping excitedly about future re-
leases from Yuga Labs, the creators of Bored Apes. "*Mecha* apes, man,"
he said. "Apes that are completely mechanized."

Another man, a shy forty-year-old engineer in a black BORED TO
DEATH T-shirt with his hair in a topknot, told me he owned a mega
mutant robot, also worth millions of dollars. He said he'd won it in a
kind of lottery after buying a Bored Ape for about $45,000. "I don't
flaunt," he told me. "No one in my real life knows."

Another member of the cartel, who went by PTM, told me that
on this very night his ape would "slurp" a "mega mutant serum," generating a new mega Mutant Ape. One of these serums had sold for
$5.8 million three months earlier, which meant this was a true degen
move. It would only pay off if the new mutant was even more valuable.

There was talk about "IP" and "culture" and, of course, "community." Messika said anyone could use their apes to create new games or
merch. The Mutant Cartel was his effort to build a community around
the Mutant Apes, which he felt had been a bit overlooked by their creators. "It's all the good stuff about being in a cult without any of the
negative," Messika said. "It's genuinely beautiful to see this deep ca-
maraderie." I wasn't sure about what he was saying, but I have to
admit it felt cool to be part of his crew.

WE WALKED TO the pier together and up to the rooftop concert
venue. Two giant neon ape skulls lit the stage, and orange apes were
painted on the walls, graffiti-style. "Welcome to the ApeFest," the DJ
called out. "Let's go!"

I'd heard that at last year's ApeFest people carried bananas and
gibbered like apes, but the crowd seemed to be trying to play it cool, or
at least as cool as you can look while wearing clothes covered in cartoon apes. It was mostly men. I saw men in Bored Ape T-shirts and
men in backward Bored Ape caps. I saw men carrying Bored Ape shopping bags stuffed with Bored Ape T-shirts and caps. I saw men with
tattoos of their apes. Many were passing out ape patches, pins, or
stickers, trying to raise the profile of their apes.

It seemed like everyone was wasted or high. Some told me they'd
taken mushrooms. A man from Florida with ombré dreadlocks and a
CRYPTO & COCAINE T-shirt told me he'd brought two hits of LSD, a
gram of ketamine, two Valiums, and some weed. A short, heavyset guy

from Miami in a neon jumpsuit and matching bucket hat kept repeating himself whenever anyone tried to talk to him. "Everything is a fairy tale," he said, over and over.

No one knew who'd be performing, but there were rumors about an appearance by Bieber or Eminem. Comedian Amy Schumer's set early in the evening was not a hit. She seemed embarrassed to be there and called the attendees nerds. "I don't know what NFT stands for," she said. "I'm assuming it's, looking out, not fucking tonight, is that correct? Do I have that right?"

I'd been warned that anyone I met might be trying to steal my ape. NFT collectors told me not to download any apps or scan any QR codes. I'd heard a rumor about an ape-stealing QR code on a billboard in Times Square. The best way to store my ape, I was told, was to transfer it to an encrypted thumb drive. This sounded tricky. I didn't want to screw it up and accidentally lose Dr. Scum forever. Instead I left him in the fox head on my computer and turned it off. I wasn't sure if this actually provided any protection. And it also meant that on my phone, I had only a screenshot of Dr. Scum, and no way to prove he was mine.

I had worried this might be a problem, but no one asked to see him, or to hear the story I'd invented for him. The people I did show thought it was lame that I didn't have a more expensive ape. "I try to stay away from those ones with the snot face," a man in camo cargo shorts with blond spiked hair and a goatee told me. A nineteen-year-old shamed me by displaying a gold ape he said was worth $1 million. Another teenager told me his parents had bought him a better mutant for $50,000. "I'm not too serious about it," he said.

Stone, my host, didn't seem to like the scene either. He left early in the night. The rest of the Mutant Cartel gathered near the stage to see PTM's ape slurp its serum. A special cartoon had been commissioned for the occasion, in the style of *He-Man*. PTM was rapt. He called his wife on Facetime. When it was revealed that his ape had turned into a gold mutant, he let out a long, orgasmic moan. "Holy fucking shit," he screamed. He wiped away a tear.

ACROSS FROM THE stage, in VIP booths, I spotted the founders of the Bored Ape Yacht Club. Originally anonymous, they'd been outed by *BuzzFeed* two months earlier.

Wylie Aronow, thirty-five, six-foot-two and buff in a ratty T-shirt, with a lifelike portrait of Charles Bukowski tattooed on his right arm, towered over Greg Solano, a bookish-looking thirty-three-year-old who once reviewed poetry for a small literary journal. A little more than a year earlier, when the two friends started texting about creating an NFT, Solano was working in publishing and Aronow was unemployed. Now, based on their company's valuation and their crypto holdings, I figured both were billionaires.

Their company, Yuga Labs, took in $2 million from the original sale of Bored Apes in April 2021. Personally, I would have absconded to Dubai with the proceeds before anyone caught on to my scam. But Solano and Aronow didn't. Instead, they moved quickly to capitalize.

Beeple, the famous NFT artist, introduced Aronow and Solano to Guy Oseary, Madonna's manager, who took them on as a client. Oseary was the one who connected many of the celebrities to the Bored Ape Yacht Club.

Most didn't go through the whole ridiculous Coinbase–Ethereum–fox icon process. A company called MoonPay, which Paris Hilton had mentioned on Jimmy Fallon's show, had provided what it called a "white glove service for high net worth individuals who want to purchase NFTs in the simplest way without all the hassle." (MoonPay took advantage of its celebrity ties to raise money at a $3.4 billion valuation.)

Aronow, Solano, and their colleagues started producing more ape-related NFTs. They made $300 million selling plots of land in an online game for the Bored Apes—they called it a metaverse—that didn't exist yet. Then they created ApeCoins, a currency for that imaginary world, gave some to Ape owners, and kept about $1 billion worth for their company and themselves. (Yuga Labs claimed ApeCoin was cooked up independently by something called a DAO.) And no one complained that they'd been tricked. For some reason, people just wanted to pay real money for ugly ape cartoons. They essentially had a license to print money.

A presentation to venture capitalists projected that Yuga Labs would take in $455 million of net revenue for 2022, with an unheard-of 84 percent profit margin. Of course the venture capitalists bought in, led by *Axie Infinity*–backers Andreessen Horowitz and Sam Bankman-Fried's FTX, which seemed to have so much money it was backing almost every crypto start-up. The investment round, announced in March 2022, valued Yuga Labs at $4 billion. That was as much as Disney paid to acquire Lucasfilm and the *Star Wars* and *Indiana Jones* franchises. The Bored Apes, of course, were not the stars of a popular movie, or the stars of anything at all. But in an amazing bit of chutzpah, NFT promoters claimed that was a good thing.

Yuga Labs said that each person who bought a Bored Ape would own the rights to them as "intellectual property"—meaning they were free to license them for use in products or movies. Ape owners liked to use this to justify the prices, but a Bored Ape movie seemed like a stretch to me. Even assuming one was made, the licensing fees would likely be barely enough to cover the cost of one Bored Ape. To make everyone's investments pay off, 10,000 movie studios would have to make 10,000 deals to make 10,000 cartoons about 10,000 similar-looking animals.

Most Bored Ape buyers made nothing from licensing. Stone was one of the few who did. He got the giant Hollywood talent agency Creative Artists Agency to represent him and his NFT collection. The deal was announced in *The Hollywood Reporter* in October 2021. It didn't reveal his real name, only his Twitter pseudonym "0xb1." It showed a large picture of his demon Mutant Ape, the NFT he bought for $1.1 million and used as his avatar.

There was an initial wave of interest. He said his agents met with *Family Guy* creator Seth MacFarlane's team, and the director M. Night Shyamalan, but nothing came of it. Plans to hire Rihanna to burn a Beeple artwork on camera with a flamethrower fell through, as did a planned Bored Ape party at Snoop Dogg's house. "What is wrong with these people?" Stone said to me. "They just think the world revolves around them." The only deal brokered by CAA was a onetime $33,000 payment for action figures that would be sold at Target.

Other efforts to monetize apes were even sadder. In addition to the food trucks outside, there was a Bored Ape DJ duo; Bored Sauce (branded hot sauce); and "Ape Shit," a music video released by Ape-In Productions ("the NFT-based record label"). Someone started trying to sell "Ape Water"—regular spring water in a can with a Bored Ape on it—which it called "the first cool, sustainable water beverage crafted for the Web3 community."

The bestselling writer Neil Strauss wrote an impenetrable ape-themed book that was itself released as a limited-edition NFT. At least 2,000 copies sold for about $250 each. "Captain Trippy lay in his hammock at the back of a room, holding a Shaving Ape cigarette loosely in his right foot," he wrote. "Some say it's the reason for his brightly colored psychedelic skin and captain's hat, so that he can be seen through the smoke." I'm not sure if anyone has actually read the whole thing, but I made a $300 profit when I sold my copy.

EVEN THOUGH I flashed Dr. Scum at ApeFest to prove I was a member of the club, and spent hours talking with their public relations representatives beforehand, Aronow and Solano declined to be interviewed. They seemed to be on edge. Bored Ape prices had been falling. Some explained the decline with a conspiracy theory that the Bored Ape cartoons contained hidden Nazi imagery.

The theory was created by Ryder Ripps, a thirty-six-year-old conceptual artist and prankster who'd collaborated with Kanye West and shown his work in New York galleries. He was clearly a skilled troll. (He'd once claimed credit for the CIA's website redesign, since no one would believe their denials.) That January, he'd registered a new website, named it after Aronow's pseudonym, "Gordon Goner," and laid out his theory.

On the site, he showed a Nazi emblem next to the Bored Ape Yacht Club's skull logo. They did look similar. But the other connections ranged from tenuous to far-fetched. Yuga Labs, he argued, was a reference to Kali Yuga, a term from Hindu mysticism popular with the alt-right. "Gordon Goner," he claimed, was an anagram for *Drongo Negro,* and he said "drongo" was Australian slang for *stupid.*

"It's extremely apparent to anybody who knows our history how absurd this is," Solano later told another reporter. "That said, the persistence, the maliciousness of the troll—frankly, how fucking evil the whole thing is—it's hard."

The strongest part of Ripps's theory was that ape cartoons played on racial stereotypes. Ripps said there was a long history of using ape images to insult racial minorities, which he called "simianization." And there was something gross about a big-lipped cartoon monkey wearing a hip-hop-style gold chain. "Don't you think that's a little condescending to our culture?" said Damon Dash, who co-founded Roc-A-Fella Records with Jay-Z. "Is that the way a nerd is trying to get cute and laugh at us? Why is everything an ape or a gorilla or a monkey—something that's been used to disrespect us for years."

A month before ApeFest, Ripps had started to sell his own NFTs. He called them RR/BAYC. They were exact replicas of Bored Apes—in fact, since NFTs don't actually contain images, just links to them, Ripps's NFTs contained links to the exact same images. He offered his for way cheaper, about $200 each. Ripps told me he hadn't ripped off Bored Apes—he'd created a new artwork by placing them in a new context.

"The NFT isn't the image," Ripps said. "The NFT is a cell in the spreadsheet that's in the blockchain that links to an image. No one is mistaking their apes for my apes."

Whether it was because there was a kernel of truth to his Nazi theory, or because anyone who paid hundreds of thousands of dollars for ape cartoons because Paris Hilton told them to was inherently gullible, Ripps found a receptive audience. Several Bored Ape owners told me they'd purchased RR/BAYC NFTs as a way to hedge their bets. And after the first night of ApeFest, I found more than a thousand people in a Twitter audio chat discussing Ripps's theories, many of them displaying apes as their avatars. RR/BAYC would eventually sell out. Ripps told me the project took in $1.1 million. (Yuga Labs would later sue him for ripping off their brand, which its lawyers called, misquoting someone, "the epitome of coolness." In April 2023, a judge ruled in the company's favor.)

DID I TELL you that ApeFest was a four-night festival? On one of the evenings, Snoop Dogg DJ'd. He was not concerned about simianization. He wore a white sweatshirt with his ape on it, Dr. Bombay, and performed with a dancer wearing a large Dr. Bombay head. By the time he brought Eminem out as a surprise guest, the stage was shrouded in weed smoke. "Yo that's fucking Eminem over here bro!" someone yelled.

"It's been a minute since me and Snoop did an actual song together again. So we came here tonight to play it for y'all and debut it here," Eminem said. He flipped off the crowd with both hands and walked off the stage, looking down. The video that played afterward showed Bored Apes rapping and smoking blunts.

At another point during the show, two poles were set up on the stage and women in bikinis started spinning around them. One of the dancers grinded on Dr. Bombay's crotch as Snoop spun a song about

ApeCoin. "If you've got some ApeCoins make some motherfucking noise," Snoop yelled. "ApeCo-oi-oin," the chorus went. "I ain't tripping on that Dogecoin shit."

I later learned from a legal document that Snoop allegedly owned a stake in Yuga Labs. I was almost relieved to find out he may have been shilling his own investment. The alternative—that one of my favorite rappers actually thought the Bored Ape Yacht Club was cool—would have been worse.

LATE ON THE first night of ApeFest, I saw Jimmy Fallon standing in the back of the VIP section. Fallon looked tan and smooth, almost waxen. He was wearing a baby blue cardigan over a vintage-looking polo shirt. Questlove, part of The Roots, who became the house band for Fallon's show, was DJing. Fallon nodded his head to '90s hip-hop.

The recent decline in Bored Ape prices meant that almost anyone I'd spoken to at ApeFest had just lost hundreds of thousands of dollars. They mostly didn't complain about it—anyone who had lost faith would have sold their ape and not come. But I felt angry on their behalf. I wondered if Fallon felt any responsibility for promoting Bored Apes in his segment with Paris Hilton. It might be pocket money for the two of them, but some people had sunk their life savings into these cartoons.

I approached Fallon and told him I was working on a book about crypto and had bought a Mutant Ape. Fallon feigned interest as I whipped out Dr. Scum. I feigned interest as he told me he thought of Bored Apes as a "cool art experiment."

"I wanted to come see the community, see what happens," he said.

"I feel like you really helped NFTs go mainstream," I said, reminding him of how influential his interview with Paris Hilton had been.

"Oh really?" Fallon said.

"You know people have lost real money," I said.

"I have no idea about investing," he said. "I bought it for the community."

THE MORNING OF the last day of ApeFest, I told my four-year-old twins what I was working on and showed them my ape. Even the twins—who found *My Little Pony* mesmerizing—were underwhelmed.

"Why don't you write about people who build machines to go to space?" my daughter Margot asked.

The time had come to sell Dr. Scum. People outside the club didn't know they should be impressed, and people inside the club could tell that he wasn't a winner. When I went to click SELL, the tiny fox in my browser popped up to say, mysteriously, "Nice function here," and then asked me to click SIGN on a long string of gibberish. Was I being hacked? I didn't care. All I wanted was to be rid of the JPEG ape. I only worried no one would be dumb enough to buy it.

For most of the day, I turned on my computer every few hours to check if he had sold, balancing my anxiousness to unload Dr. Scum with my fear that I would be hacked. These were some of the worst hours of my life. That evening, I realized the website hadn't been working properly and someone had already paid me $19,896.20 worth of Ethereum. Then I had to repeat the excruciating process of sending those coins to Coinbase and converting them back to dollars without losing my money due to typos or hacks. At one point, Coinbase's access to the Ethereum network went down. My money was in limbo for hours.

Had I been trading apes in U.S. dollars, I would have lost about $800. But in crypto, there's a fee associated with every transaction. I ended up wasting at least another $1,160: $36 to Coinbase, $497 to Yuga Labs for their 2.5 percent cut on all ape sales, another $497 to the NFT marketplace, $90 to Bank of America, and about $40 in Ethereum fees.

Because some people tag their blockchain address with their real name, I could see that Dr. Scum's new owner was an Armenian man named David Movsisyan. On Twitter, he said he'd thought Dr. Scum would get him into ApeFest. He had tried and failed to get into the last night of the festival a few hours after buying the Mutant Ape. I started to feel guilty. I'd lost money, but I'd also taken advantage of the Bored Ape hype to sell an ugly cartoon that I knew no one liked to some poor guy for $20,000.

I contacted Movsisyan, and when we spoke three weeks later, the Armenian wasn't angry. He told me that he was a freelancer who would generate cartoons for people who wanted to sell NFT collections. His first project was called Gambling Apes—an obvious Bored Ape rip-off—and the creators had sold them out for at least $2 million. Owning a real ape would help him generate more business. He told me he'd make a collection of ten thousand cartoons for me for as little as $15,000. When I apologized, he told me that Dr. Scum had actually gone up in value by $5,000 in the weeks since I sold him.

"You didn't scam me," Movsisyan said. "I was the one that scammed you."

ON ONE OF the nights of the festival, I met up with Stone again outside. As we sat on a park bench together, he told me why he'd been feeling so down. Between bumps of ketamine, he explained that crypto prices had been falling and Celsius was refusing to pay him the compensation he felt he was owed. He'd also deposited a bunch of crypto into an exchange run by teenagers in California and it had been stolen. His net worth, once near $100 million, had collapsed. He explained he'd slunk away from ApeFest's opening-night festivities because he felt like the people there were poseurs.

"These aren't real crypto people. Real crypto people were worth ninety million and now they've got three million and they feel like they want to kill themselves," he said.

We went to a side party on a different rooftop, hosted by the Mutant Cartel. At one point, he excused himself to take a phone call and came back looking whiter than I'd ever seen someone look.

"Shit's going down," Stone said to me. "I'm a wreck. I need to do more drugs."

He told me and one of his friends that the call had been from his lawyer. Investigators were looking into Celsius, he was told.

"Is it federal?" the friend asked.

"It's the FBI," Stone said.

CHAPTER SEVENTEEN

Blorps and Fleezels

A week before ApeFest, Celsius had made an announcement that customers would no longer be able to withdraw their funds. The crypto bank euphemistically termed it "pausing all withdrawals" but it was the digital equivalent of a bank branch locking its doors to keep people from taking their money out—the primitive technique some actually used during 1920s bank runs. Celsius founder Alex Mashinsky had assured me that his company was safer than any bank. When I'd asked why his interest rates were so much higher than banks paid, he'd said that bankers were dishonest and greedy.

"Somebody is lying," Mashinsky had said. "Either the bank is lying or Celsius is lying."

Now it was clear the liar was Mashinsky. That's why federal agents were calling Jason Stone, the former trader for Celsius who'd taken me to ApeFest. After meeting with U.S. authorities, Stone told me they weren't after him. They wanted to know whether Mashinsky and other Celsius executives had stolen money or lied about the company's finances. He was excited to tell the feds what he'd been telling me—that Celsius lost track of huge amounts of customer money and gambled it on all kinds of inappropriate bets.

"The real reason people give money to Celsius is they expect it to be safe," Stone said. "They're supposed to be this organized professional organization. What they're getting are snake oil salesmen."

THE RUN ON Celsius was part of a crisis that engulfed almost the entire crypto industry in the summer of 2022. It took months to unfold. Watching it was like seeing a house of cards collapse in slow motion. The whole time, I was watching Tether prices to see if a run would start on the stablecoin.

The crisis started in May. Token prices had been falling, along with tech stocks and other day-trader favorites. Then a crypto company run by an obnoxious thirty-year-old South Korean named Do Kwon exploded. It wasn't obvious at the time, but this would bring down a huge portion of the crypto economy.

Kwon's main coin was called TerraUSD. It was a stablecoin like Tether, intended to always trade for one dollar. But Kwon didn't promise to back his coins with dollars in a bank account. Instead, TerraUSD was backed with a second coin that Kwon made up, called Luna. Since Kwon controlled the supply of Luna, he could simply create as many as needed out of thin air.

If you're having trouble following this, that's actually a good sign about your investing instincts. Comedian John Oliver later summarized Do Kwon's nonsensical business plan: "One blorp is always worth one dollar. And the reason I can guarantee that is I'll sell as many fleezels as it takes to make that happen. Also, I make the fleezels."

The reason people bought into Kwon's Terra-Luna plan is that TerraUSD coins could be deposited in a special crypto bank called Anchor, also controlled by Kwon, which paid a 20 percent annual interest rate. This raised obvious questions, such as "Where does the money to pay those interest rates come from?" and "This is a Ponzi scheme, right?"

Kwon didn't really have good answers. Instead, he insulted anyone who questioned him. "I don't debate the poor on Twitter," he wrote to one critic. His plan, if you can call it that, was to make so much money that he could eventually have good assets to back TerraUSD.

Kwon wasn't some crackpot. His company was backed by some of crypto's top venture capitalists. One of them, ex-Wall Streeter Mike Novogratz, even tattooed his left shoulder with the word LUNA, next to a wolf howling at the moon.

Kwon's scheme made many people rich. Before the crash, the combined value of Terra-Luna topped $60 billion. But starting on May 7, after traders were spooked by a large sale of TerraUSD, many started cashing in their stablecoins for Luna tokens and selling them, driving down the price. The lower the price of Luna went, the more Luna tokens Kwon had to issue.

On May 9, Luna fell by more than half, to less than thirty dollars, then lost another two-thirds in value the next day. Kwon exhorted followers to hold on. "Getting close . . . stay strong, lunatics," he tweeted.

But there was no stopping the death spiral. By the morning of May 13, 6.5 trillion Lunas were in circulation, and the price had dropped to $0.00001834. TerraUSD's price dropped below 20 cents, because even if one TerraUSD coin could be redeemed for an immense pile of Luna tokens, there was no one to buy them. Nobody wanted blorps or fleezels. The $60 billion was gone.

FOR A SHORT time, it looked like Tether would be the next domino to fall. The coins almost always traded at close to a dollar because of the company's promise to redeem them at that price. Any decline below that level suggested a loss of confidence. On May 12, as Kwon's scheme unraveled, so many people rushed to dump Tether that the price of a token dropped below ninety-five cents on some exchanges. It seemed like the run might be on.

The Tether critics were getting excited. Bitfinex'ed, the anonymous critic who asked me to call him Andrew when we met at the bayside pool, tweeted more than sixty times that day. Hindenburg's Nate Anderson told me that he felt like his skepticism would soon be vindicated.

"The past two years have felt like this perpetual gaslighting of anyone who expresses caution," he said. "Now it's all unraveling very quickly."

Tether's tech chief, Paolo Ardoino, vowed in interviews at the time to defend the $1 peg and assured investors the company had more than enough available cash and easy-to-sell investments. He promised that anyone who wanted their money back could get it. "The worst-case scenario, Tether just shrinks," he said.

Because blockchain transactions are public, I could watch as investors sent back more and more Tethers to be redeemed—$3 billion worth within a day. As far as anyone could tell, Tether was able to come up with the money to pay them, and the token's price climbed back to $1. But it didn't seem like redemptions were slowing down. "Is this the beginning of a slow-motion bank run," I wrote in a note to myself, "or evidence that things are working as planned?"

· · ·

BY THEN, CELSIUS was in trouble too. Rumors were flying about whether the company really had the money it claimed. On May 13, the day after Tether fell below its $1 peg, Mashinsky tried to reassure his customers that their funds were safe. "Celsius is stronger than ever," Mashinsky said on a livestream. "We're open for business and we continue to do what Celsius does best: serve the community, protect the community, make sure your assets are there when you need them."

But behind the scenes, the situation was dire. Celsius had lost much of the money that its customers had deposited, and it hadn't told them. It turned out that giving money to Stone to gamble in DeFi was one of its safer investing activities. In fact, the company had no reliable way of generating money to pay the interest rates it promised. It had been secretly buying up large amounts of its proprietary cryptocurrency, CEL token, in an attempt to keep its price high, even while Mashinsky was dumping his own holdings. And it had been making unsecured loans to big traders who wanted to gamble on crypto. On a corporate Slack channel, one Celsius executive had joked that his job title should have been "Ponzi Consultant." Another executive explained the company's problematic business model. "Pay unsustainable yields so you can grow [assets under management], forcing you to take on more risk, experience losses bc of those risks + bad controls / judgment and you are where you are," he wrote on June 9. (Mashinsky and his lawyers have called allegations of fraud "baseless." They said Celsius was undone by "a series of calamitous, external events.")

Even as Mashinsky maintained publicly that all was well, Celsius went looking for a bailout. Among the companies it approached was Tether. The two companies were deeply entwined. There was the loan of a billion dollars' worth of Tether tokens that Mashinsky had told me about. And Tether was one of the biggest investors in Celsius. But Tether rebuffed Celsius's request for new money. In fact, instead of bailing Celsius out, Tether liquidated its loan to Celsius, further depleting Mashinsky's reserves.

Then Celsius tried a Hail Mary. It turned to Sam Bankman-Fried. Since his Bahamas conference, he'd become the most famous man in crypto. His supply of money was seemingly limitless. Celsius executives approached him about possibly buying their company. He met with them on June 12. Caroline Ellison, the head of his hedge fund Alameda, joined the call. The two of them had a lot of questions about Celsius's balance sheet and decided to pass on the deal.

"There are companies that are basically too far gone and it's not practical to backstop them," he later told a reporter.

Celsius's withdrawal pause came a few hours after Bankman-Fried turned the company down. It would prove permanent, and Celsius would later file for bankruptcy.

THE NEXT COMPANY to collapse was a hedge fund called Three Arrows Capital, long regarded as one of the best investors in crypto. Co-founder Su Zhu had promoted an influential theory that he called the "supercycle," which boiled down to a belief that crypto prices were going to reach unimaginable heights because crypto was taking over the world.

Zhu predicted the price of a single Bitcoin would rise to more than $2.5 million. On Twitter, where he had more than 500,000 followers, he once compared the invention of crypto to the creation of folkloric poetry, books, or photography. "Most are aware that crypto is the 4th computing paradigm, but it is also the 4th Epoch of Augmented Memory," he wrote. Comments like these made him, by crypto standards, a powerhouse intellectual.

Zhu's theories might have been stupid, but it was hard to argue with his results. When he founded Three Arrows in 2012 with a friend from the Massachusetts prep school Phillips Academy, the fund had $1 million, some of which came from their parents. Now the two thirty-five-year-olds were rumored to control as much as $10 billion. The fund was an early backer of Do Kwon's Terra-Luna scheme and *Axie Infinity*.

Zhu had earned enough to buy two houses in Singapore for about $57 million. And to friends, he liked to show off photos of the 171-foot superyacht he had ordered. It was to be named *Much Wow*, an inside joke about Dogecoin.

I'd seen Zhu at Bankman-Fried's Crypto Bahamas conference in April. Our experiences at the conference were a bit different. I'd flown commercial and been ridiculed by a man who owned a knock-off monkey NFT for asking to attend his party. He'd arrived on a private jet and posted a picture on Instagram of himself standing next to Katy Perry.

It wasn't widely known, but much of the money Three Arrows used for its supercycle bets was borrowed from Celsius and several other crypto companies that also offered high-yield accounts. The hedge fund was willing to pay a high interest rate, which was convenient, because the lenders needed to find some way to earn money to meet the promises they'd already made to depositors. Kyle Davies, Zhu's high school friend and co-founder, later said the lenders were so desperate to make loans that they asked for almost no proof that Three Arrows would be able to pay. "One of the last calls we did someone lent me almost a billion, off a phone call," he said. "That was uncollateralized. That's where the system was. People needed to get dollars out the door."

And Three Arrows had funneled much of that money into Terra-Luna. When it collapsed, the hedge fund lost $600 million. (The founders later said they were swayed by their friendship with Kwon, who lived near them in Singapore.) On May 11, one of the lenders to Three Arrows messaged an executive at the hedge fund asking for repayment, saying he would accept payment in Tether or other stablecoins. "Yo," the Three Arrows executive wrote back. "Uhh, hmm." The fund did not repay the loan.

On June 14, two days after Celsius's "pause," Zhu took to Twitter to address rumors that his fund was in trouble. "We are in the process of communicating with relevant parties and fully committed to working this out," he wrote, not very reassuringly. Two weeks later, Three Arrows filed for bankruptcy. Court documents showed that the fund's holdings included a portfolio of NFTs. Among them were a Bored Ape with a vaguely racist "sushi chef headband," and a pixelated image of a cartoon penis, called a CryptoDickButt, which, incredibly, was worth about $1,000 at the time. (Davies told me that one was sent to him unsolicited, apparently by some kind of crypto flasher.)

The fall of Three Arrows caused big losses for all of its lenders. Celsius had advanced them $40 million. Celsius competitors BlockFi and Voyager Digital revealed that they'd made even bigger loans to the hedge fund. Even companies that hadn't lent to Three Arrows themselves took a hit. Gemini, a well-regarded exchange, turned out to have lent users' money to a company called Genesis Global, which lent it to Three Arrows.

This was not at all what the users of Celsius and the other companies expected. They thought their accounts were low-risk—instead, their money was being lent to Three Arrows, the drunkest gambler at the crypto casino, who swapped it for Do Kwon's blorps and fleezels.

Some compared crypto's credit crisis to the 2008 financial crisis, when many U.S. banks had bet big on risky mortgage securities. But I felt like that was giving crypto too much credit. It reminded me more of the network of "feeder funds" that collected money from investors and pushed it into Bernie Madoff's Ponzi scheme, skimming off fees for themselves. As crypto skeptics David Gerard and Amy Castor wrote, the industry was like an inverted pyramid whose tip rested on a box of hot air—Kwon's Ponzi scheme. When the box crumpled, the pyramid came falling down.

THE LOSSES HIT everyone in crypto. Michael Saylor, the laser-eyed crypto prophet who was the star of the Bitcoin conference in Miami, stepped down as CEO of his company, MicroStrategy, after it lost almost $1 billion on its Bitcoin bet. Miami hoteliers and nightclub promoters complained about the disappearance of the big-spending crypto bros who would drop hundreds of thousands of dollars on champagne, hand stacks of cash to 50 Cent to toss into the crowd, and show off their account balances in their little fox-icon wallets on their phones. "You wouldn't normally show your bank account, but people do show their crypto wallets," a partner at the nightclub E11EVEN told a reporter. "I've seen more crypto wallets in a year than I've seen bank accounts in a lifetime."

After Three Arrows failed, Davies moved to Bali, where he painted, tried shrooms, and read Hemingway. "You eat very fatty pork dishes, and you drink a lot of alcohol, and you go to the beach and you just meditate," he told a reporter. He and his co-founder had saved enough money that they'd never need to work again. The real losers were the regular people who trusted their savings to Celsius's Mashinsky or Terra-Luna's Kwon. They gathered to commiserate on Twitter and on Reddit, where some forum administrators posted links to suicide hotlines.

"It felt to me like I was watching my own house burn down or something," one investor said on an audio chat on Twitter. "You're not an idiot, you're not unloveable," the host said. "Please don't make any rash decisions guys."

Newspapers filled with stories about people who'd lost their life savings. I spoke to Odosa Iyamuosa, a twenty-eight-year-old who lived in Abuja, Nigeria, who told me he'd thought Terra-Luna was his best hope to get out of a city where he said many jobs paid just two dollars a day, or less. He'd scraped together a little money selling knockoff Nike and Adidas sneakers to local buyers he found on Instagram. He wanted to increase his savings to $16,000 and enroll in a data-analytics program at a college in Toronto so he could get a job at a big American company, like Netflix or Google. For a few months, it looked like his plan was working. But after the crash, he was down to his last twenty dollars. He told me he was still on Twitter and the chat app Discord, hunting for a crypto project to make his money back. "There's literally nothing else for me again," he told me. "I don't know, man. Honestly, there's no job. There's no nothing."

Many investors wrote letters to the judge overseeing Celsius's bankruptcy, pleading for access to their funds. They didn't understand the money was gone, gambled away by Mashinsky. A thirty-six-year-old regional bank manager in Lancaster, Pennsylvania, with two small children, said that he'd lost $205,000, his entire retirement savings. A shepherd in Ireland said he had lost his farm. And a stunt double in Los Angeles said he was facing eviction. "No person would ever allow a financial company to hold their money under the pretense they could take it permanently," he wrote.

I called up another one of the angry Celsius customers: Chapman "Chappy" Shallcross, a fifty-seven-year-old retired fire captain for the city of Orange, California. Chappy got interested in crypto during the pandemic when he had a lot of time on his hands. His son Zach (who happened to have been the star of the 2023 edition of *The Bachelor*) was also playing around with trading small amounts of Bitcoin, Ether, and Dogecoin, and they liked talking about new coins together.

"We just bonded over trying to figure out what crypto is and how the blockchain works," Zach told me. "To this day I can't figure it out."

Chappy didn't tell his son he was cashing in about $200,000 of his retirement savings for Ether and Cardano, which he deposited at Celsius in December 2021. "I think decentralization is good, and I think blockchain technology and cryptocurrency can be great," Chappy said to another reporter. "But when you get slapped in the face with losing your whole retirement savings, you can't help but go, 'Hey I sure wish there was some kind of regulation that would have prevented this.'"

Like Chappy, many of the investors I talked to said they were still committed to crypto. It seemed to me like they just didn't want to admit they'd been wrong. "To me it's not about the money at all, it's about the future," an emergency room doctor in Lafayette, Louisiana, told me after he lost $800,000. He said he still believed Bitcoin would go up, calling it "the most pure digital asset that you can buy that's going to inevitably increase in value."

FOR HIS PART, Sam Bankman-Fried came out of crypto's summer of crisis looking like a hero. In June 2022, he bailed out BlockFi and Voyager with emergency loans after their Three Arrows losses, though Voyager succumbed to bankruptcy anyway. The bailouts were great for his public image. Already crypto's golden boy, now he was the industry's savior.

Fortune put Bankman-Fried on its cover, with the headline "The Next Warren Buffett?" In the accompanying article, he was called "crypto's white knight" and "a trading wunderkind whose ambition knows no limits." *The Economist* and CNBC host Jim Cramer compared Bankman-Fried to the financier John Pierpont Morgan, Sr., credited with using his own funds to avert a stock-market panic in 1907. Bankman-Fried did yet another round of interviews and TV appearances to talk about how he'd saved crypto.

"I do feel like we have a responsibility to seriously consider stepping in, even if it is at a loss to ourselves, to stem contagion," Bankman-Fried told NPR. "Even if we weren't the ones who caused it or weren't involved in it. I think that's what's healthy for the ecosystem."

Bankman-Fried did say something ominous in an interview for *Forbes* that June. While he assured the magazine that FTX was doing great, he said that some other crypto exchanges had already lost their customers' money and just weren't telling anyone. "There are some third-tier exchanges that are already secretly insolvent," he said.

I COULDN'T BELIEVE it, but even as crypto company after crypto company failed, Tether survived. It was more than a little frustrating. Back in 2021, I could have picked a company to investigate by tossing a dart at a wall full of crypto logos, and whichever one I'd hit would have probably blown up by now. Instead, I'd spent more than a year investigating one of the few that hadn't.

I still thought Tether was questionable. In fact, the more I looked into it, the less I trusted the company and its principals. But by July,

Tether had redeemed $16 billion of tokens and averted a full-on bank run.

Skeptics like Anderson pointed out to me that this was not proof the company had all the money it claimed. Redeeming 16 billion coins only proved Tether had $16 billion. The company could have lost $5 billion or $10 billion, but unless all the tokens were redeemed, there would be no way to know. Of course, by that standard, it was pretty hard for Tether to prove it was backed too. When I started investigating Tether, I thought it was the kind of mystery I could solve. Now it was starting to seem like a bottomless pit.

I wondered why more people hadn't cashed in their Tethers. There was clearly at least a small chance Tether might fail. Even someone who mostly trusted the company, despite all the reasons not to, would have reason to cash theirs in. Investors wouldn't even have to leave the crypto world. Tether could be easily swapped for a competing stablecoin, called USDC, which was based in the United States and didn't have the same checkered past.

I read that in some countries with high inflation, such as Turkey or Lebanon, some locals were buying Tether as a way of getting access to U.S. dollars, stable by comparison. Tether itself promoted this explanation, but I'd seen little evidence that these uses were actually widespread enough to account for a meaningful chunk of Tether's giant size.

Another theory I'd heard was that Tether's biggest clients could be shady characters, who might prefer to deal with an offshore entity that might be less willing to share information with U.S. law enforcement. Money launderers wouldn't care what exactly was backing Tether—they would just use it to move their dirty cash quickly.

At least some people were using Tether to launder money. One of its most prominent early promoters, a Chinese currency trader named Zhao Dong, pleaded guilty in 2021 to criminal charges in China for using Tether to launder $480 million for illegal casinos. I saw the coin mentioned from time to time in other cases. When North Korea sent workers overseas to earn cash, it would have them paid in Tether or other stablecoins. The nonprofit Transparency International Russia found that many crypto exchanges in Moscow would accept Tethers from users, with flimsy ID checks, and, in exchange, have a courier in London hand off stacks of cash.

I came across another intriguing mention of Tether in a criminal case against a Russian money launderer. U.S. prosecutors accused him of orchestrating a vast scheme that included, among other things, stealing American military technology. Amid the court papers, I saw messages the authorities had intercepted in which the money launderer discussed the best way to pay for Venezuelan black-market oil. He recommended Tether, saying it "works quick," like text messages. "That's why everyone does it now," the money launderer wrote. "It's convenient, it's quick."

But I wasn't sure if the money launderer was telling the truth that Tether use among criminals was widespread. It would take a city full of crooks moving huge sums of money to account for even a fraction of Tether's size. I wasn't sure how to investigate that. Then, one evening in August 2022, my phone buzzed with a message from an unknown number with a Southern California area code. It was from a beautiful woman I'd never met. And she'd end up delivering the clue I didn't know I needed.

CHAPTER EIGHTEEN

Pig Butchering

The mysterious text message arrived one night in August 2022, while I was out at a bar with a friend. It read: "Hi David, I'm Vicky Ho don't you remember me?"

This was strange, because my name is not David, and I couldn't remember anyone named Vicky. But in recent months I'd been getting a lot of seemingly misdirected messages on my phone. Usually I ignored them, but this time, maybe because I'd had a spicy watermelon margarita, I decided to write back.

After I told Vicky she had the wrong number, she apologized. Then, she awkwardly tried to continue the conversation. "Instead of apologizing for the wrong number can we be friends? lol," she wrote.

When I asked where she was writing from, she replied with a selfie. It was edited so heavily that she looked like an anime character: a pretty young Asian woman with porcelain-smooth skin, a narrow chin, and big round eyes with long lashes.

"Nice to meet you," I wrote. "My name is Zeke Faux. I live in Brooklyn."

"You have a very cool name," she said. "I am 32 years old and a divorced woman."

I showed my phone to my friend and explained that I was stringing Vicky along because I'd heard about a new kind of investment fraud that often started with a random text message. I had a hunch that this was why "Vicky" was texting me. The scam was called "pig butchering" because the scammers liked to build up the victim's confidence with a pretend romantic relationship and made-up investment gains before stealing all their money in one fell swoop—like how hogs are fattened up before their slaughter. My friend said he'd been getting, and ignoring, texts with similar nonsensical come-ons too.

I sent back a selfie of my own. Vicky told me I looked great and asked how old I was. But I let the conversation drop after we left the bar and went out for dumplings. When I woke up the next morning, I had a string of messages from Vicky waiting for me:

"What are you doing"

"good night"

"have you slept"

"What is your profession?"

"where is my dear friend"

"it seems you are very busy"

Vicky seemed thrilled when I wrote back. I knew that she just saw me as a potential mark, and that she wasn't who she said she was, but it was kind of fun to have an attractive new pen pal, even a made-up one. She told me she lived in New York too, where she ran a chain of nail salons, and that she'd moved from Taiwan five years ago at the advice of her uncle, a rich man who she said was "very good in financial fields."

Vicky told me she had a lot of free time and rattled off a long list of upscale hobbies: traveling, yoga, scuba diving, and golf. Amid the small talk, she dropped a hint about where the conversation was heading, saying she also liked to "analyze cryptocurrency market trends."

I knew that Vicky's job was to use social engineering to defraud me. But she wasn't very good at it. For one thing, she informed me it was raining in New York when I could see for myself that it was sunny. She said she was attending the Met Gala, but it had happened three months earlier. When she sent a suggestive photo of her legs in bed, the view from her window didn't look anything like New York. Her attempts at flirting sounded robotic: "I like to pursue romantic things like a healthy body and the surprise and preciousness of love."

After a day, Vicky revealed her true love language: Bitcoin price charts. She started sending me graphs of prices going up. She told me that she had figured out how to predict market fluctuations and make quick gains of 20 percent or more. The screenshots she shared showed that during that week alone she'd made $18,600 on one trade, $4,320 on another, and $3,600 on a third. The trades, she explained, hinged on a cryptocurrency called Tether. She told me it was safe, because

Tether is a "1:1 cryptocurrency with the US dollar, also known as a stablecoin."

But Vicky told me I wasn't ready to trade like her and recommended I read a few books about Bitcoin first. For days, she went on chatting with me, without asking for me to send any money. I was supposed to be the mark, but I felt like I had to work her to get her to scam me.

I tried flirting. "Very cute," I wrote, after she sent me pictures from a golf course. I tried asking directly: "I am curious to try the technique you explained," I said. To show her I was already primed for crypto trading, I even told her about my friend Jay.

"Some of my friends made a lot of money on crypto," I wrote. "One bought Dogecoin and made enough to take his whole family to Disneyworld."

But for an entire week, she stuck to chitchat, brushing off my attempts to redirect the conversation to her scam. Her restraint was remarkable. I was getting impatient to be scammed.

When I woke up to yet another text saying "Love Did you sleep well last night," I tried another way to show her I was a good prospect. I told her I wanted to buy a new car, and I sent her a photo of the $142,000 gull-wing Tesla I coveted—the one I'd daydreamed about buying if I struck it rich on Bored Apes.

"I see the price is 142,200," Vicky wrote.

"Yeah they are costly," I said.

"As long as you like this, money is nothing," she said.

Then she sent me a Bitcoin price graph and told me that the next day she was going to make a new trade based on her data analysis. Her explanation of how it worked involved lots of made-up jargon, but it sounded just as plausible as the other crypto mumbo-jumbo I'd been hearing. "I invest in short-term contract node trading," she told me. "Sharing with you tomorrow."

Finally, I was in. The next day, Vicky sent me a link to download an app called ZBXS. It looked pretty much like the other crypto exchange apps I'd tried, though it didn't come from Apple's official app store. "New safe and stable trading market," a banner read at the top. It displayed prices for different cryptocurrencies, all in terms of Tether.

Then Vicky gave me some instructions. She explained that I should use a U.S. exchange to buy the Tethers and then send them to ZBXS's deposit address, a 42-character string of letters and numbers. I decided to start with $100, and ended up with eighty-one Tethers after paying a series of fees. Sure enough, after I transferred them to the address, they appeared in my account in the ZBXS app.

But Vicky said that was not enough. She told me I'd have to deposit $500 in Tether to make the "short-term node" work. When I didn't send the money right away, she sent me a voice memo. "Okay Zeke, what are you doing?" she said, in a soft and silky high voice, with an accent I couldn't place. "I see you got my message. Why you not reply me back, huh?"

At this point, I decided I had played this out long enough. "I have to tell you something," I wrote. "I'm an investigative reporter. The reason I've been talking with you is I wanted to learn more about how these things work."

"ohoh it's not what you think," Vicky wrote.

Then I saw her WhatsApp profile picture turn from a doe-eyed woman into a white dot. That was the last I would hear from Vicky.

VICKY'S ATTEMPTS AT a fake friendship were pretty weak. But lots of people were falling for pig-butchering scams. It seemed like if the scammers texted enough people, they eventually found someone lonely enough to take the bait.

News stories revealed that people were losing huge amounts of money. A project finance lawyer in Boston with terminal cancer handed over $2.5 million. A divorced mother of three in St. Louis was defrauded of $5 million. A twenty-four-year-old social media producer in Tennessee lost $300,000 she inherited from the sale of her childhood home. "You hear all these stories about people becoming millionaires," she told a reporter. "It just felt like, oh, well, cryptocurrency's the new trend, and I need to get in."

My short-lived texting flirtation with Vicky confirmed something that I had suspected: The scammers were using Tether to move the money. I spoke with several other pig-butchering victims, and they said they'd been asked to send Tether too.

WHILE I WAS looking for people who'd lost money to the scam, I came across a group that claimed to be raising money dedicated to helping victims. It was called the Global Anti-Scam Organization. The group said it had helped a huge number of pig-butchering victims: 1,483 worldwide, who'd lost more than $250 million combined. If this figure was accurate, it likely represented only a tiny fraction of pig-butchering losses. I realized the total amount of Tethers used in this scam could be huge.

Global Anti-Scam's website said that it was a nonprofit run by victims of pig butchering who volunteered to help others. But its generic name and clip-art-filled website made me suspect it was itself a scam. Another detail I read on its site raised my eyebrows even higher: The group claimed to fight "human trafficking," a seemingly unconnected phenomenon—and a buzz phrase among Pizzagate-style conspiracy theorists.

"All over the world, thousands of men and women in the prime of their lives are victimized, impoverished, and devastated by online scams," the group wrote. "Help us to end this global crisis by lifting up victims, raising cybercrime awareness, and fighting human trafficking."

I was made more suspicious when I contacted the group and was told all of its members went by code names. When I told them I was looking into Tether's role in these scams, they told me to talk to the group's crypto expert, who went by "Icetoad." We set up a Zoom.

Icetoad turned out to be a thirty-eight-year-old with messy brown hair named Jason Back, who called in from his basement in Ontario, Canada, wearing a blue Phish T-shirt. His LinkedIn profile showed he'd recently been working as a "cannabis concierge." And Icetoad wasn't some kind of dark-web alias. It was the screen name he'd used since third grade.

Icetoad said that he'd joined Global Anti-Scam after getting scammed himself. His specialty was following the money. He said that, using publicly available blockchain analysis tools, he could track the crypto a victim sent. And he confirmed that in most cases, the bad guys used Tether. He said he'd personally traced several hundred million dollars' worth of Tether that were the proceeds of pig-butchering scams.

"It always starts with Tether," he said. "They're basically facilitating money laundering."

. . .

ICETOAD WASN'T SURE why the scammers always used Tether. And at first, I wasn't sure either. After all, the crypto trading apps that they had the victims download were completely fake, like Vicky's made-up crypto exchange ZBXS. In theory, I could have sent in my deposit via credit card, PayPal, or bank wire, before placing my pretend crypto trades. It would have saved the scammer from teaching the victim how to acquire and send Tethers.

But then I thought about how scammers moved money before Tether existed. One thing I'd learned from reporting on financial fraud is that money transfers, not persuasion, were often the hardest part of ripping someone off. When I thought through the mechanics of Vicky's swindle, I realized it was almost identical to a con-man tactic that was popular in the early 1900s, called "the Big Store." Even back then, swindlers had to go to great lengths to get the money out of their victims' bank accounts and into theirs.

A century ago, the railroad stations, transatlantic steam liners, and saloons of the United States were plied by confidence men. Lesser grifters rigged dice games or played three-card monte. But the most skillful specialized in long cons, spending days or weeks building the trust of the victim, or "mark," before disappearing with their cash.

The Big Store was one of these long cons. The traveling con man—called a "roper"—would befriend a mark and tell them they had a relative with a surefire money-making trick, just as Vicky Ho told me. Back then, it was generally a way to pick winning racehorses or stocks. Then they'd lead the mark to the Big Store—a rented suite that was dressed up to look like a betting parlor or a stock brokerage, complete with fake stock tickers and actors playing customers, flashing wads of cash.

After being allowed to place a few winning bets or trades, the victim, feeling emboldened and thus vulnerable, would be convinced to make a really big gamble. That one they'd lose. Once the mark was gone, the store would be packed up. If the police came, they'd only find an empty room. It was, as the linguist David Maurer wrote in his 1940 classic *The Big Con,* "a carefully set up and skillfully managed theater where the victim acts out an unwitting role in the most exciting of all underworld dramas."

Big Stores could take in as much as $100,000 at a time—a huge sum back then. Top practitioners became famous, like Joseph "Yellow

Kid" Weil. "I have never cheated any honest men, only rascals," Weil once told the writer Saul Bellow. "They wanted something for nothing. I gave them nothing for something."

Back then, one of the hardest parts of running a Big Store was transferring such large sums of money without arousing suspicions. It usually required the cooperation of a local banker. Con men had to find one willing to accept bribes to cash large checks from out-of-towners and to keep their mouths shut.

The way Vicky approached random strangers like me also reminded me of a more recent con: the "Nigerian Prince" scams of the 1990s. In the early days of email, people posing as Nigerian royalty spammed inboxes with "urgent solicitations" seeking "honest and reliable partners" to help reclaim family fortunes. The recipients were always told that they'd first have to send money to cover expenses. But no matter how much they paid, they'd always be told that another obstacle stood in the way of their windfall.

Those scammers would ask victims to send a wire transfer to a co-conspirator with an account at a U.S. bank. Because these "money mules" had to give banks their real name, they were often eventually arrested.

From the scammer's perspective, Tether was a clear improvement on bribing bankers or money mules. It was instant, there was no recourse for refunds, and it didn't ask for anyone's name or address. And unlike other cryptocurrencies, its value didn't fluctuate from hour to hour, making it less scary for potential victims and easier to manage for criminals.

SCAMMING WAS THE one industry where the blockchain was living up to the limitless potential touted by crypto bros.

Icetoad and other volunteers from the Global Anti-Scam group told me that Tether refused to help them by freezing accounts or seizing stolen money, even when presented with evidence that an account held the proceeds of fraud. Tether clearly had the capability to help. In some cases, like hacks, Tether had frozen accounts and seized money. But when contacted about pig butchering, Tether would fall back on the excuse that it didn't control the blockchain. Another Global Anti-Scam volunteer provided copies of several victims' email exchanges with Tether.

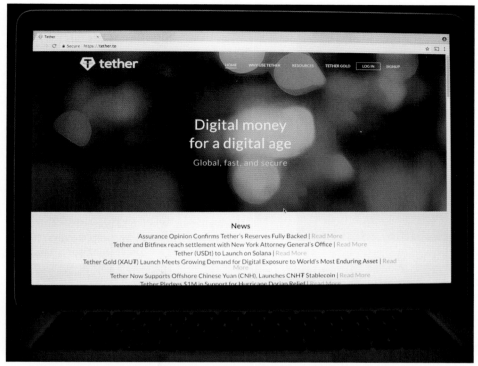

Tether's website as of May 2021. By then, there were $55 billion worth of Tether coins in circulation—an amount that would have made the cryptocurrency company one of the fifty largest banks in the United States.   *(Tiffany Hagler-Geard/Bloomberg)*

Engineers on a cherry picker inspect cryptocurrency mining rigs at the CryptoUniverse mining operation in Nadvoitsy, Russia, in 2021. That year, by some estimates, Bitcoin mining consumed as much energy as the entire country of Argentina, population 46 million.   *(Andrey Rudakov/Bloomberg)*

Sam Bankman-Fried, founder of the crypto exchange FTX, in the Bahamas in the spring of 2022, a few months after he relocated there. FTX had recently raised funding from venture capitalists at a valuation of $32 billion. *(Melissa Alcena)*

Four crypto companies aired ads during the NFL's Super Bowl in 2022. FTX's spot featured *Curb Your Enthusiasm*'s Larry David as a time-traveling Luddite who scoffs at major inventions in human history—from the wheel, to toilets, to the Walkman. When he's presented with FTX's cryptocurrency trading app, he says, "Ehh, I don't think so." *(YouTube)*

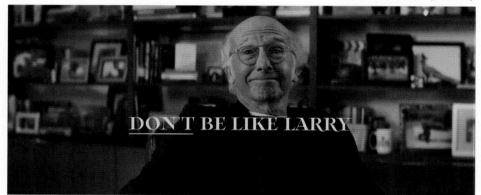

DON'T BE LIKE LARRY

In this ad for the exchange Crypto.com, actor Matt Damon strides through a virtual "Museum of Bravery," past astronauts, an early aviator, and a climber scaling an icy mountain, before looking into outer space, where he sees the Crypto.com logo. "Fortune favors the brave," he intones. *(YouTube)*

Brock Pierce played the younger version of Emilio Estevez's character, Gordon Bombay, in *The Mighty Ducks*. He was one of the first to realize the potential of cryptocurrency, thanks to his experience with massively multiplayer online games, and claims that he came up with the idea for Tether. "I'm a doula for creation," he said. *(Christopher Gregory-Rivera)*

Tether boss Giancarlo Devasini was formerly a plastic surgeon. In an essay accompanying this photograph—shot for an exhibition at an art gallery in Milan in 2014—he explained his decision to walk away from medicine. "All my work seemed like a scam, the exploitation of a whim," he said. *(Alberto Giuliani)*

Jean Chalopin, the chairman of Deltec Bank & Trust in the Bahamas, was the co-creator of the beloved children's animated TV series *Inspector Gadget*. By the summer of 2021, Deltec was the only financial institution I could find that was willing to say it was working with Tether. *(Rebecca Sapp/WireImage via Getty Images)*

Alex Mashinsky was an indefatigable salesman for the crypto quasi-bank he founded, Celsius Network. He claimed to have accumulated $18 billion in assets by 2021, by paying implausibly high interest rates—as much as 18 percent a year. *(Piaras Ó Mídheach/Sportsfile for Web Summit via Getty Images)*

Jason Stone, a thirty-four-year-old DeFi trader, was entrusted by Celsius with hundreds of millions of dollars' worth of cryptocurrency to invest. "I'm just like click, click, click, make money, make money, make money," Stone explained of his trading strategy. *(Dave Krugman)*

Sam Bankman-Fried poses with supermodel Gisele Bündchen at FTX's Crypto Bahamas conference in April 2022. The unlikely pair also starred in a glossy magazine advertising campaign for FTX. *(Joe Schildhorn/BFA.com)*

Razzlekhan was the rap persona of Heather Morgan. She and her husband were charged with conspiracy to launder $4.5 billion in cryptocurrency in connection with the 2016 hack of the exchange Bitfinex. The seizure was the largest in U.S. history.

People using their mobile phones to play the cryptocurrency game *Axie Infinity* in an alley in suburban Manila. Players had to buy teams of cartoon blobs and earned tokens by using them in battles. The game became a get-rich-quick craze in the Philippines. By October 2021, about two million people were playing the game every day. *(Above: Jam Sta. Rosa/AFP via Getty Images; left: Zeke Faux)*

Nayib Bukele, El Salvador's president, announced plans to build "Bitcoin City" at a November 2021 crypto conference near El Zonte Beach. El Salvador's infrastructure budget could barely cover a single skyscraper, but he said he would fund the construction of the futuristic metropolis through Bitcoin investments, including volcano-powered crypto mining. *(Jose Cabezas)*

A demonstrator in San Salvador holds a sign during a protest against President Nayib Bukele and Bitcoin in September 2021. That month, El Salvador became the first country to adopt Bitcoin as legal tender. *(Camilo Freedman/Bloomberg)*

Celebrity heiress Paris Hilton and host Jimmy Fallon showed off their Bored Ape Yacht Club NFTs on *The Tonight Show* in January 2022. NFTs, digital images tracked on the blockchain, were marketed as the future of art, but many of the most popular collections were derivative cartoons that sold for ridiculous sums. Fallon's, shown here, cost him $216,000.   *(YouTube)*

A yacht-sized inflatable ape reclines outside ApeFest, a four-day Bored Ape festival at a pier in the East River in downtown Manhattan. Snoop Dogg and Eminem, both Bored Ape owners, were the headliners.   *(Zeke Faux)*

Jason Stone's demon Mutant Ape NFT cost the unbelievable sum of $1.1 million. The trader used it as an avatar on Twitter, where his pronouncements would move markets.   *(Jason Stone)*

I purchased this Mutant Ape NFT for more than $20,000 in cryptocurrency. The process was a convoluted and horrifying ordeal. I named him Dr. Scum and imagined that he was a private detective who gains superintelligence from smoking weed. No one cared.   *(Zeke Faux)*

In "Chinatown," a vast compound of derelict office towers in Sihanoukville, on Cambodia's western coast, thousands of migrants worked as online cryptocurrency scammers. Workers who have escaped say they were held against their will and forced to send spam text messages day and night. Some say they were beaten, tortured, and worse. This drone photograph shows the section known as Kaibo and the KB Hotel.   *(Danielle Keeton-Olsen)*

Buildings in the Kaibo section of Chinatown at night. The Cambodian publication *Voice of Democracy* wrote about a string of suspicious deaths in the area—one body was found hanging from a construction site, and a handcuffed corpse was dug up from a shallow grave in a field nearby.   *(Zeke Faux)*

In August 2022, I received a mysterious text message that read: "Hi David, I'm Vicky Ho don't you remember me?" Vicky later sent me this photo from a room that she said was in Manhattan, the view from the window notwithstanding. She tried to scam me using the cryptocurrency Tether.

Thuy, a twenty-nine-year-old photographed in Ho Chi Minh City, Vietnam, escaped from the Kaibo section of Chinatown in 2022 after suffering severe beatings and torture. He proved a valuable source of information about the scam compound where he was held captive. *(Zeke Faux)*

Sam Bankman-Fried lived in a $30 million penthouse at this condo building, called the Orchid, in Albany, a resort in the Bahamas. Bankman-Fried's supposed thriftiness was part of his public persona, so this wasn't part of the typical tour he gave to visiting journalists. *(Zeke Faux)*

Sam Bankman-Fried being walked in handcuffs to a plane in Nassau in December 2022 after FTX's collapse. He was flown to New York after agreeing to be extradited to the United States to face criminal charges. *(Royal Bahamas Police Force via Reuters)*

In December 2022, after crypto markets had collapsed, I spotted a sign of the times in a garage in Midtown Manhattan: a Toyota Supra with an "NFT" vanity plate that had been booted due to unpaid bills. *(Zeke Faux)*

"We do not issue all the addresses in use and are not in control of them nor of every transaction made on-chain," a Tether customer service representative wrote to one victim in Singapore. "We also do not have identifying information about the persons who use addresses which we do not control."

"As I am sure you can appreciate, we do not wish to be drawn into a possible dispute between two parties," the company added.

To me, that sounded like a cop-out. When I sent my eighty-one Tethers to Vicky Ho's platform, there was an entry in Tether's database representing how much money I had, and another one representing how much Vicky Ho had. Another way of looking at it would be that Vicky Ho had an anonymous, numbered account at the Bank of Tether.

In another exchange provided by Global Anti-Scam, Tether told a Hong Kong police official that it *did* have the ability to intervene. But the company still refused, saying the case was too small.

"We must sometimes decline fraud cases involving relatively small amounts of stolen USDT," the Tether representative wrote, using the ticker symbol for the cryptocurrency. It said they would only intervene if the case was "directly connected to acts of violence."

I couldn't believe that Tether was getting away with making its own rules for when it would cooperate with police. Imagine if the cops told a bank that it was holding stolen money and the bank said it wouldn't return it because the thief didn't shoot anyone.

And, from what Icetoad and other members of his group were telling me, the criminal syndicates who ran pig-butchering scams were actually extremely violent. They told me that many of the people sending spam texts to potential victims like me were themselves victims of human trafficking.

According to Global Anti-Scam, most pig-butchering scams were orchestrated by gangsters based in Cambodia or Myanmar. These bosses would lure young men and women from across Southeast Asia to move abroad with the promise of well-paying jobs in customer service or online gambling. Then, when the workers arrived, they'd be held captive and forced to work on online scams.

Icetoad and his colleagues told me there were thousands of people who'd been tricked this way. Entire office towers were filled with floor after floor of people forced to send spam messages around the clock, under threat of torture or death. These were the people using Tether to move their money.

I wasn't sure if I believed Icetoad and his friends at first. But when I dug into it, details that seemed to corroborate their far-fetched story had been trickling out in other news outlets—Cambodian newspapers, *Al Jazeera, Nikkei,* and *Vice.* I wondered if the person who called themselves Vicky Ho was a slave. Maybe they were still trapped. But they had stopped responding to my messages. The best clue I had to go on was their Tether deposit address, a 42-character string of seemingly random letters and numbers.

Of course, sometimes those 42-character addresses did lead somewhere—as the cringey rapper Razzlekhan learned when the IRS traced the funds from the giant Bitfinex hack to her Wall Street apartment. I needed a blockchain detective of my own.

AFTER RESEARCHING SEVERAL crypto security firms, I contacted the lead investigator at one called CipherBlade. His name was Rich Sanders and his firm's website advertised that he was an expert on recovering money from crypto scams. What sold me was that he'd gone as far as posing as a teenage girl—using a voice changer and a collection of suggestive photos—to trick a crypto thief into revealing his identity. Surely a man with this level of dedication could help me trace my eighty-one Tethers.

I emailed Sanders and he offered to help. We met at his house in West Mifflin, an old steel mill town near Pittsburgh. He greeted me outside. At his side was his dog Havoc, a husky-retriever mix. Sanders, thirty-two, was wearing jeans covered in dog hair and a gray T-shirt that read T-SWIFT'S NEXT ALBUM. On his left arm he had a tattoo of the lyrics of a French Foreign Legion song, and on his right a sword with wings, a tribute to a soldier he'd served with in Afghanistan.

Sanders invited me into his office, and as Havoc slobbered on me, he told me that he'd tracked $500 million lost to pig-butchering schemes, and that he estimated at least $10 billion had been lost to crypto romance scams overall.

"We've been getting cases like this pretty much since the onset and a massive uptick of them around the time Covid hit," he said.

I'd provided Vicky Ho's address to Sanders before the meeting. Sanders pulled up a flowchart he'd made tracking transfers to and from the numbered account.

Near the center, a small dark circle represented Vicky Ho's wallet.

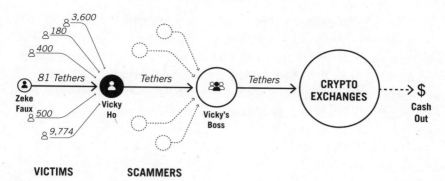

This was where I'd sent the eighty-one Tethers. Sanders explained that the wallet was active for about two months and received many deposits from addresses that were known to be associated with U.S. and Canadian crypto exchanges. There were transfers of $3,600, $180, $400, $500, and $9,774, always in Tether. These were other people who'd been scammed by the same operation, Sanders said. In other words, I wasn't Vicky's only love interest.

Once Vicky Ho had collected the money, they sent it to another numbered address, represented on the screen by a larger white circle. This one was likely controlled by the scammers too, Sanders said, and it held $9.4 million in Tethers.

From there, many of the Tethers were sent to addresses associated with the crypto exchange Binance, and to others that belonged to Sam Bankman-Fried's FTX. Sanders said that was typical. Scammers would send their Tethers to exchanges, trade the crypto for local currency, and withdraw the cash to a bank account.

Sanders told me the transfer to Binance was as far as he could trace Vicky's money. The exchange would have an identity on file for whoever received the transfer, but they wouldn't reveal it, except to law enforcement. (He was right—when I asked Binance, a representative said the exchange wouldn't help me.)

Even if Binance did give me the name, it might be fake. Sanders said that it was easy to open exchange accounts using false identification. He'd even signed up for accounts of his own under the name "Taylor Swift." As verification, he'd sent in a photo of himself in drag, wearing a blond wig, heavy blue eye shadow, and a glittering silver dress, which displayed his abundant chest hair. He said crooks who prefer not to dress in drag can buy accounts registered by other people for as little as $20.

"Why don't people trust crypto? It's shit like this," Sanders said.

I noticed what looked like a toy submachine gun sitting on a table behind his desk. He told me it was a very real Scorpion semiautomatic pistol, with laser sights. He said he kept it handy because he'd received credible threats from some of the people he'd investigated. I told him I was going to keep trying to trace my Vicky Ho payment back to its source.

"I'd be careful if I were you," he said. "Money makes people lose their humanity."

ICETOAD HAD GIVEN me another contact who might be able to help: a Vietnamese hacker named Ngô Minh Hiếu. He'd been one of the first to gather intel on pig butchering, both by interviewing victims of human trafficking and by breaking into some of the scammers' computers.

Hiếu had quite the résumé. By the time he was in his early twenties, he'd stolen so many people's identities that a U.S. Secret Service agent said he'd caused the most financial harm of any hacker ever. Lured to Guam in a sting operation, he was arrested and sentenced to fifteen years in an American prison. After he was released in 2020 and deported to Vietnam, he switched from crime to law enforcement. He was now a "threat hunter"—a white-hat hacker—for Vietnam's National Cyber Security Centre, and a minor celebrity there.

We spoke via Zoom. Hiếu told me that because he was well-known for exposing fraud, he was contacted by a Vietnamese victim of human trafficking. That man introduced him to other victims. They'd responded to ads offering good pay for work in customer service at casinos in Cambodia. But when they'd arrived, they found they couldn't leave. And instead of customer service, they were forced to work as scammers.

Hiếu showed me pictures and videos he'd obtained from inside the scam compounds. A worker with a deep gash across their forehead. Tall apartment blocks ringed by concertina wire, each window blocked with steel bars. In a video, a man trying to escape leaped from the third floor of a building, crumpling when his legs hit the sidewalk.

"These are super dangerous areas, controlled by Chinese mobsters," he told me. "You can get inside, but you can't get outside. It's like a prison."

I asked Hiếu if he could gain any intel from ZBXS, the fake crypto trading app that Vicky had told me to download. He looked at the source code and said it was similar to other apps he'd seen that he'd traced to Cambodia. Hiếu said it was likely that whoever was posing as Vicky Ho had sent the messages from Cambodia. But when he tried to break into the website, it seemed like its owners noticed. Within a few hours, it had been wiped from the internet. It was so easy to set up a new one, he said. It was an insidious problem.

"Multiple scam websites get eliminated every single day, but new websites are coming up," he said.

I FELT LIKE I'd hit a dead end trying to find Vicky Ho. But their message had, in a weird way, led me to what had to be one of the biggest and most illicit uses of Tether. Even as I tried to move on to other things, I kept thinking about the people trapped in Cambodia forced to pose as Vickys, sending spam text messages in hopes of earning Tether for their bosses.

The Vietnamese hacker gave me a list of people who'd escaped scam compounds in Cambodia, and, working with a translator, I started interviewing some of them over video chat. Most said they'd responded to legitimate-seeming job ads, or were contacted by recruiters. These job-seekers were convinced that plum positions in customer service or sales were waiting for them in Cambodia. Once they arrived, they were told they'd be working as scammers instead. Armed guards prevented them from leaving.

The people I spoke with described abuses that were worse than I could have imagined. Workers who didn't meet quotas for scamming were assaulted, starved, made to hit each other, or sold from one compound to another. One said he'd seen people forcibly injected with methamphetamine to increase their productivity. And several said that they'd seen workers murdered, with the deaths passed off as suicides.

"I was really scared every day," one nineteen-year-old girl from Vietnam's Mekong Delta region who'd been enslaved in Cambodia told me. Her family paid a ransom of about $3,400 to secure her release.

Bilce Tan, a square-faced, outgoing forty-one-year-old from Malaysia, told me he'd answered an ad on a website called JobStreet seeking someone to work in "telesales." The ad promised free roundtrip tickets to Cambodia, $1,000 to $2,000 a month plus bonuses, a "cozy, welcoming office with friendly colleagues," and "attendance incentives." In an interview over video chat, the recruiter told him that the company was in telecommunications, and he was offered a better position, in business development. He was told the position was based in Sihanoukville, on Cambodia's western coast, and that he would be given housing near the company's offices. In May 2022, he flew to Phnom Penh.

A middle-aged man picked him up at the airport in a black van, and, at a gas station, three others jumped in. When Tan tried to chat with them, he could tell right away something was off. "They were silent and told me to shut up," he said. "I felt like I was a criminal and they're the police."

It was night when he arrived at his new job. The office turned out to be a compound of buildings, at the top of a hill. It was dark, but what little he could see didn't seem like a normal company. The road was lit with spotlights. Guards patrolled with batons and long rifles. The buildings were surrounded by barbed-wire fences. There were surveillance cameras everywhere.

"It's my first time in Cambodia," Tan said. "I'm thinking, What the hell kind of place is this?"

A manager met him at the gate and walked him to a dormitory, where he spent a restless night. This was not the kind of housing he had imagined. The next day, another manager took him to the office where he'd be working. The room held ten workers. Each had two computer monitors and ten phones, loaded with fake accounts, with pictures of a man or a woman, depending on the gender of the target. Two of his false identities were women named Lily and Angelina. He was given scripts, lists of potential marks, and trained how to approach different types of people. Single parents were said to be the best targets.

"We start to make introduction by telling what we've gone through," Tan told me. "Then they'll start to give back their own story."

Instead of pushing people to download an app, he was told to drop hints about how much money he was making, and wait for the mark to bring it up themselves—just like Vicky did with me. "If he asks us the question, this is the time we strike," Tan said. "We start to show the website of this cryptocurrency and how to register."

Tan said that, like Vicky, he'd always asked victims to send Tether. The bosses used it to avoid detection. "It's more safe," Tan told me. "We are afraid of people will track us, for money laundering. It's untraceable."

Tan didn't want to scam anyone. But workers who didn't meet quotas were shocked with an electric baton, or locked in a room for punishment, or even sold to another compound.

Tan had traveled to Cambodia with three cellphones, which he'd hidden in his dorm when he arrived, and one night, he called his family. But somehow, his employer found out. They threw him in a chair, pointed a gun at his head, and slapped him around; then he was locked in a closet. For what seemed like days, he was kept in the dark. His leg was bleeding and he lay on the floor. He was not let out to use the bathroom, and he was given only white rice to eat. He couldn't stomach it. "It's very difficult to breathe," he said. "You feel very dizzy and faint."

After Tan was let out of the room, he was given a final warning to shape up or else. Then, with help from someone whose identity he doesn't want to disclose, he was able to escape. He asked me not to share the details, to protect his rescuer's identity. But he did say the escape involved hiding under a pile of cardboard boxes. "It was like a kidnapping out of a Hollywood movie," he said. As soon as he could, he flew back to Malaysia. He'd only been in Cambodia for three weeks; he felt lucky to get out alive.

"I need the whole world to know what is happening," Tan said. "We need more people to be aware of this and save the people inside."

THE SCALE OF the problem was vast. Many of the victims were held in one giant compound, called "Chinatown," also in Sihanoukville, a few miles from where Tan escaped. From news reports, interviews with victims, and postings on social media, I learned that Chinatown held as many as six thousand people.

I started researching Chinatown, as best I could from nine thousand miles away. From photos, it looked as large as a city's downtown. It had dozens of tall and drab office towers, arrayed around a few courtyards, surrounded by high gates, security cameras, concertina wire, and armed guards dressed all in black. "It's one of the most haunted places on earth," the hacker Hiếu told me.

At street level were noodle shops, convenience stores, and barber shops, many of them with signage in Chinese, rather than the local Khmer. Photos posted by one confused tourist showed that the shops were bisected by metal gates, preventing anyone who entered from the back door from escaping through the front.

One of the best sources of information was a Cambodian publication called *Voice of Democracy*. There I read accounts from workers who'd been abused in the Chinatown compound. Some had been beaten, tased, or tortured, and others handcuffed in confined spaces and starved. They said the scam bosses would buy and sell them like animals. On social media, I saw videos where handcuffed workers were tortured with electric shock batons, and mercilessly kicked and beaten with bats.

Voice of Democracy also described a string of suspicious deaths near Chinatown—one body was found hanging from a construction site, and another handcuffed corpse was dug up from a shallow grave in a field nearby. A local vendor told a different Cambodian outlet that there had been many suicides at the complex. "If an ambulance doesn't go inside at least twice a week, it is a wonder," he said.

And the problem was large enough that it could account for a serious amount of Tether transactions. If Chinatown held six thousand people scamming like Vicky Ho, and each had to meet a quota of $300 a day—the number I'd heard from some victims—that one compound alone would generate more than $600 million a year in illicit proceeds.

From what I had learned, it seemed that this scam slave complex would not be able to operate without crypto. And the benefits of crypto to the rest of the world seemed to be limited to enabling a zero-sum gambling mania.

Crypto bros routinely claimed that anonymous, untraceable payments on the blockchain would somehow help the world's poor. But it seemed like none of them had bothered to look into what their technology was actually being used for. Tricking Filipinos into going into debt for a pipe dream based on Smooth Love Potions was bad enough. But aiding and abetting enslavement?

There was only so much I could learn about Chinatown over video chat. I had to see it for myself.

CHAPTER NINETEEN

"We Have Freedom"

The video opens with a man driving on a highway. The man is wearing a polo shirt and a button with his nickname on it, Phong Bui, and he's holding his cellphone in one hand, talking on speakerphone. On the other end of the line is a man who sounds panicked, speaking in Vietnamese. That man, whose name is Thuy, is calling from just outside the Chinatown scam compound, in Sihanoukville. He'd been tricked into traveling to Cambodia like many people I'd interviewed and read about, forced to scam, and abused for months.

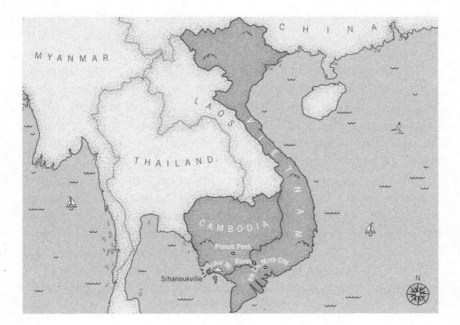

The man driving on the highway is a famous Vietnamese YouTuber, who has just paid a $5,000 ransom to free Thuy.

"I just got electrocuted a few more times before I got out," Thuy says. "I gave them the ransom," Phong Bui says. "Why did they electrocute you?" "I don't know either," says Thuy. "They took my phone and smashed it. They beat me up and asked who paid the ransom."

"How brutal," the YouTuber says.

Videos like these captured millions of views in Vietnam and turned Phong Bui into a local star. They had gruesome pictures of victims' injuries and lurid titles like "The Story of Thuy Escaping from Hell on Earth and the Midnight Screams." I'd paid to have them transcribed and translated. It seemed distasteful to turn human suffering into YouTube content. But they were one of the best sources of information on crypto-fueled human trafficking that I'd found. That's how I located several of the victims I'd been interviewing.

Before going to Cambodia, I stopped in Vietnam to meet Phong Bui and the man he rescued. I'd contacted Thuy via text, and I had spoken with him almost a dozen times by video chat over months. He told me he was living in an industrial town with his aunt and uncle about an hour's ride from Ho Chi Minh City. I took a taxi there with my translator, and he met us on the side of a dusty highway lined with car shops. Thuy was a young-looking twenty-nine-year-old, with wavy bangs that covered his forehead and a thin mustache. When he opened his mouth to light a cigarette, he revealed he was missing at least four of his front teeth—knocked out, he told me, by his captors in Cambodia.

Thuy led us down an alley shaded by blue tarps to the unmarked door to his aunt's apartment, where he was living. The entire place was ten-foot square, including a kitchen and a lofted mattress. We sat cross-legged on the green-tiled floor. It was a languid day. Above us, an oscillating fan mounted on the bottom of a sleeping platform squeaked back and forth, failing to keep us cool.

Thuy was eager to tell me more about his ordeal in Chinatown, where he was held for months and suffered brutal abuses. He showed me a ragged scar behind his ear, and one on his arm. And he brushed his bangs aside to point out a long lump on his forehead, a fracture that was still healing. He said he'd seen workers beaten to death, and that others had committed suicide.

After interviewing so many absurd and frivolous crypto characters, Thuy's story was sobering. But even though his accounts were consistent with news reports, I was still not sure how much I could trust him. He told me he'd spent two stints in prison, for assault and drug trafficking, and some of what he told me about his personal life didn't check out. But he was still a valuable source of intelligence. He provided photos he'd taken inside Chinatown and the most detailed description of the compound of any of the escapees I interviewed.

Thuy's ordeal sounded like a sequel to *Taken,* the Liam Neeson action movie. The most unbelievable part was how he'd been able to find Phong Bui's YouTube videos and contact him to arrange for his rescue. Thuy told me that he stole a guard's iPhone and secreted it inside his rectum, a trick he'd learned in prison. When the phone ran out of battery, he took it apart, without using any tools, peeled out the dead battery, and charged it by hot-wiring it to a fluorescent light fixture.

"I was very calm, no fear at all, because I thought that I would die either way," Thuy told me in Vietnamese. "If they found out I was the one stealing that phone, I would either be beaten up or killed. But if I managed to hide it, I would have a chance to live."

I was skeptical. And the next day, when we met again in Ho Chi Minh City, where I was staying, I told Thuy that I harbored some doubts about his ability to hot-wire an iPhone. Thuy said he could demonstrate. We found a shop, where I bought a used phone for fifty dollars. We went to my hotel, where, without hesitation, Thuy took apart an LED bulb in the lamp in my room. Then, using a USB cable he stripped with his teeth, he wired the bulb to the iPhone's battery. When he reinstalled it, the phone powered on. I was amazed.

We went over satellite photos of Chinatown to prepare for my trip. Thuy showed me the gates that were manned by guards, and the areas that the captive workers couldn't leave. He pointed out a hotel with a gilded facade within the complex where he said the scam bosses were serviced by prostitutes.

In Ho Chi Minh City, I arranged to meet Phong Bui at a restaurant near my hotel. A waiter there recognized him right away. Phong Bui told me that he'd started out making happier videos about his travels throughout Southeast Asia. But in Cambodia, he'd heard about the travails of Vietnamese migrant workers. And the videos he started posting about their ordeal generated lots of views, and donations. Victims like Thuy started contacting him from within scam compounds. Phong Bui said he'd already paid ransoms to free more than fifty people who had been held against their will. The YouTuber said the work was dangerous. He'd started using intermediaries to arrange rescues after receiving threats from gangsters.

We went over maps of Chinatown together too. Phong Bui showed me the building where he'd sent a driver to deliver the ransom and pick up Thuy. He said that while the stories were extreme, he believed them. Another young woman who'd been held in Chinatown told him she'd seen two people killed in front of her. He warned me not to go poking around.

"Hire a taxi and sit inside to take pictures," he told me. "Don't get out of the car."

IN CAMBODIA, I made plans to meet up with two reporters from *Voice of Democracy* who had helped expose the scam-slavery problem. If they were in the United States, they would have won journalism awards. In Cambodia, things didn't work that way.

Ahead of the national elections, Prime Minister Hun Sen, the country's longtime authoritarian ruler, was jailing opposition leaders on trumped-up charges and harassing union leaders. The rampant human trafficking in the country had become an international political issue. In February 2023, he ordered *Voice of Democracy* to close. He said he was angered by a reference to his son in an article, but many suspected it was because the publication's stories about scam compounds had become an embarrassment.

"You always say I use my power, so I'll use my power for you to see," Hun Sen said in an angry speech on February 20, about closing the publication.

"Foreigners, I remind you, do not get involved. This is Cambodia," he added.

Three days later, I was riding in a bus from Ho Chi Minh City, bouncing past cow pastures, shacks with rusty tin roofs, and neon-colored stucco mansions, on my way to Cambodia's capital, Phnom Penh.

I made a pit stop in Bavet, a dusty casino town in southeastern Cambodia, just over the border from Vietnam. I'd seen Vietnamese news reports that said several of the casinos were fronts for scams and forced labor. I'd even seen a video of workers fleeing from one of them in the rain, chased by guards who beat those who slipped and fell.

Once I was there, I realized there was little I could learn by myself. But in the parking lot, a sign on a little booth caught my eye. It advertised money-transfer services in Vietnamese and Chinese. On it, I spotted a white "T" encircled in green: Tether's logo. It didn't prove anything, but it seemed odd that the first time I'd seen the symbol outside of crypto conferences was at an alleged human-trafficking hub.

In Phnom Penh, I linked up with the former *Voice of Democracy* reporters: Danielle Keeton-Olsen, a twenty-eight-year-old from the Chicago suburbs who'd been reporting in Cambodia since college, and Mech Dara, a thirty-five-year-old known for his fearless reporting, and for flouting the unofficial dress code by wearing flip-flops and jeans to government press conferences.

Dara rumbled up to my hotel on a janky moped older than he was. The bike's purple body was cracked and its mirrors had been lost to accidents. When I asked the two if they were nervous to continue reporting after the prime minister's edict, they told me they weren't. "If they want to get you, they will get you, no matter what you do," Dara told me.

DANIELLE TOLD ME that in Phnom Penh, in a Chinese district, there were many money-exchange shops that advertised Tether on their facades, similar to the one I had seen near the border in Bavet. She was as curious as I was to see what that meant. She took me to one, across from a shiny condo tower that advertised luxury apartments in Chinese.

Parked outside, I saw two sleek black SUVs with tinted windows: a Range Rover and a Chinese-made Zotye. On an LED sign, above ten-foot brass doors, there was a continuous scroll of Chinese characters. Among them we spotted the ticker symbol for Tether again: USDT.

When we went in, a clerk invited us to sit down at a large marble desk, in white leather chairs that were embroidered with the Bentley logo. I was the only customer in the office, which had polished marble floors. In niches in the wall, I saw a statue of a stag and blue-and-white porcelain vases.

I told the clerk, a friendly young Cambodian man in a football jersey, that I wanted to exchange Tether for U.S. dollars. He told me I could have cash on the spot, or money deposited in a Chinese bank account, and asked me to wait for the boss to come back from lunch. He told me Tether was popular with Chinese businessmen.

"When they want to send to overseas, it's convenient to send USDT," he said. "It's anonymous and it's quite safe."

As we waited, a hungover-looking Chinese man in flip-flops and pajama pants strolled in, walked behind the desk, and unwrapped a bundle wrapped in black plastic to reveal a lunchbox-sized brick of $100 bills wrapped in rubber bands—$50,000 in all, the clerk later told me—then walked out with it stuffed under his arm. *This guy doesn't care if Tether is backed by Chinese commercial paper, or anything at all,* I thought. *He just wants to trade crypto for bricks of cash, and not tell anyone about it.*

The boss turned out to be a different surly Chinese man who arrived soon after, wearing a white T-shirt over his big belly. "ERC-20 or TRC-20," he grunted at me. During my ape-buying ordeal, I'd learned what this meant—he was asking which blockchain I wanted to use for the transaction.

I'd come prepared, with a few hundred Tethers loaded into my fox-head app, which I'd installed on my iPhone. The boss texted me his wallet address—the string of random numbers and letters. I pasted it into the fox head and zapped him 105 Tethers—five of them to cover his fee. Then, without asking for identification or even a name, he handed me a crisp $100 bill. I'd turned my crypto into cash, with no paper trail.

Using blockchain analytics, I saw that over the next few days, other customers sent him $2,990, $5,000, and $20,000. And this was only one of four currency exchanges that advertised Tether in the neighborhood.

NEWS REPORTS HAD tied the Chinatown scam compound to Xu Aimin, a Chinese magnate who'd developed the property. Aimin was, at least technically, an international fugitive, subject of an Interpol "red notice," which was supposed to alert police around the world to arrest him. He was sentenced in 2013, in absentia, to ten years in prison in China for running an illegal gambling operation with more than $1 billion in turnover.

But when I asked Danielle and Dara whether he was on the run, they scoffed. The avenue that runs through Chinatown is named for him. And in Phnom Penh, down the street from *Voice of Democracy*'s shuttered office, I could see the cranes constructing a new building for Aimin's company. It was a fifty-three-story tower, which if completed would be one of the tallest buildings in the capital. Inquiries to Aimin's company went unanswered.

BEFORE GOING TO Chinatown, I decided to go with Danielle and Dara to visit a different scam compound closer to Phnom Penh. This was attached to a casino complex in southern Cambodia, about a hundred miles southwest of the capital, on the Gulf of Thailand. It was on top of a mountain called Bokor, in the middle of a national park.

There were reports that dozens of people were being held there, forced to work in online scams, beaten, and threatened with death if they tried to contact the outside world. In 2022, a Taiwanese gangster who went by the nickname "Big Fatty" had been arrested in his home country for trafficking dozens of workers there to work in online scams. But the mountaintop compound was reportedly still open. It was an ideal location for traffickers. Surrounded by forest, it was impossible to escape.

Before we left, I spoke with Richard Jan, a veteran Taiwanese police officer who worked on the Big Fatty case. He said the Taiwanese government had rescued more than four hundred victims of human trafficking in Cambodia in 2022. He traveled to Bokor to exfiltrate some victims himself. One of the young women his agency had rescued from the mountain had been beaten so badly she was nearly blinded. Jan said other workers there were killed.

"I've heard from people who came back alive that some victims were thrown from the rooftop, but the abuser pretended that these victims jumped to their death," Jan said.

Jan told me that in addition to using crypto for scamming, the Big Fatty gang demanded payment in Tether when it sold its victims into slavery. Jan had been investigating human trafficking for a long time. He told me crypto was making his work more difficult. Before, gangsters had used bank accounts to move money. The banks would turn over customer information, which often provided leads. Tether didn't even collect information on the holders of its coins.

"It's extremely difficult to investigate," he said in Chinese. "It doesn't require any identification and documents at all."

I was a bit nervous to visit a human-trafficking gang's mountain hideout. But Danielle explained that it was not as risky as it sounded. Bokor was a tourist attraction, which drew visitors to admire the ruins of French colonial mansions and the view from the mountaintop. Someone could pose for selfies only a hundred yards from the scam compound and never have any idea that anyone was trapped inside.

Bokor Mountain was shrouded in clouds as we approached. We stopped at a gate manned by guards who asked our destination. Then, for half an hour, we drove up a twisty road blasted through rock, past palm trees and white-faced monkeys. Near the top of the mountain, we came to a giant hotel, with a yellow facade so weathered and dirt-streaked that it looked like it had survived a zombie apocalypse. Behind it, a row of about fifty empty townhouses with chrome fences snaked up to the summit. I could see weeds growing between the cobblestones of their unused sidewalks.

A century-old Buddhist monastery stood at the summit, where I saw three monks in orange robes sweeping up around golden Buddhas, listening to a recording of chanting. Outside, a dog picked through trash, looking for something to eat.

The 500-room hotel, called Thansur Sokha, was spookily silent and empty—apart from one bemused French couple who must not have read the online reviews, and dozens of staffers whose heads swiveled to follow me like a family of owls. There was nobody in the casino, the spa, the wine bar, the restaurants, or the playroom for children. A parking lot built for hundreds of cars had just six. I felt like I was visiting the amusement park for ghosts from the Hayao Miyazaki movie *Spirited Away*.

A cluster of nine dilapidated office buildings stood behind gates about a hundred yards behind the hotel. It was the purported scam compound. I decided to get a closer look. To accentuate my dumb tourist getup, I snapped on my fanny pack and bought a cup of strawberry ice cream, which was so freezer-burned and chalky that it seemed months old. A gate separated the public areas of the hotel-casino from the compound. As I walked up, I conspicuously licked strawberry ice cream off my tiny spoon. A German shepherd emerged and barked at me furiously, straining on a heavy chain. A guard indicated to me that I couldn't pass. Through the buildings' windows, I could see rows of bunk beds.

While I was getting barked at, Dara chatted up another guard. That man told him the buildings were rented to Chinese companies and that the workers inside couldn't leave. I wanted to do something, but Danielle and Dara had told me it was useless to report forced labor to the authorities. Local potentates were generally getting paid off by the traffickers. Rather than aid escapees, Cambodian officials would detain them for immigration violations.

The Taiwanese cop told me it seemed to him that local police seemed to be in league with the gangsters. They'd been willing to help him arrange the release of some Taiwanese victims, but hadn't made any arrests or forced the scam compound to close. He had gone undercover, posing as a sketchy businessman, and met with a group of scam bosses. While they were at dinner, one had gotten a tip-off about an upcoming raid.

"The police are purposely covering up these compounds," he said.

AFTER MY EERIE but inconclusive visits to Bavet and Bokor, it was time to head to the most notorious purported scamming site of all: Chinatown. The drive from Bokor to Sihanoukville, only seventy-five miles, took several hours over dusty roads, giving me plenty of time to talk with Danielle and Dara about their investigations.

Sihanoukville was named for the Cambodian king who was ousted in a 1970 coup five years before the genocidal Khmer Rouge seized power. Its white-sand beaches had long made it an attractive if slightly seedy destination for European backpackers, who stayed in bamboo huts and smoked cheap marijuana.

Then, starting around 2017, the city was transformed by a casino-building boom fueled by Chinese investors. Gambling is illegal in mainland China, outside of the state-run lotteries, but Sihanoukville was only a short flight away. A questionable legal loophole allowed betting over livestreamed video.

Skyscrapers and new apartment blocks rose along dirt roads. Downtown filled up with domed structures with flashing neon signs. Tens of thousands of Chinese workers flooded into Sihanoukville to staff the casinos and to gamble at them. By 2019, Chinese immigrants outnumbered Cambodians. There were ninety-three licensed casinos and hundreds more illegal ones, which generated as much as $5 billion a year in revenue. On the gaming floors and from offices hidden away upstairs, women in ballgowns and tiaras would livestream games like baccarat to gamblers back in China. Rolls-Royce and Hongqi limousines parked outside the nicer casinos.

"The typical customer at the baccarat table in the Golden Sand seemed to be a young Chinese man wearing a T-shirt and shorts, rough-looking, smoking, and cradling stacks of $100 bills in his palm, betting upwards of $1,500 per hand," a visitor wrote in *The New York Review of Books* in 2019.

With gambling came crime. Sihanoukville became infamous for prostitution, score-settling shoot-outs, kidnappings, and money laundering. Local officials blamed Chinese gangsters. In one viral video, a man wearing a bloodied white T-shirt runs down the street, chased by two guards wielding shock batons, then falls to his knees, holding scissors to his own neck and yelling for help. In another, a loan shark's lifeless body is pushed out of the backseat of an SUV in broad daylight.

But at the end of 2019, Cambodia's prime minister effectively made online gambling illegal by saying he wouldn't renew licenses for online casinos. The ban, combined with Covid-19 travel restrictions, tanked Sihanoukville's economy. About half of the casinos closed and construction froze, leaving more than 1,100 buildings unfinished. Most Chinese workers left. The casino bust pushed criminal gangs to evolve. They turned the casinos into bases for online scam operations.

When we got to Sihanoukville, I saw the city was dotted with the concrete skeletons of hundreds of abandoned high-rise construction projects. Through the gaps between their floorplates, staircases to nowhere cut through the sky. The skyline looked eerie, like a city-sized sculpture meant to illustrate the excesses of speculation.

As we drove through Sihanoukville, Dara and Danielle pointed out scam compounds everywhere, telling me stories about abuses that happened at each one. Some would have been easy to miss—a regular office tower behind a casino, but with bars on the windows and security guards standing outside, or a gate off an alley that advertises a casino but doesn't allow anyone to enter. Others were conspicuous. Dara pointed out a high tower painted black with windows barred, high fences topped by broken glass and barbed wire, and security cameras facing inward.

. . .

CHINATOWN WAS OUTSIDE the city center, near one of Siha-noukville's beaches. When its gray towers appeared on the horizon, I almost couldn't believe they were real. It had been almost two years since *Businessweek*'s editor had asked me to look into Tether. I'd spent most of that time investigating its laughably weird founders and try-ing, and failing, to find the billions of dollars of reserves that it claimed it had. I had thought Tether might be a giant scam. But I never could have imagined the money trail would lead to someplace like this.

Chinatown was just as the human-trafficking victims had described it, except many of the towers appeared to be empty. Five months ear-lier, the authorities had announced that they'd shut down one of the area's biggest operations, after the stories by Danielle and Dara and other outlets had made it the most famous symbol of the government's apparent tolerance of human trafficking.

The first cluster of buildings in Chinatown were vacant. But when we reached the second, we saw more activity. It was a massive com-plex of at least twenty shabby, two-tone gray buildings surrounding a gold-faced hotel, on a wide avenue flanked by streetlights each shaped like a bouquet of a dozen flowers. Guards clad in all-black stood out-side large black-and-gold gates topped with gold spikes. Each unit in the building had been built with an airy deck. But bars had been welded on to convert the balconies into cages.

I saw a steady stream of cars passing by the guards, who would check to make sure they had proper placards—chrome-accented Toy-ota Alphard vans and Range Rovers with tinted windows. Several young women in skin-tight party dresses approached on scooters and were waved through too. Had activity in the compound restarted after the unwanted attention had passed?

Inside the gate, I could see what looked like a whole neighbor-hood: a barber shop, restaurants, and a store with stuffed animals in the window. But when I asked if I could enter, I was turned away. One of the guards said something to the other five and everyone cracked up.

Next to the compound was the hotel with the golden facade, called the KB Hotel. I'd been told it housed sex workers. But now, it appeared to be open to the public. Its doors were flanked by coconut palm trees and manned by bellhops clad in black-and-gold knee pants, vest, and loafers. I checked Booking.com and saw that, incredibly, the hotel was listed. A superior king room went for $98 a night, with breakfast in-cluded.

Outside, I saw five men dressed in black polishing a black Maybach limousine, and a Chinese man with a red mohawk and big belly wearing a Gucci T-shirt pacing back and forth. A man handed me a business card advertising prostitutes.

I decided to go inside. Danielle and Dara agreed it would appear less suspicious if I went alone. One of the bellhops gave me a tour. A highlight was a twenty-foot-tall golden pineapple in the lobby. The halls were just as empty as the hotel on top of Bokor Mountain. At its casino, where Chinese soft rock played and elegant cups held free Chinese cigarettes, dealers outnumbered players three to one.

A sweeping marble staircase led me from the lobby to an elegant restaurant upstairs, where a small buffet of Chinese food was set out in metal chafing dishes. The host appeared surprised that a tourist had come there to eat, but invited me to come in. "It's free for you, sir," a waiter said.

The massive dining room could have hosted a wedding, but there were only a few people eating. Among them were the Maybach-polishing minions and a buff Chinese man in a T-shirt, who was watching TikTok videos on his phone at an obnoxious volume. He appeared to be their boss, because he peeled off cash for each of them from a wad he pulled from his pants pocket.

Everyone seemed right at home there, except for me. I took a Budweiser from a fridge set up on the side of the room and sipped it, trying not to look too nervous or too interested in what was going on. But I was fascinated. Was this a scam compound boss sitting right next to me, eating roast duck? But because everyone was speaking Chinese, I couldn't pick up any hints.

One hostess spoke English. I asked her why the hotel was so empty. She said that it had only opened to the public a few months earlier. Before that, she said, it had only been for people from the surrounding buildings. I asked her why the buildings had such tight security.

"This is Chinatown, don't you know?" she said.

I played dumb. She explained that the workers were not permitted to leave, trying her best to explain it in a palatable way. When I made a face, she tried to reassure me that I was not being served by slaves.

"The staff here, we have our freedom," she said.

I walked to the back of the restaurant, where large windows looked out onto the inner courtyard. The sun had set and the lights in some of the gray office buildings made it clear they were occupied again. I could see T-shirts and shorts hanging to dry off some of the balcony cages. I shuddered thinking about what the people inside might be going through and hurried back outside.

Dara picked me up, and as we drove out of the complex, I saw a shuttered currency exchange. Its sign had been taken down, but the outline was still visible. I saw four letters in English: USDT, the ticker symbol for Tether.

EVEN BEFORE I went to Cambodia, I knew I wasn't going to find Giancarlo Devasini on top of Bokor Mountain, slurping noodles with Big Fatty at the ghost hotel. The beauty of Tether as a way of moving money is that it can operate with little oversight from the company itself. Tether says that it knows the identity of all of its customers, but those are just the small group of crypto traders who buy or redeem coins from the company directly. I was able to use Tethers on my fox-head app to get cash in Phnom Penh without providing any personal information. If law enforcement asked Tether for identifying documents for Vicky Ho or Big Fatty, the company wouldn't have any. It could completely disclaim responsibility.

Since the summer of 2022, when I first learned about pig butchering, I'd been operating on two tracks. While I was researching how Tether was fueling scam compounds in Cambodia, I also started investigating a place where Devasini *had* shown his face: El Salvador. The country's president, Nayib Bukele, had proudly announced his adoption of Bitcoin as a national currency at Bitcoin 2021, the conference in Miami I had attended. In February 2022, a member of El Salvador's ruling party had posted on Twitter a photo of himself alongside a Bitcoin proponent and other party officials, taken at the legislative assembly. Standing in the back was Devasini.

I read in a Salvadoran publication called *El Faro* that Devasini and other Tether officials were advising El Salvador's government on Bitcoin. Tether couldn't distance itself from the place. And neither could the rest of the crypto bros, who'd been telling me that Bitcoin had miraculously transformed the country, even after most reports in the media made the experiment sound like an unpopular flop. The Central American nation had been turned into a referendum on whether Bitcoin could be used in the real world.

CHAPTER TWENTY

No Aceptamos Bitcoin

When Nayib Bukele, the president of El Salvador, announced in May 2021 that his country would adopt Bitcoin as a national currency, I didn't really believe he would do it. The country was on the brink of defaulting on its foreign debts, and the persistent gang violence that had once made it the murder capital of the world was flaring up anew. Was the answer to El Salvador's problems to go all-in on a volatile digital currency that nobody else in the real world was using?

But Bukele really did follow through. He gave thirty dollars in Bitcoin to each citizen—a few days' wages for a farmworker—plunked down Bitcoin ATMs in every town plaza, and told businesses to accept Bitcoin as payment. And with the country on the edge of a debt crisis, Bukele told off international creditors, saying he'd solve El Salvador's financial problems with Bitcoin instead. "#Bitcoin is FU money!" he tweeted.

El Salvador became a country-sized advertisement for Bitcoin, and many of the crypto enthusiasts I interviewed told me that the plan was such a success that other countries would soon follow suit. And, of course, entire countries buying the cryptocurrency would be sure to send its price up and up. "There's probably a big part of the future happening in El Salvador right now," Twitter co-founder Jack Dorsey said in an online talk in February 2022.

I wanted to see the effects of Bitcoin in El Salvador myself. Before going, I met with Jack Mallers, the boyish crypto executive who'd introduced Bukele's Bitcoin plan for El Salvador on stage at Bitcoin 2021 in Miami. Only ten months had passed since he burst into tears and told the crowd: "I'll be there. We die on this hill. I will fucking die on this fucking hill!" But when I asked him how the experiment was working out, he said he couldn't remember the last time he visited. He didn't seem to be too torn up about it. "It's very important to know that it's not my project, you know," he said.

Bukele was more committed to the bit. The forty-one-year-old president had become a crypto influencer, with four million followers on Twitter, where he dubbed himself "The Coolest Dictator." He used government funds to buy $100 million worth of the cryptocurrency, and promptly lost half of it when the price of Bitcoin fell. Despite his trading losses, he would still post about buying more, sometimes bragging that he traded on his phone while sitting naked in his bathroom.

"The Coolest Dictator" was supposed to be a joke, but it was too close to the truth to be funny. Bukele was becoming increasingly authoritarian. In March 2022, he'd declared a state of emergency, suspended due-process rights, and ordered the police to round up anyone suspected of gang ties. More than 60,000 people were detained—about one in a hundred Salvadorans. Most were held without charges. Bukele reveled in the brutality, posting humiliating pictures online of the detainees stripped to their underwear. They were all gangsters, he said, who would die in prison. At least 150 people did die in custody, some showing signs of torture, according to the human rights group Cristosal.

Bukele's oppressive policies did not turn off the Bitcoin faithful, who, to be fair, did not have a lot of Bitcoin-loving presidents to choose from. They turned El Salvador's Pacific Coast into a destination for crypto pilgrims. One of the first was, of course, Brock Pierce, the child actor turned Tether co-founder, who arrived on his private jet in September 2021, threw a party for crypto bros and influencer Logan Paul, and flew out the next day.

Another Bukele booster was Tether's Giancarlo Devasini. I learned that he had come in February 2022 in support of the second phase of Bukele's crypto plan: Bitcoin City. This was to be a futuristic metropolis like Dubai, which the president claimed he would build in the country's east. Bukele said it would have a new airport, no taxes, free power from a Bitcoin-mining volcano, and a giant plaza shaped like the Bitcoin logo, so large it would be visible from space.

What didn't make much sense was how a country with an infrastructure budget that would barely cover a single skyscraper was going to pay for all this. That was where Devasini was supposed to come in. His crypto exchange, Bitfinex, had promised to raise the money to build Bitcoin City with a special Bitcoin bond offering. But what was in it for Devasini?

MY FIRST STOP was El Zonte, the beach town where the Bitcoin experiment started. In 2019, a surfer from San Diego started handing out small amounts of Bitcoin to locals in the hopes of creating what he called a "Bitcoin circular economy." His supposed success was cited by Bukele as inspiration for the national Bitcoin policy.

El Zonte had been swarmed by Bitcoin influencers, travel bloggers, and TV crews, who dubbed it Bitcoin Beach. Bitcoiners liked to tell me that the town's adoption of Bitcoin was a crucial proof of concept, a first step on the cryptocurrency's inevitable path to global acceptance. They seemed a little too excited by the idea that there was finally a store or two where tourists could use their Bitcoins to buy regular stuff. "Okay, guys, we are about to order here at Minutas Mario, and we can pay with Bitcoin," a German Bitcoin YouTuber said in a video I found. Standing at a rusty-wheeled pushcart, he got a *minuta*— a fruit-flavored shaved ice—and spent more than three minutes scanning QR codes to transfer 13,418 hundred-millionths of a Bitcoin (about five dollars at the time) to the vendor's digital wallet.

El Zonte proved to be a genuinely beautiful but tiny tourist town about an hour south of the capital, where I saw chickens hopping down rutted dirt roads, and residents living in corrugated-metal shacks next to hotels for foreign surfers. What I did not see was anyone using Bitcoin for anything. When I mentioned Bitcoin at the first store I entered, the clerk snatched the bottle of water I was trying to pay for out of my hands. "Trash," he said. "I will never use it." My hotel wouldn't accept it either, and a beachfront restaurant next door displayed a handmade sign saying NO BITCOIN. Its owner told me he got sick of telling visitors he didn't want to handle such a volatile currency. "The tourists think everybody accepts Bitcoin," he said.

I walked out onto the black-sand beach, where I saw surfers cutting through the waves and two muscular influencers flexing and posing for pictures with their baby. I quickly spotted the beat-up pushcart where the German Bitcoiner had filmed his video. The proprietor, Mario García, was wearing a fuzzy white cap, an Adidas fanny pack, and a dirt-streaked orange polo shirt. His ACCEPTAMOS BITCOIN sign was so faded I could barely see the "B" logo. Nearby, his wife was stirring a giant pot of potatoes to make dumplings.

García didn't have much to say about Bitcoin. It was a way of drawing in tourists, he said. He converted their payments to dollars as quickly as possible. But he did have a story to tell about a different Bukele initiative: the gang roundup. It turned out being an unofficial Bitcoin mascot was not enough to protect him.

One morning in April, four soldiers and two police officers approached him on the beach as he started work. He was ordered, at gunpoint, to strip to his underwear. García only later learned he'd been accused of being part of the Chiltiupanecos Locos clique of MS-13, the country's largest gang. He told me he spent almost a month in prison, where he was beaten and pepper-sprayed. He pulled up his shirt to reveal a V-shaped scar and a bruise. Other prisoners fared worse—he recalled seeing five inmates die. "They arrested half the world so they could have a number and say, 'We arrested so many people,' regardless of whether the person committed any crime," García said.

He asked if I could share the QR code on his sign, in hopes of getting donations so he could pay his electric bill and bank loans. But when I went to buy shaved ice using Bitcoin myself, the code didn't work.

TETHER'S LISTED ADDRESS in El Salvador proved to be an office tower in San Salvador housing a law firm that I wasn't permitted to enter. And I had no luck getting information about the company from Salvadoran officials. Bukele had yet to break ground on his Bitcoin City project, so there wasn't much to see there—though I visited and met some farmworkers who were livid they were being evicted to make room for the president's pipe dream.

Bukele refused to speak with me. I texted with the legislator who'd posted the photo with Devasini, but he refused to talk about Tether, sticking to praising the president for his successful Bitcoin project, all the evidence to the contrary notwithstanding. "Our president is a brave visionary," wrote the legislator, William Soriano. "El Salvador now leads the monetary revolution that will transform the world as we know it. Not just economically, but culturally as well."

It was strange to hear. I was seeing even less Bitcoin use elsewhere in El Salvador than I'd seen in the revolution's birthplace, El Zonte. In downtown San Salvador, I spent an afternoon walking through a market looking for someone who accepted Bitcoin. I saw soldiers holding rifles or shotguns on street corners, a wall spray-painted with anti-Bitcoin graffiti, and stands hawking white prison uniforms, which family members have to buy for the incarcerated. I didn't find anyone who said they used Bitcoin. "Sometimes it's up, sometimes it's down. For me it doesn't work," said a man running a small pharmacy. Even at upscale restaurants catering to tourists, cashiers accepted Bitcoin only reluctantly, often going to a back room to look for a device loaded with a Bitcoin app, the way a waiter at a French restaurant might pull a dusty bottle of ketchup out from under the counter to humor an ignorant American.

If El Salvador was meant to be the proving ground for Bitcoin's application to everyday life, the plan was a total bust. All it was proving was that no one wanted to use Bitcoin, even when their government incentivized it heavily. Salvadorans didn't understand it, they didn't trust it, and they certainly didn't see it as a way to raise up the poor.

"I don't have any money," one woman told me, laughing. "How am I going to use it?"

THE CLOSEST I could get to Tether in El Salvador was speaking with some of the Bitcoiners who appeared to be in the company's orbit. But that only led to more interminable conversations about Bitcoin's greatness and the supposedly amazing things Bitcoiners were doing for the country. One American Bitcoiner I met in San Salvador told me, semi-seriously, that he'd stimulated the economy by buying a refrigerator for the family of a stripper he was dating. A Bitcoin evangelist turned Bukele adviser pulled out an actual ruler to make some kind of argument about how the price of Bitcoin was sure to go up, even though it was going down dramatically at the time. "Think of Bitcoin like a ruler," he said. "The reason number goes up is the ruler is a fixed size."

Bukele's most prominent, if unofficial, Bitcoin advisers appeared to be Max Keiser, the podcaster who'd screamed "Fuck Elon!" on stage in Miami in 2021, and his wife and co-host Stacy Herbert. A few years earlier they were producing a conspiracy-theory-heavy news show on Russia's state-owned RT network. Now, judging from social media, they were living large as champions of the state, eating at El Salvador's best restaurants and flying in military helicopters to tour government crypto projects. Before my trip, I'd watched a segment on YouTube where they celebrated El Salvador's Bitcoin law.

"It's volcano energy, yeah!" Herbert, a pink-haired former TV producer, yelled, as she flexed her biceps.

"Cheap and clean volcano energy from the balls of the Mother Earth's own testicles, exploding in a jism of free power that's going to make us all fucking rich down here!" Keiser yelled.

Keiser and Herbert seemed to be close with Devasini. On social media, they posted about handing out money across the country from a $2 million Bitfinex-backed charity fund. I asked Herbert to meet me for coffee at a café in an upscale San Salvador mall.

Herbert was cheerful and slightly less unhinged in person. She called Bitcoin "perfect money," Bukele a "super-genius-like mathematician," and said that Bitcoin City was part of how he would transform El Salvador into the next Singapore. But she wouldn't share much about Tether and Devasini.

She did mention there was one tangible sign of Tether's presence in El Salvador: a mural that featured a Bitcoin volcano eruption and a tree with leaves shaped like Bitfinex's logo. It was designed by Devasini's much younger partner, an artist named Valentina Picozzi, and it was painted on a large wall near the entrance to a gang-controlled neighborhood. She said this was a sign of the commitment by Devasini and Tether's other executives to helping the Salvadoran people.

"They're just quiet, humble, and very charitable guys," she said.

This wasn't much of a lead. But back in New York, I looked up Picozzi's work. She was a painter and a sculptor, whose art, like most other Bitcoin-related work, tended toward the kitschy and extremely literal. There were grenades with the Bitcoin logo painted on them, and plexiglass boxes full of shredded dollars with quotes from Satoshi Nakamoto printed on them. Sometimes I couldn't help but imagine she was sending a message about Tether itself, like one piece that had a red sign that read, SORRY YOU'RE FUCKED, and a blue one that said, SORRY WE'RE NOT FEDERAL AND HAVE NO RESERVE.

PICOZZI APPEARED TO have only a small following of crypto faithful. The month after my trip to El Salvador, in August 2022, I saw on Twitter that she was finally going to show all the Bitcoin art she'd been working on at a mainstream art fair. It was going to be in Lugano, Switzerland.

My first reaction was to wonder how terrible Bitcoin art got into a mainstream art fair. But when I thought about it some more, I realized this might be my best chance to meet the reclusive Devasini and confront him about the nefarious actors that Tether seemed to be enabling around the world. I wanted to ask the former plastic surgeon about pig-butchering scams and Bukele's failed Bitcoin policy, but it was hard to imagine he'd be eager to talk with me. Tether's CEO, Jean-Louis van der Velde, had not responded to my messages after our enigmatic meeting in the Bahamas. I figured if I wanted candid responses, I'd need to engineer an informal conversation with Devasini.

Devasini seemed to avoid crypto conferences, presumably to duck pesky reporters like me. But who wouldn't show up to support his partner at the biggest show of her career? And he wouldn't be expecting any reporters there—what kind of reporter goes to an art fair in Switzerland on the off-chance they'd get an interview with the boss of a cryptocurrency company?

It was time to go look at some Bitcoin art.

CHAPTER TWENTY-ONE

Honey Is Better

I arrived in Lugano on the trail of my elusive Milanese quarry, Tether boss Giancarlo Devasini, in a bus full of Italian art critics. The junket was arranged by WopArt, the fair where Devasini's partner, Valentina Picozzi, was exhibiting her work. The fair's theme was "The paper and its mirror, NFT," and the event's press representative said I was welcome to come along when I told her I was working on a book about cryptocurrencies.

The bus took us from Milan past Lake Como, across the Swiss border, then to Lugano, which proved to be a sleepy and rich town, on the banks of a placid lake ringed by undulating green mountains. Its cobblestone streets were so steep that a funicular train pulled people up and down one of them.

Lugano, like El Salvador, claimed to have adopted Bitcoin as a payment method. The mayor had announced the plan earlier in the year, which he said he'd developed in partnership with Tether. I figured that was why Picozzi was showing her work in the alpine town, of all places.

The critics and I walked inside the cavernous convention center hosting the fair. We were greeted by a giant poster created by Picozzi of a man drawing a lightbulb in yellow paint, illuminating a series of Bitcoin logos, painted in a graffiti style. Dozens of her other pieces hung on a thirty-foot-long wall.

I spotted Picozzi right away, adjusting a frame. She was a tiny, elegant woman, wearing a leather jacket, flowing black pants, and black stilettos, her blond hair pinned back. On her ring finger, she had a large diamond ring and a small band. I had decided not to approach her, figuring it would be better to wait for Devasini.

As I waited, the Italian critics and I respectfully contemplated Picozzi's work: a blister pack of large orange pills with the Bitcoin logo on them—Bitcoiners like to say they've "taken the orange pill"—and a piece of white paper embossed with the phrase "Son of a bit." There was also a Venezuelan bill, but with a black eye on Simón Bolívar, and a dollar bill with George Washington holding his head in his hands—references to inflation.

The fair's artistic director, an ebullient man with neon orange glasses, brought the critics and me over to hear about her work. She seemed thrilled to have an audience. I don't speak Italian, so the only word I caught in the moment was "Bitcoin," but I smiled while holding out my tape recorder so I could have her remarks translated later.

"Fundamentally it is super-ethical in that it can't be corrupted," she told the critics. "Suddenly I create the opportunity for mathematics to print currency. And there are laws which are mathematical laws."

The tour went on for a few hours, and I kept ducking out and peeking at Picozzi's booth, hoping I'd see Devasini. But I didn't. I stayed after the critics left and waited for hours more, wandering the fair. The wait was interminable. Where was he? I figured he would at least come to the opening-night dinner for artists and VIPs, but I didn't see him there either. Picozzi attended with her assistant. After a second day of hanging around the fair, waiting for him in vain, I returned to Brooklyn, feeling like a failure. But I would soon have a second chance.

AS IT HAPPENED, the next month, Lugano was holding a conference about its Bitcoin plan. Tether was listed as the event's co-host. Still, I didn't think Devasini was likely to attend. He wasn't listed among the many speakers on the agenda. And if he wanted to avoid reporters and other investigators, skipping big public events would make sense. I hadn't seen him at Sam Bankman-Fried's conference in the Bahamas or either of the Bitcoin conferences in Miami. Still, I felt like I was in so deep, I had to go. I wasn't sure what they'd talk about at the conference. I knew from my first trip that Bitcoin had not exactly taken off in Lugano. In fact, if El Salvador's Bitcoin experiment was an overhyped publicity stunt, Lugano's was pretty much nothing at all. Locals mostly weren't even aware of the Bitcoin plan. I had trouble finding stores other than McDonald's that accepted crypto. And buying a Big Mac with Bitcoin was not that exciting. It was slower than my credit card, charged me fees instead of earning me rewards points, and the burger still tasted rubbery.

Some local politicians had come out against the Bitcoin plan, and one of them recommended I speak with the most vocal opponent: Paolo Bernasconi, a muckraking former prosecutor. He invited me to meet him on the morning of the first day of the conference. His office was right across the street. A secretary brought me into a conference room at his law office. From the hallway, I heard someone whistling a chipper tune from Vivaldi's *Four Seasons*. In walked a handsome man with thick gray hair in a blue blazer and a preppy purple-and-white-striped tie.

"We started the practice of follow the money," Bernasconi said. "It is quite frustrating, you know, after sixty years fighting against criminality, today I have to look at it just in front of my desk."

Bernasconi turned and pointed through double glass doors at the convention center, where we could see Picozzi's red, blue, and green Bitcoin flags. He smiled and raised his eyebrows. The lawyer was exaggerating his credentials only slightly. As state attorney for the south district of Switzerland in the '70s and '80s, Bernasconi, seventy-nine, had investigated Swiss banks that moved dirty money for the mafia. His most famous case was called "The Pizza Connection," because U.S. pizza parlors were used as fronts to move billions of dollars of drug money to Lugano or to the Bahamas or Bermuda. The work was dangerous. An Italian judge who worked with Bernasconi was assassinated by the mafia in 1992, his motorcade blown up by a remote-detonated bomb. The investigation was also opposed by the local banking industry, which was built on money from shady sources in Italy. But in 1990, with Bernasconi's help, money laundering was finally made a crime in Switzerland.

"We achieved the goal to neutralize organized crime, and now they are coming with cryptocurrencies. Thank you very much," he said.

As a lawyer, Bernasconi said, he'd represented companies that were victims of hacks and had been asked for ransom. The hackers always ask for payment in crypto, he told me. "You have a lot of criminals giving us the evidence that the best way to launder money is crypto," he said, smacking his hands on the table. "It's so simple. Why? Because it's impossible to follow the money."

I told Bernasconi what I'd learned about Tether's use by organized crime in Southeast Asia. Criminals were likely using the stablecoin to move billions of dollars anonymously. American retirees were being tricked into sending huge sums of Tether to scammers across Southeast Asia. And I explained how the scammers themselves were often held against their will, in vast office parks like Chinatown. Tether executives might not even know about any of this, because no identity documents are required to hold or send Tether, I explained. I imagined the company would disclaim responsibility. Bernasconi interrupted. He told me that was the same attitude Swiss bankers had, back when he was fighting the Mafia. He covered his eyes with his fingertips, then pulled them away and stared straight at me.

"If you're blind, intentionally blind, then you're responsible," he said. "If you don't care, then you are responsible."

ACROSS THE STREET, I found a mix of Bitcoin cultists, crypto second-raters, students, and curious locals. Bitcoin prices had been one of the main topics of previous crypto conferences, but with the value down about two-thirds to $20,000, the topic seemed to be taboo.

I was worried this second trip might be a waste of time. But to my surprise, Devasini did come. I saw him in the audience, but he walked out before I could approach him. Then, around midday, I spotted him walking into the conference center, flanked by Stacy Herbert and her flamboyant broadcast partner and husband, Max Keiser.

Devasini was tall, with unruly curls that hung to his shoulders and tufted out around his ears. By then he was fifty-eight, and he dressed like an aging rocker in a black-hooded leather jacket and jeans that hung off him. On his right hand he wore a black ring, and on his left hand he had three bracelets. He had an angular face, a prominent nose, and a jutting chin. He walked stooped forward, swinging his long arms. Perhaps because of his screen name, Merlin, wizards came to mind. He reminded me more of a different one: Gargamel, the power-hungry archnemesis of the Smurfs.

The group paused just inside the doors to the bustling conference hall. I rushed over to catch Herbert, hoping that our coffee in San Salvador meant she'd make a friendly introduction. But she gave me a stern look and pretended she didn't know me.

I tried to tell Devasini who I was and what I was working on, but he brushed me off too.

"Everything is okay, thank you very much," he said, strangely, in a light Italian accent. "Good luck with your book."

Devasini walked to the main auditorium, took a seat in the front row, and settled in to listen to the conference programming. I won't bore you too much with the content. Suffice it to say, you'd be surprised how much people could find to say about the new payment method at the town McDonald's.

I preferred to stand out in the lobby, despite the moody electronic music that played on a five- or ten-minute loop. A metal statue of a bull designed by Picozzi was on display. I saw a man in black ski mask and sunglasses being dragged out in a headlock by a security guard. "People with privacy are being removed!!" he yelled.

I also overhead two buff, tan men talking loudly. Their accents sounded like they were from the New York City area, so I went over to introduce myself. They told me they were traders for Bitfinex. But when I asked them if they had flown in from Brooklyn like me, they suddenly got shy. "No, no, we don't have any U.S. presence," one of them said. "We've already been instructed not to speak to anybody."

Nearby, I spotted Tether's chief technology officer, Paolo Ardoino, who was explaining his diet to another attendee. He looked fit, in a tight T-shirt tucked into slim gray dress pants. "I eat once a day. Only red meat," he said. But he wasn't willing to speak with me, even about the wonders of beef.

"He's the one that is writing bad things about us," he told his wife, who was standing next to him.

"Hello!" I said. She wouldn't talk with me either.

The next day, bored of speech after speech about the Salvadoran Bitcoin miracle, I went to a bar down the street and composed a message to Devasini on Telegram, where he still used his old screen name MerlinTheWizard. I thought there was at least a chance he'd be willing to speak with me in private, if his friends didn't see.

"I introduced myself yesterday—I'm the one writing a book about cryptocurrency in which you are a major character," I wrote. "Why not have a conversation? I would love to hear your story in your voice, which would carry weight. I am at Bar Laura near the conference if you would like to meet."

By then, I'd spent more than a year pursuing Devasini and there was so much I wanted to talk with him about. It wasn't that I thought he'd suddenly open up to me and discuss his plastic surgery career, his divorce, and the old blog I'd found. I didn't expect him to reveal new information about Tether's reserves either. But I wanted to tell him about scam compounds in Cambodia. Perhaps from his reaction, I could get a sense of whether he knew anything about what Tether was enabling around the world.

For a few hours, I sat and waited for a reply. I picked at a zucchini panini and looked at the empty red chair in front of me. At the next table, a Swiss family played with their toddler and drank espresso. A tiny brown bird landed on the table, looked at me for a few seconds, then flew away.

But he never showed. That night, at 12:38 A.M., while I was sleeping, a one-sentence reply from Devasini arrived: "Bees don't waste their time explaining to flies that honey is better than shit."

I WAS DISAPPOINTED. I'd come all the way to Switzerland—twice—for an interview that was not going to happen. My attempts to get Devasini and the other Tether leaders to open up were being stonewalled. I didn't know where to go next.

But a week after I got back to New York, a seemingly innocuous tweet sent by Sam Bankman-Fried set off an unpredictable chain of events that would finally reveal the rot at the center of crypto. The tweet was directed at the richest man in crypto: Binance founder Changpeng Zhao. And it was meant to be a joke.

CHAPTER TWENTY-TWO

Assets Are Not Fine

"Excited to see him repping the industry in DC going forward! uh, he is still allowed to go to DC, right?" Sam Bankman-Fried wrote on Twitter on October 29, 2022.

He was responding to an obsequious message posted by one of his deputies praising Changpeng Zhou, better known as CZ, the head of rival exchange Binance. The joke was that CZ might not want to visit the United States, given that Binance was reportedly under investigation by the Justice Department, the IRS, the SEC, and the CFTC. The two men had long had a complicated relationship. A thin forty-five-year-old with a buzzcut, CZ was one of FTX's early investors. But Bankman-Fried envied his onetime benefactor's success. When I'd visited FTX's offices, he'd shown me a dashboard that tracked his market share against Binance's. Bankman-Fried might have been worth more than $20 billion. But Bloomberg once estimated CZ's fortune at $96 billion, making the Chinese-born immigrant to Canada one of the richest people in the world, and the richest man in crypto.

CZ also ran one of the shadiest operations in crypto. Binance had long refused to say where it was headquartered, making it tough for any country to claim jurisdiction. The U.S. investigations into Binance related to evading sanctions on Iran and Russia, trading unregistered securities, and violating money-laundering rules. Reuters called Binance "a hub for hackers, fraudsters and drug traffickers." In 2018, Binance's own chief compliance officer admitted bluntly in a message to a colleague, "we are operating as a fking unlicensed securities exchange in the USA bro." Pig-butchering scammers also liked to use the exchange to cash out the proceeds. Some of the eighty-one Tethers I sent to "Vicky Ho" had ended up there. (Binance and CZ have denied the allegations.)

But regardless of whether there was any truth to SBF's joke, his poke at CZ would prove to be ill-timed. On November 2, an article on crypto news site *CoinDesk* raised questions about Bankman-Fried's finances, revealing that his hedge fund, Alameda Research, held nearly $6 billion of a cryptocurrency he'd created, called FTT, and owed billions of dollars to lenders. Though the article suggested Bankman-Fried's fortune might rest on a shaky foundation, most people initially shrugged off the report. After all, Bankman-Fried's exchange had been checked out by auditors and top venture capitalists. Of all the people in crypto, he seemed most open to U.S. regulation. He'd been called the J. P. Morgan of crypto. He didn't seem like he had something to hide.

But on Twitter, CZ decided to twist the knife, suggesting the article was cause for concern. He announced on November 6 that because of "recent revelations," Binance would be selling off its stash of FTT tokens, which it had acquired due to its early investment in Bankman-Fried's company. "We won't pretend to make love after divorce," he wrote on Twitter. "We won't support people who lobby against other industry players behind their backs."

Other investors piled on, dumping their FTT tokens and withdrawing their money from Bankman-Fried's exchange. Rumors flew that FTX might not have enough money to cover users' deposits. The withdrawals—some of which were publicly trackable on the blockchain—accelerated like a snowball. The more money was pulled, the more other investors decided it might be a good idea to withdraw theirs too. It was a case of reverse FOMO. It wasn't so much that investors were sure FTX was in trouble. It was more that they figured they might as well pull their money in case CZ was right. They'd seen what happened to investors who left their money at Celsius or the other crypto firms that failed.

Bankman-Fried took to Twitter to try and stem the withdrawals. "FTX is fine," he posted, a bit feebly. "Assets are fine. We don't invest client assets (even in treasuries)."

But that didn't stop the withdrawals. The bank run was on. CZ's tweet came on Sunday. By that Tuesday, $6 billion had been withdrawn from FTX, a large percentage of all the money investors had deposited at the exchange.

. . .

I WAS WATCHING all of this unfold from Brooklyn, a bit stunned. The chain of events that short sellers had long hypothesized might take down Tether seemed to be ravaging Bankman-Fried's company instead. FTX had seemed to me like a crypto casino, which lured investors to gamble on made-up coins and scams. But I hadn't suspected that the casino's counting room was short on cash.

From the Bahamas, Bankman-Fried desperately tried to raise money from new investors. To them, he presented the problem as one of "liquidity"—he claimed FTX had plenty of assets, but it couldn't sell some of them fast enough to cover customers' withdrawals. But the rivals he called to ask for a loan were surprised by how much he was seeking. Lennix Lai, an executive at the exchange OKX in Hong Kong, later told a reporter that Bankman-Fried said to him on Tuesday morning he needed a few billion dollars immediately to avoid "very serious consequences." On a conference call, Bankman-Fried reportedly told investors FTX would go bankrupt if he didn't raise at least $4 billion.

"I fucked up," Bankman-Fried reportedly said on the call, adding that he would be "incredibly, unbelievably grateful" to anyone who could help.

This didn't really make sense. An exchange like FTX was supposed to hold onto customers' deposits and return them if asked. Like a casino, it made its money by collecting a small cut of every bet. It wasn't supposed to gamble itself, and no matter how many gamblers wanted to cash in their chips at once, it shouldn't have had any trouble paying out. Amid the crisis, U.S. regulators opened investigations into whether FTX had misused customer funds.

Later on Tuesday, Bankman-Fried made a shocking announcement: He was selling the exchange. And the buyer would be CZ. "I know that there have been rumors in media of conflict between our two exchanges, however Binance has shown time and again that they are committed to a more decentralized global economy while working to improve industry relations with regulators," Bankman-Fried wrote on Twitter. "We are in the best of hands."

But the next day, CZ backed out of the deal. "As a result of corporate due diligence, as well as the latest news reports regarding mishandled customer funds and alleged US agency investigations, we have decided that we will not pursue the potential acquisition," the

Binance founder wrote on Twitter. Some speculated that the potential deal was a ploy by CZ to ensure FTX's demise.

That Friday, just five days after CZ's tweet announcing Binance's divestment of FTT tokens, FTX filed for bankruptcy. The company, valued at $32 billion earlier in the year, was finished. Anyone who had left money on the exchange was completely wiped out.

THE SHOCKING REVERSAL was the biggest news that crypto had ever seen. It was as if Satoshi Nakamoto's identity was finally revealed—and it was Janet Yellen, the central banker hated by Bitcoiners. FTX's bankruptcy made the front page of *The New York Times*. "Sam Bankman-Fried Went From Crypto Golden Boy to Villain," wrote *The Wall Street Journal*.

On Twitter, crypto followers were debating whether it was a bank run set off by CZ or a massive fraud. Some called for Bankman-Fried's immediate arrest. His rivals gloated. Anything tied to him became toxic. The venture capitalists who once hailed FTX as the future of finance wrote their investments down to zero. Politicians who took Bankman-Fried's donations started distancing themselves from him.

The effective-altruism community collectively freaked out. Philosophers and activists were dismayed that their biggest funder was broke, and that the face of their movement had been discredited. Some were asking if Bankman-Fried had ever intended to give his billions of dollars away, and if they'd been co-opted by him for publicity. Will MacAskill, the philosopher behind the movement who'd years earlier recruited the young Bankman-Fried at Au Bon Pain, denounced him.

"I had put my trust in Sam, and if he lied and misused customer funds he betrayed me, just as he betrayed his customers, his employees, his investors, & the communities he was a part of," MacAskill wrote on Twitter.

CoinDesk reported that many of FTX's top executives lived with and dated each other, which prompted a wave of social media speculation that they were partying it up in a "polycule." Conservative media seized on Bankman-Fried's huge donations to Democratic political candidates. "How is this guy not shackled?" ranted Fox News anchor Jesse Watters. "The guy's a financial hand grenade and he blew up just after he bought the Senate for the Democrats. How about the fact that he's sleeping with his entire staff, at the office?"

. . .

I WAS AS obsessed as anyone. One of the first times I'd spoken with Bankman-Fried, I'd asked him if he would ever consider running a scam to raise money for charity. To me, the logic of effective altruism and utilitarianism would have justified such a move. Set aside little things like morals and ethics, and focus instead on Bankman-Fried's favorite metric: expected value. If you embezzle $1 billion from cryptocurrency gamblers, give it to the poor, and save thousands of lives, wouldn't that be a net positive?

But Bankman-Fried had told me back then that running a scam—"rugging" everyone, in crypto slang—wouldn't make sense. He didn't cite a moral law against scamming. Instead, he argued that running a scam would destroy his credibility, and that of the charities he funded. A scam might be a surefire way to raise a few billion dollars for charity, but in the long run, the expected value of running an honest business was higher.

That explanation had made sense to me at the time. But now it seemed like he might have pursued my scam-for-charity idea. And, of course, there was the possibility he'd only acted philanthropic to gain the credibility he needed to run a massive fraud.

Late one night, a few days after the bankruptcy filing, I emailed Bankman-Fried and reminded him of that early conversation.

"In our first conversation you told me it wouldn't be +EV to rug everyone, given the second-order effects, and I have to imagine you would have thought that through," I wrote to him at 1:09 A.M. (+EV means positive expected value, i.e., a good bet.) I asked if he'd be willing to meet to discuss this.

"I might be up to speak in person—if not happy to have a call," Bankman-Fried replied a few minutes later. "Nothing's ever as black and white as it looks."

The next day, I bought a ticket to Nassau. New stories kept appearing that looked worse and worse for Bankman-Fried, and I figured I didn't have long before he would be arrested. That morning at breakfast, I explained the situation to my kids.

"The bad guy is in big trouble, and I'm worried he'll get sent to time-out before I get there," I told them.

"But why would somebody do bad things if they were trying to do good things?" my daughter Margot asked. It was a good question.

. . .

I HAD GONE out on a limb. Bankman-Fried hadn't actually agreed to an interview. Once I landed, I started sending him emails and texts. But he was noncommittal. I passed the time by visiting places associated with FTX. The island was teeming with reporters. At least two camera crews were filming documentaries, hoping to get deals from Netflix or HBO. Outside the windswept lot of weeds and gravel where FTX was planning to build its giant headquarters, I ran into a friend on assignment for *New York* magazine. A caterer who'd serviced FTX told me he'd already been interviewed by the *Financial Times*. Two guards were posted at the gate to the office park where I'd interviewed Bankman-Fried in February. "I'm sorry, the boss is not allowing entry," one told me. Outside, a CNBC anchor recorded a segment, a Bloomberg camera crew packed up its van, and a photographer shot from across the street with a telephoto lens.

A photo posted on Twitter showed Bankman-Fried at a convenience store. I could tell from the logo he was at Albany, the resort where he lived on the southwest side of the island. Non-residents were barred from entry. So many reporters were trying to get in that the resort had stopped selling day passes to its spa. From what I heard, no one had been able to get an interview with Bankman-Fried.

I called a member of the resort, and he agreed to sneak me in, on the pretense that I'd be joining him for a game of the racket sport padel. I figured Bankman-Fried would be more likely to agree to the interview if I said I was waiting right downstairs. Just as I was driving into Albany, he wrote back to say he'd meet.

IT WAS A muggy Saturday afternoon. Bankman-Fried's apartment was at the top of one of the luxury condo buildings that border the Albany resort's marina. Outside, deckhands buffed the stanchions of a 200-foot yacht owned by a fracking billionaire. Even larger superyachts were docked nearby.

A bronze replica of Wall Street's *Charging Bull* statue stood on the pristine lawn, which was as manicured as the residents I had seen strolling by. The resort was so silent I could hear the gentle lapping of the water. Somehow, it even smelled expensive. I felt like I had crash-landed on an alien planet populated solely by the very rich and the people who work for them.

I walked to Bankman-Fried's building, "the Orchid," which was decorated with intricate arches in the style of a Venetian palazzo. He greeted me in the lobby.

Bankman-Fried was shoeless, in white gym socks, a red T-shirt, and wrinkled khaki shorts. His standard uniform. It had been eight days since FTX filed for bankruptcy. I had imagined his mood would be grim. I'd even worried that he might be suicidal. But he seemed surprisingly upbeat.

"It's been an interesting few weeks," Bankman-Fried told me.

Together we rode the elevator up to his penthouse. Then the doors opened.

CHAPTER TWENTY-THREE

Inside the Orchid

Sam Bankman-Fried's $30 million Bahamas penthouse looked like a dorm after the students have left for winter break. The dishwasher was full. Towels were piled in the laundry room. Bat streamers from a Halloween party were still hanging from a doorway. Two boxes of Legos sat on the floor of one bedroom. And then there were the shoes—dozens of sneakers and heels piled in the foyer, left behind by employees who'd fled the island of New Providence when FTX imploded.

This wasn't part of the typical tour Bankman-Fried gave to the parade of reporters who came to the island to tell the tale of the boy-genius crypto billionaire who slept on a beanbag chair next to his desk and only got rich so he could give it all away. It was easy to see why. This wasn't the domain of an ascetic so thrifty he drove a Toyota Corolla.

Bankman-Fried led me down a marble-floored hallway to a small bedroom, where he perched on a plush brown couch. Always jittery, he tapped his foot so hard it rattled a coffee table, smacked on a piece of gum, and rubbed his index finger with his thumb like he was twirling an invisible fidget spinner. But he seemed almost cheerful as he explained why he had invited me into his 12,000-square-foot bolt-hole, against the advice of his lawyers, even as investigators from the U.S. Department of Justice scrutinized whether he'd used customers' funds to prop up his hedge fund Alameda Research, a crime that could send him to prison for years. (To me, it sure looked like he had.)

"What I'm focusing on is what I can do, right now, to try and make things as right as possible," Bankman-Fried said. "I can't do that if I'm just focused on covering my ass."

But he seemed to be doing just that. My visit to the penthouse marked the beginning of an apology tour that would, in the coming days, include a video appearance at a *New York Times* conference and an interview on *Good Morning America*. In Bankman-Fried's telling, nobody had been intentionally defrauded. He blamed his firm's failure on a hazy combination of comically poor bookkeeping, wildly misjudged risks, and complete ignorance of what his own hedge fund was doing. In other words, an alumnus of both MIT and the elite Wall Street trading firm Jane Street was arguing that he was just dumb with the numbers—not pulling a conscious fraud. Talking in detail to journalists about what was certain to be the subject of extensive litigation seemed like an unusual strategy, but it made sense: The press helped him create his only-honest-man-in-crypto image, so why not use them to talk his way out of trouble?

He didn't say so, but one reason he might have been willing to speak with me was that I was one of the reporters who helped build him up. After my trip to FTX's offices in February, I flew past the bright red flags at his company—its lack of corporate governance, the ties to his hedge fund, its profligate spending on marketing, the fact that it operated largely outside U.S. jurisdiction. I wrote a story focused on whether Bankman-Fried would follow through on his plans to donate huge sums to charity.

It wasn't the most embarrassingly puffy of the many puff pieces that came out about him. ("After my interview with SBF, I was convinced: I was talking to a future trillionaire," one writer said in an article commissioned by a venture capital firm.) But my tone wasn't entirely dissimilar. "Bankman-Fried is a thought experiment from a college philosophy seminar come to life," I wrote. "Should someone who wants to save the world first amass as much money and power as possible, or will the pursuit corrupt him along the way?" Now it seemed pretty clear that a better question would've been whether the business was a scam from the start.

In the bedroom, I told Bankman-Fried I wanted to talk about the decisions that led to FTX's collapse, and why he took them. Earlier in the week, in late-night DM exchanges with a Vox reporter and on a phone call with a crypto influencer, he had made comments that many interpreted as an admission that everything he'd said was a lie. ("So the ethics stuff, mostly a front?" the Vox reporter asked. "Yeah," Bankman-Fried replied.) He spoke so cynically about his motivations that to many it seemed like a comic book character was pulling off his mask to reveal the villain who'd been hiding there all along.

I set out on this visit with a different working theory. Maybe I was feeling the tug of my past reporting, but I still didn't think the talk about charity was all made up. Since he was a teenager, Bankman-Fried had described himself as utilitarian—following the philosophy that the correct action is the one likely to result in the greatest good for the greatest number of people. He said his endgame was making and donating enough money to prevent pandemics and stop runaway artificial intelligence from destroying humanity. Faced with a crisis, and believing he was the hero of his own sci-fi movie, he might've thought it was right to make a crazy, even illegal, gamble to save his company.

To be clear, if that's what he was thinking, it was the logic of a megalomaniac, not a martyr. The money wasn't his to gamble with, and "the ends justify the means" is a cliché of bad ethics. But I figured that if it was what he believed, he might still think he had made the right decision, even if it didn't work out. It seemed to me that this was what he meant when he messaged Vox, "The worst quadrant is sketchy + lose. The best is win + ???" I wanted to probe that, in part because it might get him to talk more candidly about what had happened to his customers' money.

I decided to approach the topic gingerly, on terms I thought he would relate to, as it seemed he wasn't exactly in a crime-confessy mood. I began by posing a question using his favorite metric, expected value: "Should I judge you by your impact, or by the expected value of your decision?"

"When all is said and done, what matters is your actual realized impact. Like, that's what actually matters to the world," he said. "But, obviously, there's luck."

That was the in I was looking for. For the next eleven hours—with breaks for fundraising calls and a very awkward dinner—I tried to get him to tell me exactly what he meant. He denied that he had committed fraud or lied to anyone, and blamed FTX's failure on his sloppiness and inattention. But at points it seemed like he was saying he got unlucky, or miscalculated the odds.

Bankman-Fried told me he still had a chance to raise $8 billion to save his company. He seemed delusional, or committed to pretending this was still an error he could fix, and either way, the few supporters remaining at his penthouse seemed unlikely to set him straight. The grim scene reminded me a bit of the end of *Scarface,* with Tony Montana holed up in his mansion, semi-incoherent, his unknown enemies sneaking closer. But instead of mountains of cocaine, Bankman-Fried was clinging to spreadsheet tabs filled with wildly optimistic cryptocurrency valuations.

WHAT EXACTLY HAD happened to all the money? By the time I arrived at Bankman-Fried's penthouse, multiple news reports had emerged alleging that FTX had secretly lent billions of dollars of customer money to Alameda Research, which had lost it in some mix of bad bets, insane spending, and perhaps something even sketchier. John Ray III, the lawyer who was appointed CEO of the bankrupt exchange, alleged in court that FTX covered up the loans using secret software.

Bankman-Fried denied this again to me. Returning to the framework of expected value, I asked him if the decisions he made were correct.

"I think that I've made a lot of plus-EV decisions and a few very large boneheaded decisions," he said. "Certainly in retrospect, those very large decisions were very bad, and may end up overwhelming everything else."

To explain what happened, we had to go back to Hong Kong, where Bankman-Fried had moved in 2018 with Caroline Ellison, Nishad Singh, Gary Wang, and a small group of other friends from the effective-altruism community to run their hedge fund, Alameda Research. (The name itself was an early example of his casual attitude toward rules—it was chosen to avoid scrutiny from banks, which frequently closed its accounts. "If we named our company like, Shitcoin Daytraders Inc., they'd probably just reject us," Bankman-Fried told a podcaster in 2021, using the crypto slang for random obscure tokens. "But, I mean, no one doesn't like research.") At the time, they were considering starting their own exchange—what would become FTX.

The way Bankman-Fried later described this decision reveals his attitude toward risk. He estimated there was an 80 percent chance the exchange would fail to attract enough customers. But he said one should always take a bet, even a long-shot one, if the expected value is positive, calling this stance "risk neutral." But it actually meant he would take risks that to a normal person sound insane. "As an individual, to make a bet where it's like, 'I'm going to gamble my $10 billion and either get $20 billion or $0, with equal probability,' would be madness," Rob Wiblin, host of an effective-altruism podcast, said to Bankman-Fried in April. "But from an altruistic point of view, it's not so crazy."

"Completely agree," Bankman-Fried replied. He told another interviewer that he'd make a bet described as a chance of "Fifty-one percent you double the earth out somewhere else, forty-nine percent it all disappears."

Starting an exchange while already running a hedge fund was a huge conflict of interest. And it wasn't as if Bankman-Fried kept FTX and Alameda separated. On the exchange, Alameda was one of the biggest traders, or "liquidity providers" in Wall Street parlance. Imagine if the top executives at an online poker site also entered its high-stakes tournaments—the temptation to cheat by peeking at other players' cards would be huge. But Bankman-Fried assured customers that Alameda would play by the same rules as everyone else, and enough people came to trade that FTX took off. I asked Bankman-Fried if allowing Alameda to trade on FTX was his original mistake. He disagreed.

"Having Alameda provide liquidity on FTX early on was the right decision, because I think that helped make FTX a great product for users, even though it obviously ended up backfiring," Bankman-Fried told me.

Part of FTX's appeal was that it was mostly a derivatives exchange, which allowed customers to trade "on margin," meaning with borrowed money. That was a key to his defense. Bankman-Fried argued that no one should be surprised big traders on FTX, including Alameda, were borrowing from the exchange, and that his fund's position just somehow got out of hand.

"Everyone was borrowing and lending," he said. "That's been its calling card."

But FTX's normal margin system, crypto traders told me, would never have permitted anyone to accumulate a debt that looked like Alameda's. When I asked if Alameda had to follow the same margin rules as other traders, he admitted the fund did not.

"There was more leeway," he said.

That wouldn't have been so important had Alameda stuck to its original trading strategy of relatively low-risk arbitrage trades, like its big score on Bitcoin prices in Japan. But in 2020 and 2021, as Bankman-Fried became the face of FTX, a major political donor, and a favorite of Silicon Valley, Alameda faced more competition, and the easy trades disappeared. It shifted its strategy to, essentially, gambling on shitcoins.

As Caroline Ellison, then Alameda's co-CEO, explained in a March 2021 post on Twitter: "The way to really make money is figure out when the market is going to go up and get balls long before that." She added that she'd learned the strategy from the classic market-manipulation memoir, *Reminiscences of a Stock Operator*. Her co-CEO said in another tweet that a profitable strategy was buying Dogecoin because Elon Musk tweeted about it.

I couldn't believe it. This was more or less the trading tactic my friend Jay had recommended I pursue with what he called "doggie coin." Just multiplied by about a billion. Bankman-Fried's fortune was partly built on the same ideas that funded Jay's trip to Disney World.

THE REASON ELLISON was bragging about such an asinine strategy was that it was working better than anyone knew. When we spoke in February 2022, Bankman-Fried told me that Alameda had made $1 billion the previous year. In the penthouse nine months later, he told me that $1 billion was Alameda's arbitrage profits. On top of that, its shitcoins had gained tens of billions of dollars of value, at least on paper. "If you mark everything to market, I do believe at one point my net worth got to a hundred billion," Bankman-Fried said.

Any trader would know this wasn't nearly as good as it sounded. The large pile of tokens couldn't be turned into cash without crashing the market. Much of it was even made of tokens that Bankman-Fried and his friends had either spun up themselves—such as FTT, Serum, and Maps (the official currency of a nonsensical crypto-meets-mapping app)—or were closely affiliated with, like Solana. While Bankman-Fried acknowledged the pile was worth something less than $100 billion—maybe he'd mark it down a third, he said—he maintained that he could have extracted quite a lot of real money from his holdings.

But he didn't. Instead, Alameda borrowed billions of dollars from other crypto lenders—not FTX—and sunk them into more crypto bets. Publicly, Bankman-Fried presented himself as an ethical operator and called for regulation to rein in crypto's worst excesses. But through his hedge fund, he'd actually become the market's most degenerate gambler. I asked him why, if he really thought he could sell the tokens, he didn't. "Why not, like, take some risk off?"

"Okay. In retrospect, absolutely. That would've been the right, like, unambiguously the right thing to do," he said. "But also it was just, like, hilariously well-capitalized."

Bankman-Fried's problems had really started in May 2022, months before the *CoinDesk* article or CZ's divestment. That month, the collapse of Do Kwon's Terra-Luna scheme set off a crypto credit crisis. Some of the biggest crypto funds had invested in the $60 billion Ponzi scheme with borrowed money and went bankrupt. This made those who'd lent billions of dollars to Alameda nervous. They asked Alameda to repay the loans, with real money. But the fund didn't have enough. Alameda had invested the money in things that were hard to sell—like venture-capital deals and huge amounts of obscure shitcoins.

There were two different versions of what happened next. Ellison, by then the sole head of Alameda, had told her side of the story to her staff at an all-hands meeting amid the crisis. Ellison said that she, Bankman-Fried, and his two top lieutenants—Gary Wang and Nishad Singh—had discussed the shortfall. The honest move would have been to admit that Alameda was broke and face the consequences. But, Ellison said, they decided not to.

Instead, Ellison told her staff, Alameda borrowed "a bunch of funds" from FTX, which "led to FTX having a shortfall in user funds." She said this was possible because the way Alameda's account on FTX was set up, the fund was allowed to "go negative in coins." Essentially, instead of owning up to Alameda's failure, they decided to gamble FTX customer funds to cover it up.

If that was true, all four executives would've knowingly committed fraud. When I put this to Bankman-Fried, he screwed up his eyes, furrowed his eyebrows, put his hands in his hair, and thought for a few seconds.

"So, it's not how I remember what happened," Bankman-Fried said. But he surprised me by acknowledging that there had been a meeting, post–Luna crash, where the foursome had debated what to do about Alameda's debts. The way he told it, he was packing for a trip to D.C. and "only kibitzing on parts of the discussion." It didn't seem like a crisis, he said. It was a matter of extending a bit more credit to a fund that already traded on margin and still had a pile of collateral worth way more than enough to cover the loan. (Although the pile of collateral was largely shitcoins.)

"That was the point at which Alameda's margin position on FTX got, well, it got more leveraged substantially," he said. "Obviously, in retrospect, we should've just said no. I sort of didn't realize then how large the position had gotten."

"You were all aware there was a chance this would not work," I said.

"That's right," he said. "But I thought that the risk was substantially smaller."

I tried to imagine what he could've been thinking. If FTX had liquidated Alameda's position, the fund would've gone bankrupt, and even if the exchange didn't take direct losses, customers would've lost confidence in it. Bankman-Fried pointed out that the companies that lent money to Alameda might have failed too, causing a hard-to-predict cascade of events.

"Now let's say you don't margin-call Alameda," I posited. "Maybe you think there's like a seventy percent chance everything will be okay, it'll all work out?"

"Yes, but also in the cases where it didn't work out, I thought the downside was not nearly as high as it was," he said. "I thought that there was the risk of a much smaller hole. I thought it was going to be manageable."

Bankman-Fried pulled out his laptop and opened a spreadsheet to show what he meant. It was similar to the balance sheet he showed investors when he was seeking a last-minute bailout, which he said consolidated FTX and Alameda's positions because by then the fund had defaulted on its debt. On one line—labeled "What I *thought*"—he listed $8.9 billion in debts and way more than enough money to pay them: $9 billion in liquid assets, $15.4 billion in "less liquid" assets, and $3.2 billion in "illiquid" ones. He told me this was more or less the position he was considering when he had the meeting with the other executives.

"It looks naively to me like, you know, there's still some significant liabilities out there, but, like, we should be able to cover it," he said.

"So what's the problem, then?"

Bankman-Fried pointed to another place on the spreadsheet, which he said showed the actual truth of the situation at the time of the meeting. This one showed similar numbers, but with $8 billion less in liquid assets.

"What's the difference between these two rows here?" he asked.

"You didn't have eight billion in cash that you thought you had," I said.

"That's correct. Yes."

"You misplaced eight billion dollars?" I asked.

"Mis-accounted," Bankman-Fried said, sounding almost proud of his explanation. Sometimes, he said, customers would wire money to Alameda Research instead of sending it directly to FTX. (Some banks were more willing to work with the hedge fund than the exchange, for some reason.) He claimed that somehow, FTX's internal accounting system double-counted this money, essentially crediting it to both the exchange and the fund.

That still doesn't explain why the money was gone. "Where did the eight billion go?" I asked.

To answer, Bankman-Fried created a new tab on the spreadsheet and started typing. He listed Alameda and FTX's biggest cash flows. One of the biggest expenses was paying a net $2.5 billion to Binance to buy out its investment in FTX. He also listed $250 million for real estate, $1.5 billion for expenses, $4 billion for venture capital investments, $1.5 billion for acquisitions, and $1 billion labeled "fuckups." Even accounting for both firms' profits, and all the venture capital money raised by FTX, it tallied to negative $6.5 billion.

Bankman-Fried was telling me that the billions of dollars customers wired to Alameda was gone simply because the companies spent way more than they made. He claimed he paid so little attention to his expenses that he didn't realize he was spending more than he was taking in. "I was real lazy about this mental math," the former physics major said. He created another column in his spreadsheet and typed in much lower numbers, to show what he thought he was spending at the time.

It seemed to me like he was, without saying it exactly, blaming his underlings for FTX's failure, especially Ellison, the head of Alameda. The two had dated off and on and lived together at times. She was part of Bankman-Fried's Future Fund, which was supposed to distribute

FTX and Alameda's earnings to effective-altruism-approved causes. It seemed unlikely she would've blown billions of dollars without asking. "People might take, like, the TLDR as, like, it was my ex-girlfriend's fault," I told him. "That is sort of what you're saying."

"I think the biggest failure was that it wasn't entirely clear whose fault it was," he said.

A FEW HOURS into our conversation, Bankman-Fried told me he had to make a call. I had asked him if there was anyone who'd support his version of events, and he said I could talk with one of his few remaining supporters while I waited.

In walked a haughty man with a long, scraggly beard, a potbelly, and mismatched socks, one of them with a Pac-Man design. He was an employee of FTX who'd stuck around to help Bankman-Fried try to find an investor to rescue the exchange.

I threw out an easy question.

"Why are you still here?" I asked.

He started off by saying he wanted to help FTX's customers. Then, unprompted, he told me that he thought there wasn't much risk Bankman-Fried would ever get in trouble.

"I firmly believe once somebody becomes a certain level of rich, they're never poor again," he said. "They don't go to jail. Nothing bad happens to them."

I tried to keep a straight face as I imagined him telling that to the congressmen and prosecutors investigating FTX. His supercilious attitude and slovenly appearance reminded me of the disagreeable know-it-all Comic Book Guy from *The Simpsons*. His answer was so bad, it felt almost unfair to ask him tough questions. I gave him a second chance to say something nice about Bankman-Fried.

"Are there specific things that make you think Sam is honest?" I asked.

"Oh, I didn't say he was honest," the man said.

"Was there a separation between Alameda and FTX?" I asked.

"If you were in my position, would you answer that?" he said.

By the time the supporter had finished digging the hole as deep as he could, the sun had gone down and I was hungry. I was allowed to join a group of Bankman-Fried's supporters for dinner, as long as I didn't mention their names.

With the curtains drawn, the living room looked considerably less grand than it did in pictures. I'd been told that FTX employees had gathered here amid the crisis, while Bankman-Fried worked in another apartment. Addled by stress and sleep deprivation, they wept and hugged one another. Most didn't say goodbye as they left the island, one by one. Many flew back to their childhood homes to be with their parents.

The supporters at the dinner told me they felt like the press had been unfair. They said that Bankman-Fried and his friends weren't the polyamorous partiers the tabloids had portrayed, and that they did little besides work. Earlier in the week, a Bahamian man who'd served as FTX's round-the-clock chauffeur and gofer had also told me the reports weren't true. "People make it seem like this big *Wolf of Wall Street* thing," he said. "Bro, it was a bunch of nerds."

BY THE TIME I finished my plate of off-the-record rice and beans, Bankman-Fried was free again. We returned to the study. He was barefoot, having balled up his gym socks and stuffed them behind a couch cushion. He lay on the couch, his computer on his lap, and pulled up his favorite game, *Storybook Brawl*. The light from the screen cast shadows of his curls on his forehead.

I noticed the same skin-colored patch on his arm that I'd seen when I interviewed him in his office nine months earlier. This time I asked what it was. He told me it was a transdermal antidepressant, selegiline. I asked if he was using it as a performance enhancer or to treat depression. "Nothing's binary," he said. "But I've been borderline depressed for my whole life." He added that he also sometimes took Adderall—"ten milligrams at a time, a few times a day"—as did some of his colleagues, but that talk of drug use was overblown. "I don't think that was the problem," he said.

I told Bankman-Fried my theory about his motivation, sidestepping the question of whether he misappropriated customer funds. Bankman-Fried denied that his world-saving goals made him willing to take giant gambles. As we talked more, it seemed like he was saying he'd made some kind of bet but hadn't calculated the expected value properly.

"I was comfortable taking the risk that, like, I may end up kind of falling flat," he said, staring at his computer screen, where he was leading an army of cartoon knights and fairies into battle. "But what actually happened was disastrously bad and, like, no significant chance of that happening would've made sense to risk, and that was a fuckup. Like, that was a mass miscalculation in downside."

There was something else I needed to ask Bankman-Fried about. I'd read reports that when FTX was on the verge of failure, Bankman-Fried turned to Tether's Giancarlo Devasini for help. He asked the former plastic surgeon for a multibillion-dollar bailout. Devasini rebuffed him. I figured Bankman-Fried had nothing to lose now, and would finally be willing to tell me the truth about Tether. Before, he'd assured me that Tether really did have the money it claimed, though some of it was tied up in strange investments. I asked him if there was something more to the story. But again he said there was no big secret.

"Tether is not nearly as fucked as people say it is," he said. "It's weird how much shit they get. They don't do anything to help themselves ward it off. Like, they really don't. But yeah. There actually aren't big problems there."

I told Bankman-Fried what I'd learned about pig-butchering scams, and how crypto was fueling human trafficking in Southeast Asia. His exchange FTX seemed to have helped some of the scammers cash out their profits, and some FTX customers had fallen victim to the scam and sent funds.

"That's fucked," he said. "I just don't fundamentally know what to do about it."

I read Bankman-Fried a post by Will MacAskill, who in 2022 had joined the board of Bankman-Fried's Future Fund. The effective altruist said that Bankman-Fried had betrayed him. "For years, the EA community has emphasized the importance of integrity, honesty and the respect of common-sense moral constraints," MacAskill wrote on Twitter. "If customer funds were misused, then Sam did not listen; he must have thought he was above such considerations."

Bankman-Fried closed his eyes and pushed his toes against one arm of the couch, clenching the other arm with his hands. "That's not how I view what happened," he said. "But I did fuck up. I think really what I want to say is, like, I'm really fucking sorry. By far the worst thing about this is that it will tarnish the reputation of people who are dedicated to doing nothing but what they thought was best for the world." Bankman-Fried trailed off. On his computer screen, his army cast spells and swung swords unattended.

I asked what he'd say to people who were comparing him to the most famous Ponzi schemer of recent times. "Bernie Madoff also said he had good intentions and gave a lot to charity," I said.

"FTX was a legitimate, profitable, thriving business. And I fucked up by, like, allowing a margin position to get too big on it. One that endangered the platform. It was a completely unnecessary and unforced error, which like maybe I got super unlucky on, but, like, that was my bad."

"It fucking sucks," he added. "But it wasn't inherent to what the business was. It was just a fuckup. A huge fuckup."

To me, it didn't really seem like a fuckup. Even if I believed that he misplaced and accidentally spent $8 billion, he had already told me that Alameda had been allowed to violate FTX's margin rules. This wasn't some little technical thing. He was so proud of FTX's margining system that he'd been lobbying regulators for it to be used on U.S. exchanges instead of traditional safeguards. Bankman-Fried himself had said that exchanges should never extend credit to a fund and put other customers' assets at risk. He wrote on Twitter that the idea an exchange would even have that discretion was "scary." I read him the tweets and asked: "Isn't that, like, exactly what you did, right around that time?"

"Yeah, I guess that's kind of fair," he said. Then he seemed to claim that this was evidence the rules he was lobbying for were a good idea. "I think this is one of the things that would have stopped."

"You had a rule on your platform. You didn't follow it," I said.

By then it was past midnight, and—operating without the benefit of any prescription stimulants—I was worn out. I asked Bankman-Fried if I could see the apartment's deck before I left. Outside, crickets chirped as we stood by the pool. The marina was dark, lit only by the spotlights of yachts. As I said goodbye, Bankman-Fried pulled a plain burger bun out of a bag and bit into it and started talking with the Pac-Man sock guy about potential bailouts.

EPILOGUE

Sam Bankman-Fried's liminal period in his penthouse lasted for three more weeks. Then, on December 12, he got a call from his lawyer in New York, who warned him that Bahamian police were on their way to arrest him. Bankman-Fried was in the midst of preparing to testify before the House Financial Services Committee, where he was planning to stick to his story that this was all a massive screwup. His opening line, according to a draft of his speech: "I would like to start by formally stating, under oath: I fucked up."

Around 6:00 P.M., armed officers arrived at Albany, Bankman-Fried's luxurious condo complex. He was handcuffed and taken to a police station, where he spent the night in a cell before being moved to the notorious Fox Hill prison, on the east end of the island. Reports from human rights groups and the U.S. State Department describe the prison as dark and fetid, with little running water, and infested with rats and maggots. It is reportedly so overcrowded that inmates sleep on the bare ground.

"It's not fit for humanity," a guard once said.

Bankman-Fried faced U.S. charges of fraud, conspiracy to commit money laundering, and campaign-finance violations. He was assigned to a twenty-foot-square green and yellow room, in the infirmary, with five other inmates. Since the prison food was not vegan, he survived mainly on stale Wonder Bread and peanut butter. He took cold showers in a moldy stall with a garden hose.

But his biggest complaint was the lack of internet access. He couldn't read the latest stories about FTX, or occupy his mind with games like *Storybook Brawl*. He felt like he was going crazy. He would give his visitors lists of information he was looking for, and instructions about where to find it online, and then expect them to return to the jail with printouts the next day.

"I was trying to pretend that I had an internet connection with a latency of one day," Bankman-Fried later told a reporter.

One of the documents Bankman-Fried did have access to was a diplomatic cable the United States had attached to the request for his arrest that it had sent to the Bahamas. The document described two cooperating witnesses, both software developers.

One of them told prosecutors he'd confronted Bankman-Fried about the billions of dollars in loans to Alameda around September. The billionaire had replied that the situation was causing him concern too. Incredibly, he said it was making him "5-10 percent less productive," the documents said. Bankman-Fried said the situation could correct itself if cryptocurrency prices went up. The unnamed witness seemed pretty clearly to be Nishad Singh, the trusted lieutenant who'd once been a regular at Bankman-Fried's family dinners in Palo Alto.

The other witness told prosecutors Bankman-Fried had ordered changes to the exchange's computer code that allowed Alameda Research to borrow customer funds. The witness, who viewed this as inappropriate, said he'd raised the issue with Bankman-Fried, who'd responded that "it was okay" because the loans were backed with tokens. Bankman-Fried realized this was Gary Wang, FTX's top coder, and his friend from math camp and MIT.

He'd known Wang and Singh since they were teenagers. They'd moved to Hong Kong together to seek their fortunes, then relocated to the Bahamas, where they spent nearly every hour together. But Bankman-Fried's closest allies had apparently turned on him.

Bankman-Fried spent eight nights in Fox Hill before he agreed to be extradited to the United States. On the night of December 21, a police motorcade, led by an officer on a motorcycle, siren blaring, cut through Bahamian traffic to take him to a private runway where a jet would take him to New York. A photo from that night shows Bankman-Fried in handcuffs, flanked by two U.S. officials. The next day, he was taken to federal court in downtown Manhattan for a hearing.

The courthouse was mobbed with reporters and photographers. In a gray suit, his ankle restraints clanking, Bankman-Fried was led into the courtroom by U.S. Marshals. He sat hunched over, between two lawyers. A judge told Bankman-Fried he'd be placed on house arrest, at his parents' home in Palo Alto, until his trial. Asked if he understood the conditions, Bankman-Fried said, "Yes, I do," the only words he spoke at the hearing. I had been joking when I told my daughter that he might get grounded. But he was actually being sent to his room.

Singh and Wang were busy negotiating cooperation agreements with the government, as was Caroline Ellison, the head of Alameda Research. Each of them confessed at court hearings one by one, pleading guilty to fraud charges that carried potential decades-long prison sentences, though presumably they expected to receive shorter ones for cooperation. Wang admitted that he'd agreed to make changes to FTX's code that gave Alameda special borrowing privileges.

"I did so knowing that others were representing to investors and customers that Alameda had no such special privileges and people were likely investing in and using FTX based in part on those misrepresentations," he said. "I knew what I was doing was wrong."

Ellison said that Alameda had used those privileges to borrow billions of dollars from FTX, which came from other customers' deposits.

"I understood that FTX would need to use customer funds to finance its loans to Alameda," Ellison said. "I am truly sorry for what I did."

Singh's confession was possibly the most damning. He said that Alameda had borrowed billions of dollars of customer funds, and that he'd used that money on other expenses, including political donations, even though he knew Alameda was unlikely to be able to repay the loans. He also said that he'd helped Bankman-Fried trick potential investors by inflating FTX's revenue.

"Your Honor, I'm unbelievably sorry for my role in all of this and the harm that it's caused," he said. "I'm hoping that in accepting responsibility, assisting the government, and forfeiting assets, I can begin to make it right."

Bankman-Fried returned to the Manhattan courthouse in January 2023 to plead not guilty to all charges, then again in March to deny new charges of bank fraud and bribing a Chinese official. A spokesman for the one-time billionaire said that he disputed his friends' accounts of what happened. His trial was set for October.

Back in Palo Alto, he was sleeping in his childhood bedroom, and he was bored. He started a Substack newsletter, where he wrote a lengthy explanation of FTX's failure, complete with eight charts, which attempted to deflect much of the blame to Binance's CZ. After Bankman-Fried used a VPN—a service to conceal the user's location—to access a streaming service to watch the Super Bowl, he was reprimanded by the judge in his case, who eventually forced him to give up his smartphone, and made his parents pledge not to allow him to use the internet on theirs.

The Bankman-Frieds purchased a trained German shepherd attack dog, named Sandor. They hired armed guards, at $10,000 a week, after receiving death threats. The guards set up a barrier on their street. His lawyers claimed in court that one day a car drove into it. Three men got out and said, "You won't be able to keep us out." They left before they could be identified.

Among his visitors were the author Michael Lewis; reporters from *Bloomberg News,* the *Financial Times, Forbes,* and *Puck;* and a twenty-eight-year-old crypto influencer named Tiffany Fong. Bankman-Fried told them he was lonely and understimulated.

In his den, Bankman-Fried had a marble table with two chess sets set up side by side for Bughouse chess, one of the games he used to stay up all night playing with his FTX friends. He told one of his visitors he had no one to play with. "It is sort of there prospectively as much as anything else," he told a reporter.

FTX'S COLLAPSE IN November 2022 marked the end of the great shitcoin boom of 2020 to 2022. All cryptocurrency prices crashed. Bitcoin dropped as low as $16,000, and Solana, one of Bankman-Fried's favorites, collapsed 95 percent from its highs. The total value of all cryptocurrencies, which had topped $3 trillion two years earlier, fell below $1 trillion.

More companies failed. BlockFi, which had been bailed out by FTX, went bust, for real this time. Galois Capital, a fund that won big by betting against Do Kwon's Terra-Luna scam, failed because it kept the winnings on FTX. Others, like the makers of an NFT cockfighting game, pivoted to A.I. The friends who'd once told me about their crypto winnings grew quiet. On Twitter, few people seemed to be tweeting "WAGMI" or trying to promote coins anymore. Congress called for hearings, this time to yell at crypto bros rather than snuggling up to them to raise money. In the U.K., lawmakers called for crypto to be regulated as gambling. No crypto ads ran during 2023's Super Bowl.

"I think all that's been a waste of time, and why you guys waste any breath on it is totally beyond me," J.P. Morgan CEO Jamie Dimon, a longtime crypto critic, gloated in an interview with CNBC. "Bitcoin itself is a hyped-up fraud. It's a pet rock."

Crypto advocates said the industry had seen bad times before, and that it was only a matter of time before another cycle of hype began. But it didn't seem likely to me. It had been fourteen years since Satoshi Nakamoto mined the first Bitcoin. The technology was as old as WhatsApp or Uber, which had long since wormed their way into our everyday lives so thoroughly their names had become verbs. But no one had invented a mainstream use for cryptocurrency. So many smart people had spent so many thousands of hours working on crypto—and yet shockingly little of use had come of it. Bankman-Fried had discredited the only use anyone had come up with: semi-legal offshore gambling. If you couldn't even trust the most reputable crypto casino—FTX—who would want to play?

The idea of an instantaneous way of transferring money around the world was still appealing. But I'd tried out the fox-head icon, and the idea everyone would one day store their cash in some version of it was preposterous. Traveling around the world investigating crypto had given me a new appreciation for my Visa card. It worked instantly, with just a tap, charged no fees, and never asked me to memorize long strings of numbers, or to bury codes in my backyard. It even gave me airline miles. When my wife's account was hacked and used to book an Airbnb, we were given a full refund with just a phone call.

I didn't think the prices of all of the cryptocurrencies were about to go to zero, or that we'd never see another hot new coin mint overnight billionaires. On the stock market, pump-and-dump scams have persisted for hundreds of years, and yet there are still new suckers willing to buy shares in some shell company that claims to have struck gold.

The one coin I especially wouldn't bet against is Bitcoin. It's not that it's useful—if anything, it's more unwieldy than the others. But Bitcoin's true believers are so convinced that it's hard to imagine anything will change their minds. To them, whatever the question, the answer is "buy Bitcoin." Everything they see is evidence Bitcoin will rise, like the members of a cult certain that the apocalypse—and their salvation—is just around the corner.

. . .

EVEN AT THE peak of the boom, many of the crypto boosters I interviewed would tell me that most coins were scams—just not theirs. Now many of those same people were either in jail, awaiting trial, facing civil lawsuits, or bankrupt. It seemed like practically everyone in the industry was.

By 2023, the hot spots for crypto billionaires had shifted from the Bahamas and Miami Beach to the courthouses of Washington, D.C., and Manhattan. There was the Celsius bankruptcy, the Voyager bankruptcy, the Three Arrows bankruptcy, and the FTX bankruptcy. Do Kwon, the Terra-Luna scammer, was arrested that March at an airport in Montenegro, while trying to fly to Dubai using fake Costa Rican identity papers. (He has denied wrongdoing.) In June, the Securities and Exchange Commission filed giant lawsuits against Binance and Coinbase. The agency basically alleged that much of the crypto trading that went on openly on their websites was in fact illegal. It didn't explain why it waited out an entire boom and bust and watched countless people lose their shirts before raising any objections.

Other cases were puzzling to me too. The Feds arrested the creators of the "Mutant Ape Planet" and "Baller Ape Club" NFT collections—not for knocking off the Bored Ape Yacht Club, but for deceiving buyers. Apparently, if ape cartoons are ugly enough, they can charge you with fraud. I went to a court hearing for a twenty-six-year-old named Avi Eisenberg, who faced a long prison sentence for allegedly manipulating the price of a token called Mango on the DeFi site Mango Markets. This had somehow made him more than $100 million. His shackles rattled as he shuffled in wearing a canary yellow jumpsuit. With his head buzzed, he looked like a sullen teenager who'd been called to the principal's office for smoking weed in the bathroom. Were we really throwing the full weight and resources of the U.S. government to prosecute some kid for manipulating the price of a coin named after a fruit? The situation seemed especially ridiculous given that I didn't see any cases relating to money laundering for Chinese gangsters or facilitating human trafficking in Cambodia.

AMAZINGLY, EVEN AS the crypto industry melted down, Tether survived. No matter how hard the world stomped on crypto, Tether always seemed to skitter away, like some kind of financial cockroach. On November 16, a few days after FTX's collapse, Giancarlo Devasini returned to El Salvador, where he posed with President Nayib Bukele for a photo at the Casa Presidencial. His partner, Bitcoin artist Valentina Picozzi, and podcasters Stacy Herbert and Max Keiser came along for the visit. Devasini, wearing cropped linen pants and espadrilles, stood next to Bukele, who had a hand on the small of his back. The Tether boss was beaming.

Devasini had reason to smile. His company was hitting a financial jackpot. Throughout 2022, the U.S. Federal Reserve had been raising interest rates to combat inflation. By December, they'd hit 4 percent. This meant that U.S. government bonds, which previously paid just about nothing, were starting to pay real money.

For most banks, this also meant that they had to start paying higher interest rates to their depositors. But Tether doesn't pay interest to the people who own its coins. Whatever the company earns on its reserves is pretty much pure profit.

In May 2023, Tether announced that it had converted most of its holdings into U.S. government bonds. It said that due to the high interest rates, it had generated $1.5 billion in profits in the first quarter alone—an insane amount for an unregulated offshore company. That number would be a good quarter for corporate giants like Raytheon, Nike, or Disney. Tether had, if its numbers were trustworthy, become one of the 150 most profitable companies in the world.

At that pace, given the 40 percent stake I'd heard Devasini once held in the company, the former plastic surgeon could make more than $2 billion for himself in 2023 alone. But Tether said it would hold the profits as excess reserves, to ensure its coins were safe. And it said that it would use 15 percent of its profits to buy Bitcoins. Tether had once scoffed at critics who claimed its coins were being used to prop up the price of Bitcoin. Now the company was making that part of its business plan.

"Every single token in the market is and would remain fully backed even if the Bitcoin price were to go down to zero tomorrow," Tether's technology chief Paolo Ardoino told a reporter. "Tether could distribute the entire amount invested in bitcoin to its shareholders, and the peg to [U.S. dollars] will not be affected. In such a scenario, Tether would still have $1 billion of excess reserves."

Tether released an "assurance opinion" from the accounting firm BDO Italia, which said that it did in fact have the assets it claimed. Of course, the company had yet to produce the fully audited financial statements that it had been promising were coming any day now for years; and, as far as I knew, U.S. prosecutors were still investigating Tether's executives and considering charging them with bank fraud for the tricks they used to open bank accounts in the early days of the company. But the investigation had dragged on since 2018, and it wasn't clear it would lead anywhere.

Most of the short sellers betting against Tether gave up. Nate Anderson of Hindenburg Research, who had once tantalized me in Central Park by dangling his $1 million prize for information on Tether, failed to turn up the bombshell he was looking for.

Simply by surviving, Tether had won, at least for now. The amount of Tether outstanding, which had fallen amid the credit crisis, climbed to an all-time high of 83 billion by June. When I contacted the company one last time and sent over a detailed memo about my findings, a spokesperson declined to respond, saying only that it contained "a large number of errors and misinformation."

All I could do was laugh. I recalled a line Devasini had written in his blog: "Either I am a genius or everyone else, indiscriminately, is insulting your intelligence." One way or the other, he was right.

ON A WEDNESDAY morning in January 2023, I rode the subway to the southern tip of Manhattan to attend a court hearing in the dispute between Celsius and Jason Stone, the prototypical degenerate trader and Bored Ape aficionado. Climbing the subway stairs, I noticed a glum man ahead of me, wearing a baggy suit. As we both walked toward the federal bankruptcy courthouse, a grand building fronted with three-story Corinthian columns, I realized it was the company's founder, Alex Mashinsky. He had once so entranced his cult of "Celsians" that they had sent in billions of dollars of their savings. Now he looked like any other disgruntled commuter.

"First time here," he said, as we emptied our pockets and walked through the court's metal detector, as if he knew he'd likely be there dozens of times.

The hearing was in Room 523 on the fifth floor, a wood-paneled chamber with benches to seat hundreds of spectators. I was one of two.

Stone sat in the front, staring straight ahead. His face looked, well, like stone. He was flanked by three lawyers. Celsius had six people on its side, led by Mitch Hurley, a $1,796-an-hour partner from the law firm Akin Gump, with stiff, spiky salt-and-pepper hair and a gray suit with subtle pinstripes. It had been six months since Celsius had filed for bankruptcy, and though little progress had been made returning its remaining assets to its customers, the case had been a windfall for bankruptcy attorneys.

For the next nine hours—which cost Celsius's customers at least $43,416—the lawyers traded accusations about how Stone managed Celsius's crypto coins. Celsius accused Stone of embezzling money from its cryptocurrency wallets and using the funds to purchase rare NFTs, including the demon Mutant Ape that made him a crypto influencer. Stone said that he was told to take the ape as an advance on his management fees, and that Celsius stiffed him on the rest, which should have amounted to around $200 million.

When Mashinsky stepped up into the plexiglass witness box, one of Stone's lawyers attacked his credibility. This was quite easy. The lawyer read Mashinsky's tweets from the weeks before Celsius failed, in which he assured customers everything was fine. And he mentioned a lawsuit filed a week earlier by the New York attorney general, which accused Mashinsky of defrauding his customers by saying their funds were safe while secretly gambling with the assets.

The lawyer argued that Mashinsky should have known Stone was buying NFTs, because he bragged about it on Twitter. This prompted an argument about whether Stone's account was popular, and whether Mashinsky read his tweets.

"It's in my feed so I'm sure I, I see it once in a while, but that's—that has nothing to do with me knowing or not knowing what NFTs Jason owns," Mashinsky stammered.

The chief judge of the bankruptcy court, Martin Glenn, presided via Zoom, and he struggled with his camera, sometimes disappearing and then popping back up as a disembodied neck. "Your honor, if I could pause for a second, your camera is sort of pointed just at your chest," Hurley said at one point. The judge seemed unhappy to be refereeing a dispute about the ownership of monkey pictures. At one point, his face locked into a harsh scowl. It was hard to tell if his feed was frozen or if he'd gone stiff with frustration.

During a break, Stone and I commiserated in the hall. "This is boring," he told me. He showed off pictures of a dog he'd found on a beach in Thailand and adopted. He'd been feeling better, he said, because he'd gotten a prescription for ketamine to treat his depression.

One of the main points of contention was where Stone wrote down the password to Celsius's crypto wallet. He had kept Celsius's money—$1.4 billion in coins and another $600 million in loans—in the same fox-head icon in his browser I used to purchase my ape. Stone said he'd read the seed phrase to his father, who wrote it on a small notepad. Hurley said he had promised to return it. But Stone admitted he'd used funds from the wallet just days earlier to pay his lawyers. One of the Akin Gump lawyers mouthed "What the fuck" quite clearly, then used his hand to cover his smile.

The lawyer pulled up an Excel spreadsheet of all the transactions in Celsius's wallet. It was displayed on a large monitor at the left of the courtroom. I got up and walked over to examine it. Each line simply listed Celsius's wallet address, 0xb1adceddb2941033a090dd166a4 62fe1c2029484, another long string of characters, and an amount.

Crypto mythology had imbued these lines with meaning. Each represented an ownership stake in the future of art, the thinking went, or a DeFi investment that would revolutionize the world of finance. People paid millions of perfectly good dollars to add lines to crypto spreadsheets, to record that they owned a stash of Dogecoins, or a rare Bored Ape. By manipulating sheets like these, Sam Bankman-Fried had made himself into one of the world's richest men.

On the screen in the courtroom, the spreadsheet lost its power. It looked like any other financial document, with line after line of random letters and numbers. It was hard to fathom we had ever imagined they were anything else.

ACKNOWLEDGMENTS

The reporting of this book depended on interviews with hundreds of sources, many of them not named in the text. Most of them spoke with me at some risk to themselves and with no clear reward. Thank you for believing in journalism and welcoming me into your world. I would like to especially thank Jason Stone for his openness and generosity with his time. (Not to mention getting me into ApeFest.)

This project started with an assignment from *Businessweek*'s Joel Weber, and he and my other bosses at Bloomberg generously gave me time and support to pursue it. I wouldn't be the journalist I am today without the guidance of Robert Friedman, who has been a steadfast friend and mentor for more than a decade. Among the other colleagues who helped at various stages were Jeremy Keehn, Christine Harper, John Hechinger, Pat Regnier, Joe Light, Ava Benny-Morrison, Anthony Cormier, Alex Harris, Michael Tobin, Vildana Hajric, and Joanna Ossinger. Much of my reporting on FTX, Celsius, Terra-Luna, and El Salvador first appeared as stories that I wrote for *Businessweek* and Bloomberg Markets.

I am grateful to the intrepid reporters who helped me follow the investigation to countries where I didn't speak the language or know the lay of the land. Nelson Rauda Zablah, whose coverage of El Salvador's Bitcoin debacle has been second to none, assisted with my reporting there. It was also an honor to work with Mech Dara and Danielle Keeton-Olsen in Cambodia, whose daring reporting exposed the problem of forced labor and other abuses in scam compounds. Guill Ramos led me to the origins of the *Axie Infinity* mania in Cabanatuan City in the Philippines. Song Nguyen was a tenacious researcher in Vietnam. In Milan, Anna Momigliano and Sergio Di Pasquale contributed research and translation. The photographers

Christopher Gregory-Rivera, Jose Cabezas, and Melissa Alcena allowed me to reprint their revealing work.

Paul Whitlatch's enthusiasm kept me going. His ideas helped shape the story, and the final draft is so much better than the first thanks to his careful editing. Thanks also to Katie Berry, Gillian Blake, and everyone else at Crown and Currency.

Tina Bennett believed in this project from the first time we spoke on the phone and gave me the confidence to commit wholeheartedly to it. Her astute edits helped improve the manuscript. I can't imagine a better agent.

Many reporters have covered crypto extensively, and their work informs my own. Kadhim Shubber and his colleagues dug into Tether in a series of excellent stories for the *Financial Times,* and Frank Muci was early to point out the absurdity of *Axie Infinity* and El Salvador's economic plan. Jack Brook and Alastair McCready did superb reporting on scam compounds in Cambodia and collegially shared advice. David Jaffe-Bellany's coverage of FTX, Three Arrows, and the rest of crypto was colorful and insightful. Matt Levine's hilarious newsletter *Money Stuff* kept me sane as I descended deeper into crypto world and taught me a lot about its mechanics. He has raised the bar for everyone who writes about business.

My friends Max Chafkin, Max Abelson, Zach Mider, Nick Summers, Kit Chellel, Fais Khan, David Gauvey-Herbert, and Hugo Lindgren read parts or all of the manuscript at various stages and provided crucial guidance, encouragement, and criticism. Sam Dean went above and beyond the call of friendship to help me revise multiple drafts. My friend Jay generously allowed me to write about our group chat, Dan's Basement. Amy Reading, Rebecca Spang, and Barry Strauss shared their expertise. Gabriel Baumgaertner, Ajai Raj, Cheyenne Ligon, Madeleine Kuhns, and Ramasela Queen Molekwa all have my gratitude for carefully researching various sections.

I wrote this book while serving as a National Fellow at the New America Foundation. The members of my cohort and the staff of New America became a critical support network and critiqued a key section of the manuscript.

I am deeply grateful to my parents for more love and support than can ever be measured. My father, Russell, taught me the paramount importance of the pursuit of knowledge and instilled a skepticism of corporate marketing at a perhaps inappropriately early age. My mother,

Abby, shared her love of literature and her appreciation of words, and inspired me with her lifelong dedication to teaching and learning. My stepfather, David, showed me how to conquer any challenge with aplomb. He also helped me with a significant one: explaining Bitcoin. And, going back a generation, I am lucky to have the love and support of three of the most independent-minded and adventurous women I know: Jeri, Mary, and Carol.

The writing of this book has become a family project. Abby helped edit the manuscript and translate some Italian passages. Masha helped research and revise sections of the manuscript and workshop jokes. Percy boldly helped with some interviews. Zark and his colleague Yassmine Esteitie made the beautiful pig-butchering flowchart. Jeri was a helpful reader. Emily, who inspired me to become a journalist, came through in a pinch. I am also grateful to Sarah, Ashraf, and Diane for supporting me and my family.

My children helped me with this project more than they know. Eli's independence and determination inspired me, Margot asked insightful questions, and Fiona's exuberant spirit was a joy on the most frustrating days. I am looking forward to reading all of your stories one day. Most important, this book never would have happened without my wife, Nikki. When I started my research, Fiona was a toddler and Margot and Eli were four years old, and she spent many weeks taking care of them while I was off on research trips whose utility was not obvious. Her kindness, creativity, playfulness, and integrity are a continual inspiration to me. She takes on any obstacle with bravery and toughness. Nikki, the best adventure is the one I am on with you.

NOTES

I interviewed well over three hundred people for this book. In general, I've tried to indicate in the text when a quote or fact comes from an interview, and I have not repeated those citations in the notes that follow. In some cases, the people I spoke to have requested that I keep them anonymous.

Tether was presented with a 187-point fact-checking memo prior to publication and declined to respond to any specific questions about its history, its reserves, or its use by scammers and human traffickers. "The huge volume of corrections required would be tantamount to our rewriting Mr. Faux's book for him, which is not our job," a spokesperson for the company wrote. "Our attention is better focused on our customers and the success of the Bitcoin community."

A note on cryptocurrency prices: For coin prices, trading volumes, and market capitalizations, I generally used CoinMarketCap.com, which I checked against other sources. NFT prices came from CoinGecko and OpenSea. I converted the prices from Ether or Solana to U.S. dollars based on the prevailing exchange rate at the time of the sale.

Prologue

5 **estimated at $96 billion:** Tom Maloney, Yueqi Yang, Ben Bartenstein, "World's Biggest Crypto Fortune Began with a Friendly Poker Game," Bloomberg, January 9, 2022.

Chapter One: "I Am Freaking Nostradamus!"

9 **even Dogecoin's creator:** Jackson Palmer, "My Joke Cryptocurrency Hit $2 Billion and Something Is Very Wrong," Vice, January 11, 2018.
10 **I pulled up *Drudge Report*:** "Reddit Frenzy Pumps Up Dogecoin! Now Worth Billions!," *Drudge Report,* January 30, 2021.
12 **Janet Yellen:** Robert Schmidt and Jesse Hamilton, "Tether, Facebook Coin Spur Worry at Yellen's Closed-Door Meeting," Bloomberg, July 27, 2021.
13 **twelve thousand crypto die-hards:** Jonathan Levin, "Wall Street's Crypto Embrace Shows in Crowd at Miami Conference," Bloomberg, June 7, 2021.

Chapter Two: Number Go Up Technology

14 **"Every scheming shitwad":** Carl Hiaasen, *Skinny Dip* (New York: Grand Central Publishing, 2005), 37.

15 **CumRocket:** Anthony Cuthbertson, "Elon Musk Sends Adult-Themed Crypto Price 'to the Moon' After Tweeting Explicit Emoji," *Independent,* June 5, 2021.

15 **Suarez declared:** The mayor embraced crypto so thoroughly that he would later promote something called MiamiCoin. Suarez lost about $2,500 when the price crashed. Joey Flechas and Vinod Sreeharsha, "MiamiCoin Trading Halted. After Price Tanked, Mayor Francis Suarez Lost About $2,500," *Miami Herald,* March 22, 2023.

15 **pay city employees in Bitcoin:** Jonathan Levin, "Miami Mayor Says Plan Advancing to Pay City Employees in Bitcoin," Bloomberg, October 12, 2021.

15 **twenty-foot-high seawall across Biscayne Bay:** Patricia Mazzei, "A 20-Foot Sea Wall? Miami Faces the Hard Choices of Climate Change," *New York Times,* June 2, 2021.

19 **75 sextillion-to-1:** Matt Levine, "The Crypto Story," *Bloomberg Businessweek,* October 31, 2022. Recommended reading for anyone interested in learning more about how crypto works.

19 **six and a quarter brand-new Bitcoins:** Gabriel J.X. Dance, Tim Wallace, Zach Levitt, "The Real World Costs for the Digital Race for Bitcoin," *New York Times,* April 9, 2023.

19 **"It kind of felt like I was in the future":** Adrian Chen, "Underground Website Lets You Buy Any Drug Imaginable," *Wired,* June 1, 2011.

19 **The demand started:** Prosecutors alleged that Silk Road generated revenues of 9.5 million Bitcoins. At the time, fewer than 12 million Bitcoins existed. Tim Fernholz, "Silk Road Collected 9.5 Million Bitcoin—and Only 11.75 Million Exist," *Quartz,* October 2, 2013.

19 **Mentions of Bitcoin millionaires started:** Stephen Foley and Jane Wild, "The Bitcoin Believers," *Financial Times,* June 14, 2013.

19 **fake trades and price manipulation:** Neil Gandala, JT Hamrick, Tyler Mooreb, Tali Obermana, "Price Manipulation in the Bitcoin Ecosystem," *Journal of Monetary Economics* (2017): 5.

20 **were drowning out the sound:** Hannah Brown, "Bitcoin Mining Is Drowning Out the Sound of Niagara Falls—Here's How," AFP, July 11, 2022.

20 **from coal and natural-gas plants:** Dance, Wallace, Levitt, "The Real World Costs for the Digital Race for Bitcoin."

20 **the entire country of Argentina:** Allyson Vesprille, "Crypto Mining Is Threatening US Climate Efforts, White House Warns," Bloomberg, September 8, 2022.

22 **he told *The New Yorker*:** Larisa MacFarquhar, "Caesar.com," *The New Yorker,* April 3, 2000.

24 **one of Celsius's early backers:** "Celsius Network Secures US$10M Equity Raise with Tether as Lead Investor," *PR Newswire,* June 22, 2020.

24 **$18 billion in assets:** Zeke Faux and Joe Light, "Celsius's 18% Yields on Crypto Are Tempting—and Drawing Scrutiny," *Bloomberg Businessweek,* January 27, 2022.

27 **"way shakier":** Zeke Faux, "Anyone Seen Tether's Billions?," *Businessweek,* October 7, 2021.

27 **a Gulfstream jet:** The jet was spray-painted by the well-known artist Alec Mo-nopoly, with help from influencer Logan Paul. Paul created an NFT of a photo of the project, and, according to his website, Originals.com, sold it for about $87,000.

Chapter Three: Doula for Creation

28 **a young Bitcoiner named Dev:** Not his real name or his real hometown.

29 **sold off the vast majority:** Tabby Kinder and Richard Waters, "Peter Thiel's Fund Wound Down 8-Year Bitcoin Bet Before Market Crash," *Financial Times,* January 18, 2023.

32 **to make TV obsolete:** Joseph Menn and Greg Miller, "How a Visionary Venture on the Web Unraveled," *Los Angeles Times,* May 7, 2000.

32 **once owned by Death Row Records founder:** Andrew Rice, "DEN Board Asked Founder to Leave," *Wired,* November 1, 1999.

32 **He and his much younger boyfriend, Chad:** Ellie Hall, Nicolás Medina Mora, David Noriega, "Found: The Elusive Man at the Heart of the Hollywood Sex Abuse Scandal," *BuzzFeed News,* June 26, 2014.

32 **the ridiculous salary of $250,000 a year:** Menn and Miller, "How a Visionary Venture on the Web Unraveled."

32 **a web show called *Chad's World*:** Joseph Menn, "Teen Worker Sues DEN, Its Founders on Sex Charges," *Los Angeles Times,* July 8, 2000.

32 **a rich, older gay man:** Hunter Schwarz, "The TV Pilot with Eerie Similarities to the Bryan Singer Sexual Abuse Case," *BuzzFeed,* April 21, 2014.

32 **a viewer told *Radar* magazine:** John Gorenfeld and Patrick Runkle, "Fast Company," *Radar,* November 5, 2007.

33 **"I was passed around like a party favor":** Alex French and Maximillian Potter, "Nobody Is Going to Believe You," *The Atlantic,* March 2019.

33 **to fill two Lincoln Town Cars:** Hall, Mora, Noriega, "Found: The Elusive Man at the Heart of the Hollywood Sex Abuse Scandal."

33 **the seaside resort town of Marbella:** Ibid.

33 **The authorities caught up with them:** Joseph Menn, "Spain Arrests Fugitive in Molestation Case," *Los Angeles Times,* May 18, 2002.

33 **"None of it is true":** Nicolás Medina Mora, Ellie Hall, Hunter Schwarz, "Brock Pierce, Associate of Embattled X-Men Director, Joins the Bitcoin Foundation," *BuzzFeed News,* May 11, 2014.

33 **the dark-elf wizard Athrex:** Julian Dibbell, "The Decline and Fall of an Ultra Rich Online Gaming Empire," *Wired,* November 24, 2008.

34 **One reporter who visited:** Julian Dibbell, "The Life of the Chinese Gold Farmer," *New York Times Magazine,* June 17, 2007.

34 **a virtual-item brokerage called IGE:** Dibbell, "The Decline and Fall of an Ultra Rich Online Gaming Empire."

34 **450,000 people were playing *EverQuest*:** Andy Patrizio, "EverQuest's Long, Strange 20-Year Trip Still Has No End in Sight," *ArsTechnica,* June 6, 2019.

34 **a similar game called *World of Warcraft*:** Simon Carless, "Blizzard Announces 5 Million WoW Subscribers," *Game Developer,* December 19, 2005.

34 **a $2 billion a year business:** Dibbell, "The Decline and Fall of an Ultra Rich Online Gaming Empire."

34 **400,000 farmers in his supply chain:** Cyril Gilson, "Blockchain Tech May Allow Developing World to Leapfrog Developed World: Brock Pierce," *Coin-Telegraph,* November 20, 2017.

34 **more than $5 million a month:** Shawn Boburg and Emily Rauhala, "Stephen K. Bannon Once Guided a Global Firm That Made Millions Helping Gamers Cheat," *Washington Post,* August 4, 2017.

34 **Bannon secured a $60 million investment:** Ibid.

34 **"These guys, these rootless white males":** Joshua Green, *Devil's Bargain: Steve Bannon, Donald Trump, and the Nationalist Uprising* (New York: Penguin, 2017), 146.

35 **Willett wrote in 2012:** J. R. Willett, "The Second Bitcoin Whitepaper," https://cryptochainuni.com/wp-content/uploads/Mastercoin-2nd-Bitcoin -Whitepaper.pdf.

35 **he raised about $500,000:** Vitalik Buterin, "Mastercoin: A Second-Generation Protocol on the Bitcoin Blockchain," *Bitcoin Magazine,* November 4, 2013.

36 **inventing pop-under internet ads:** Zeke Faux, "Anyone Seen Tether's Billions?," *Bloomberg Businessweek,* October 7, 2021.

36 **They initially called the project Realcoin:** Pete Rizzo, "Realcoin Rebrands as 'Tether' to Avoid Altcoin Association," *CoinDesk,* November 20, 2014.

37 **coins with Ron Paul's face on them:** Tim Murphy, "Ron Paul Coin Minter, Pot Priest, Faces 15 Years in Prison," *Mother Jones,* March 21, 2011.

37 **an online currency called e-gold:** "Digital Currency Business E-Gold Indicted for Money Laundering and Illegal Money Transmitting," United States Department of Justice, April 27, 2007.

37 **proto-stablecoin, Liberty Reserve:** Jake Halpern, "Bank of the Underworld," *The Atlantic,* May 2015.

37 **moved to Costa Rica:** "Founder of Liberty Reserve Pleads Guilty to Laundering More Than $250 Million Through His Digital Currency Business," U.S. Department of Justice, January 29, 2016.

37 **was kept on Budovsky's servers:** *United States v. Budovsky,* United States District Court Southern District of New York, Opinion and Order, September 23, 2015, 2.

37 **eventually pleaded guilty:** "Founder of Liberty Reserve Pleads Guilty to Laundering More Than $250 Million Through His Digital Currency Business," U.S. Department of Justice.

38 **carrying on with the Tether project:** Author's interviews with Pierce, Potter, Collins, and others. Potter has also told his version of this story on various podcasts, including *Orange Pill Podcast* (March 14, 2021) and *What Bitcoin Did* (May 31, 2019).

Chapter Four: The Plastic Surgeon

40 **video that he'd made in 2009:** Bio Delitzia, "Risotto con le orteche e nano," Facebook: https://www.facebook.com/bio.delitzia/videos/100797956613 007/.

40 **from his career as a plastic surgeon:** Alberto Giuliani, "Giancarlo, l'estetica della vita," 2.18 Gallery, Facebook, https://www.facebook.com/218Gallery/ photos/giancarlo-l'estetica-della-vita-alle/425513227579095/.

40 **"the first payment for a new Porsche":** Ibid.

41 **a thesis on skin transplant techniques:** According to the university, his thesis was called "Tradition and future of esthesiology and extensiometry with particular attention to the skin and its transplant," 1989.

41 **The counterfeiting imbroglio:** Gianfranco Ambrosini, "Presa la gang informatica," *Il Corriere della Sera,* September 26, 1995.

42 **about $65,000:** AdnKronos newsroom, "Pirati informatici: Microsoft al contrattacco," AdnKronos, December 3, 1996.

42 **Devasini was unaware:** Tether, "FT Article a Selective Rehashing of Irrelevant, Inaccurate, Old 'News,'" July 15, 2021.

42 **Some of them even:** Tether has insisted that its description of Devasini's companies was accurate.

42 **destroyed in a fire:** Author's interviews with former employees of Devasini's companies. See also: Kadhim Shubber and Siddharth Venkataramakrishnan, "Tether: The Former Plastic Surgeon Behind the Crypto Reserve Currency," *Financial Times,* July 15, 2021.

43 **Tether called the lawsuit "meritless":** Ibid.

43 **a large block of wood:** Tether has claimed the goods were stolen while in transit. Tether, "FT Article a Selective Rehashing."

Chapter Five: Getting Hilariously Rich

47 **"It's enough to put the word 'bitcoin' on Google":** Comment on "Il Blog delle Stelle." December 8, 2012.

47 **programmed by a sixteen- or seventeen-year-old:** "Show HN: Bitcoinica—Advanced Bitcoin Trading Platform," *Y Combinator,* https://news.ycombinator.com/item?id=2973301.

47 **"you forgot to switch your brain on?":** User: urwhatuknow, "Re: [OFFICIAL]Bitfinex.com first Bitcoin P2P lending platform for leverage trading," *Bitcointalk.org,* February 10, 2014.

47 **he wrote to another:** User: urwhatuknow, "Re: And we have another Bitfinex Hookey THIEVING Short Squeeze!," *Bitcointalk.org,* June 22, 2014.

48 **lost 7 percent of all Bitcoins in existence:** Jeff Wilser, "CoinDesk Turns 10: The Legacy of Mt. Gox—Why Bitcoin's Greatest Hack Still Matters," *CoinDesk,* May 4, 2023.

48 **laundering money for drug traffickers:** "Russian National and Bitcoin Exchange Charged in 21-Count Indictment for Operating Alleged International Money Laundering Scheme and Allegedly Laundering Funds from Hack of Mt. Gox," United States Department of Justice, July 26, 2017.

48 **after its founder's mysterious death:** Nathaniel Rich, "Ponzi Schemes, Private Yachts, and a Missing $250 Million in Crypto: The Strange Tale of Quadriga," *Vanity Fair,* November 22, 2019.

48 **one of the largest exchanges in the world:** Charlie Richards, "Karpeles Warns of Another Mt. Gox, but BitFinex Might Have the Answer," *CoinTelegraph,* June 3, 2015.

48 **and stole 119,754 Bitcoins:** "Two Arrested for Alleged Conspiracy to Launder $4.5 Billion in Stolen Cryptocurrency," United States Department of Justice, February 8, 2022.

48 **reduced the balances of all customers:** Clare Baldwin, "Bitfinex Exchange Customers to Get 36 Percent Haircut, Debt Token," Reuters, August 6, 2016.

48 **issued IOUs to cover the losses:** Lucinda Shen, "Every User of This Hacked Bitcoin Exchange Is About to Lose 36% from Their Account," *Fortune,* August 8, 2016.

48 **enough to pay back its customers:** Garrett Keirns, "Bitcoin Exchange Bitfinex Buys Back All Remaining 'Hack Credit' Tokens," *CoinDesk,* April 3, 2017.

49 **raised a total of $6.5 billion:** Mircea Constantin Șcheau, Simona Liliana Crăciunescu, Iulia Brici, and Monica Violeta Achim, "A Cryptocurrency Spectrum Short Analysis," *Journal of Risk and Financial Management* 13, no. 8 (August 17, 2020).

49 **It raised $4 billion:** Brady Dale, "The First Yearlong ICO for EOS Raised $4 Billion. The Second? Just $2.8 Million," *CoinDesk,* September 17, 2019.

49 **"I just make a token":** Gian M. Volpicelli, "To Get Rich in Crypto You Just Need an Idea, and a Coin," *Wired,* February 3, 2018.

49 **As one *New York Times* headline put:** Nellie Bowles, "Everyone Is Getting Hilariously Rich and You're Not," *New York Times,* January 13, 2018.

49 **diamonds:** Olga Kharif, "IBM Is Tackling Blood Diamonds with Blockchain," Bloomberg, April 26, 2018.

49 **heads of lettuce:** Camila Russo, "Walmart Is Getting Suppliers to Put Food on the Blockchain," Bloomberg, April 23, 2018.

50 **"The more confusion the better":** Edward Chancellor, *Devil Take the Hindmost: A History of Financial Speculation* (New York: Farrar, Straus and Giroux, 1999), 67.

50 **"Let but Fortune favor us":** Ibid., 64.

50 **"This is going to be the largest":** Erik Schatzker, "A Crypto Fund King Says Bitcoin Will Be the Biggest Bubble Ever," Bloomberg, September 26, 2017.

50 **$2 billion a year:** Stan Hinden, "Penny Stock Fraud Toll Put at $2 Billion a Year," *Washington Post,* September 7, 1989.

50 **across from the New York Stock Exchange:** Leslie Eaton, "Ideas & Trends; Hi. My Name's Matt. I'm Selling Hot Stocks," *New York Times,* December 21, 1997.

51 **Centra raised about $25 million:** Andrew Hayward, "$25 Million ICO Backed by Floyd Mayweather Was a Fraud, Founder Admits," *Decrypt,* June 16, 2020.

51 **its crypto debit card:** "SEC Charges Additional Defendant in Fraudulent ICO Scheme," United States Securities and Exchange Commission, April 20, 2018.

51 **opioid-addled:** See transcript of Raymond Trapani's sentencing hearing at his criminal trial. *United States v. Sharma et al.,* United States District Court Southern District of New York, May 14, 2018.

51 **$100,000 for his endorsement:** "Two Celebrities Charged with Unlawfully Touting Coin Offerings," U.S. Securities and Exchange Commission, November 29, 2018.

51 **80 percent of ICOs were fraudulent:** Sherwin Dowlatt and Michael Hodapp, "Cryptoasset Market Coverage Initiation: Valuation," Satis Group, August 30, 2018.

51 **those fees added up to $326 million:** Bitfinex published some financial information in May 2019 during its "Unus Sed Leo" coin offering.

52 **They tried suing Wells Fargo:** *iFinex Inc. v. Wells Fargo & Company,* 3:17-cv-01882, (N.D. Cal.), April 5, 2017.

Chapter Six: Cat and Mouse Tricks

54 **He compared Tether to Liberty Reserve:** Bitfinex'ed, "The Mystery of the Bitfinex/Tether Bank, and Why This Is Suspicious," *Medium,* October 1, 2017.
54 **gotten arrested for money laundering:** "Founder of Liberty Reserve Pleads Guilty to Laundering More Than $250 Million Through His Digital Currency Business," United States Department of Justice, January 29, 2016.
55 **a 1989 episode of the cartoon *DuckTales:*** "Dough Ray Me." *DuckTales,* season 3, episode 7, directed by James T. Walker and Bob Hathcock, written by Brooks Wachtel and Gordon Bressack, aired November 3, 1989.
56 **"international finance entity":** Matthew Leising and Yalixa Rivera, "Puerto Rico's Noble Bank Seeks Sale Amid Crypto Slide," Bloomberg, October 1, 2018.
57 **Potter took the payment in U.S. dollars:** Zeke Faux, "Anyone Seen Tether's Billions?," *Bloomberg Businessweek,* October 7, 2021.
57 **the bank failed soon after:** Leising and Rivera, "Puerto Rico's Noble Bank Seeks Sale Amid Crypto Slide."

Chapter Seven: "A Thin Crust of Ice"

60 **Castiglione wrote in a letter:** "A.G. Schneiderman Launches Inquiry into Cryptocurrency 'Exchanges,'" New York State Attorney General, April 17, 2018.
60 **Four exchanges didn't respond at all:** "Virtual Markets Integrity Initiative Report," Office of the New York State Attorney General, September 18, 2018, 2.
60 **"Is Bitcoin Really Un-Tethered?":** John M. Griffin and Amin Shams, "Is Bitcoin Really Un-Tethered?," *The Journal of Finance* (June 15, 2020).
60 **"We've had banking hiccups in the past":** Bitfinexed, "Bitfinex Tether Phil Potter 'Solved' Banking Problems with Illegal Money Laundering Tactics," YouTube, https://www.youtube.com/watch?v=62cvxPIDBGY.
61 **called Crypto Capital:** "Attorney General James Announces Court Order Against 'Crypto' Currency Company Under Investigation for Fraud," New York State Attorney General, April 25, 2019.
61 **"any crypto exchange around the world":** "The Rise and Fall of Crypto Capital Corp, Crypto's Premiere Shadow Bank," *Protos,* August 17, 2021.
61 **By 2017, it was processing:** Damian Williams, "Memorandum of Law of the United States of America in Opposition to the Defendant's Pretrial Motions," in *United States of America v. Reginald Fowler,* Case No. S3 19 Cr. 254 (ALC) (U.S. District Court for the Southern District of New York, filed November 4, 2021).
61 **$1 billion parked in Crypto Capital's accounts:** Tim Copeland, "The Story of Crypto Capital's Dark Past and Its Deep Ties with the Crypto Industry," *Decrypt,* May 2, 2019.

61 **"I need your help":** The messages between the two men were published as part of the litigation between Tether and the New York Attorney General.

61 **waiting on withdrawals for weeks:** David Floyd and Nikhilesh De, "For Bitfinex Users, Dollar Withdrawals Are Now a Weeks-Long Struggle," *CoinDesk,* November 9, 2018.

61 **the companies had cut ties:** Leising and Rivera, "Puerto Rico's Noble Bank Seeks Sale Amid Crypto Slide."

61 **"no impact on our operations":** Bitfinex, "A Response to Recent Online Rumours," *Bitfinex Blog* [no date].

62 **"without the slightest interference":** Bitfinex, "Fiat Deposit Update—October 15th, 2018," *Medium,* October 15, 2018.

62 **actual dollars by real customers:** Letter from John Castiglione to Messrs. Miller and Weinstein, "Re: Subpoenas to iFinex Inc. and Tether Limited," State of New York Office of the Attorney General, https://iapps.courts.state.ny.us/nyscef/ViewDocument?docIndex=2CN3UUPclyTIOms93ZTYGQ==.

64 **"The market just doesn't care":** Paul Vigna, "Cryptocurrency Investors Shrug Off Tether Woes," *Wall Street Journal,* April 29, 2019.

64 **Latin for** *one, but a lion:* Pete Rizzo, "'Not a White Paper': Marketing Document Details $1 Billion Bitfinex Token Sale," *CoinDesk,* May 4, 2019.

64 **future trading revenue to buy them back:** Bitfinex, "Revenues from Tokinex Dedicated to LEO Redemptions," *Medium,* July 8, 2019.

Chapter Eight: The Name's Chalopin. Jean Chalopin.

70 **"an infinity of successive felonious larcenies":** Letter from John Adams to Thomas Jefferson, National Archives, February 24, 1819.

71 **"What a temptation was this":** Alpheus Felch, "Early Banks and Banking in Michigan," in *Report of the Pioneer Society of the State of Michigan,* vol. 2 (W.H. Graham's Presses, 1880), 111.

71 **a casual comment:** "VOX POPULI: Hurtful Rumors Can Spread Faster and Farther in Today's World," *Asahi Shimbun,* May 9, 2023.

71 **Silicon Valley Bank collapsed after worry:** George Hammond and Elaine Moore, "How Silicon Valley Learnt to Love the Government," *Financial Times,* March 17, 2023.

72 **Hindenburg Research announced:** "Hindenburg Research Announces $1,000,000 Bounty for Details on Tether's Backing," Hindenburg Research, October 19, 2021. Tether's chief technology officer, Paolo Ardoino, responded by posting a meme on Twitter depicting Anderson as a strung-out, tinfoil-hat-wearing conspiracy theorist. In his post, the imaginary Anderson whined, in internet-speak, "The regulators will shut it down bro any year or decade now."

74 **touched an all-time high:** MacKenzie Sigalos, "Bitcoin Hits New All-Time High Above $68,000 as Cryptocurrencies Extend Rally," CNBC, November 8, 2021.

74 **topped $3 trillion:** Joanna Ossinger, "Crypto World Hits $3 Trillion Market Cap as Ether, Bitcoin Gain," Bloomberg, November 8, 2021.

74 **31.7 billion Tethers in 2021:** "Tether Papers: This Is Exactly Who Acquired 70% of All USDT Ever Issued," *Protos,* November 10, 2021.

74 **$25 billion valuation:** Alexander Osipovich, "Crypto Exchange FTX Reaches $25 Billion Valuation," *Wall Street Journal,* October 21, 2021.

74 *Forbes* **estimated his personal net worth:** Steven Ehrlich and Chase Peterson-Withorn, "Meet the World's Richest 29-Year-Old: How Sam Bankman-Fried Made a Record Fortune in the Crypto Frenzy," *Forbes,* October 6, 2021.

Chapter Nine: Crypto Pirates

76 **a stolen warship:** Colin Woodard, *The Republic of Pirates* (Orlando, FL: Harcourt, 2007), 12, 15.

76 **The pirates pulled down the Union Jack:** Woodard, *The Republic of Pirates,* 230.

76 **Confederate arms runners:** Nicholas Shaxson, *Treasure Islands: Uncovering the Damage of Offshore Banking and Tax Havens* (New York: St. Martin's, 2011), 89.

76 **Bay Street Boys:** "The Bahamas: Bad News for the Boys," *Time,* January 20, 1967.

76 **covered with nameplates:** Congressional Record: Proceedings and Debates of the Fifty-Seventh Congress, Vol. 81, Part 10, United States: U.S. Government Printing Office, 1937, p. 1562.

76 **the Mafia abandoned Cuba:** Frank Argote-Freyre, "The Myth of Mafia Rule in 1950s Cuba," *Cuban Studies* 49 (2020): 277–78.

76 **Meyer Lansky develop casinos:** Charles A. Dainoff, *Outlaw Paradise: Why Countries Become Tax Havens* (Lanham, MD: Lexington Books, 2021), xii.

77 **a** *Life* **magazine investigation:** Richard Oulahan and William Lambert, "The Scandal in the Bahamas: An Exposé of an Island Paradise Corrupted by Graft, Greed and an Influx of U.S. Gangsters," *Life,* February 3, 1967.

77 **a British colonial official wrote:** Letter from W. G. Hullard, Colonial Office, to B. E. Bennett, Bank of England, November 3, 1961. Thanks to Stephen Mihm, professor of history at the University of Georgia, for pointing out this quote and many of the other details about dirty money in the Bahamas in one of his excellent columns: "FTX's Bahamas Headquarters Was the First Clue," Bloomberg, December 7, 2022.

77 **One Bahamian bank:** David Adams, "Robert Vesco: His Years on the Run," *Tampa Bay Times,* July 3, 1995.

77 **Central Intelligence Agency:** Jim Drinkhall, "CIA Helped Quash Major, Star-Studded Tax Evasion Case," *Wall Street Journal,* April 24, 1980.

77 **a megalomaniacal neo-Nazi:** His name was Carlos Lehder. Seth Ferranti, "The Nazi-Loving Drug Lord Who Revolutionized the Cocaine Smuggling Industry," *Vice,* January 9, 2016.

77 **so much dirty cash:** Guy Gugliotta and Jeff Leen, *Kings of Cocaine: Inside the Medellín Cartel—An Astonishing True Story of Murder, Money and International Corruption* (New Orleans: Garrett County Press, 2011).

77 **The corruption continued:** Edward Cody, "Probe Finds Corruption in Bahamas," *Washington Post,* December 18, 1984.

77 **"flow of criminal and tax evasion money":** Drinkhall, "CIA Helped Quash Major, Star-Studded Tax Evasion Case."

77 **$60 million headquarters:** Youri Kemp, "Crypto Exchange: Hotel to 'Im-merse' Visitors at Its HQ," *The Tribune,* March 14, 2022.

78 **an event celebrating FTX's move:** Remarks: The Rt. Hon. Philip Davis, QC, Prime Minister, The Commonwealth of the Bahamas: Office of the Prime Min-ister, October 4, 2021, https://opm.gov.bs/remarks-the-rt-hon-philip-davis -qc-prime-minister-october-4th-2021/.

79 **prime minister of Georgia:** "Meeting with SBF on FTX Crypto Derivatives Exchange," Government of Georgia, February 19, 2022.

80 **the head of Goldman Sachs:** David Solomon, then the CEO of the Wall Street bank, also liked to DJ under the name DJ D-Sol. His music was not good.

80 **Katy Perry:** The party was at the house of Michael Kives, a well-connected former Hollywood agent. The next day she told her 154 million followers on Instagram, in an unsolicited endorsement, "im quitting music and becoming an intern for @ftx_official ok."

81 **If you walked by a child drowning:** Peter Singer, "Famine, Affluence, and Morality," *Philosophy & Public Affairs* 1, no. 3 (1972): 229–43. Singer notes in the paper that he wrote it in 1971.

82 **the acknowledgments of her 2020 book:** Barbara H. Fried, *Facing Up to Scarcity: The Logic and Limits of Nonconsequentialist Thought* (Oxford: Oxford University Press, 2020), xv.

82 **$100 bills with his face on them:** Theodore Schleifer, "Keeping Up with the Bankman-Frieds," *Puck,* December 13, 2022.

82 **"the nerdiest stuff you can imagine":** Roger Parloff, "Portrait of a 29-Year-Old Billionaire: Can Sam Bankman-Fried Make His Risky Crypto Business Work?," Yahoo! Finance, August 12, 2021.

82 **Over lunch at Au Bon Pain:** Adam Fisher, "Sam Bankman-Fried Has a Savior Complex—And Maybe You Should Too," *Sequoia,* September 22, 2022.

83 **ten thousand lives:** "Want an Ethical Career? Become a Banker," University of Oxford, November 22, 2011. MacAskill later revised this estimate down be-cause it was based on an unrealistically low cost per life saved.

83 **He was a trader on the international ETF desk:** Joe Weisenthal and Tracy Alloway, "The Ex-Jane Street Trader Who's Building a Multi-Billion Crypto Empire," Bloomberg, April 1, 2021.

85 **in Oregon when they were teenagers:** Ava Benny-Morrison and Annie Massa, "From Math Camp to Handcuffs: FTX's Downfall Was an Arc of Brother-hood and Betrayal," Bloomberg, February 15, 2023.

85 **Wang joined Bankman-Fried's frat:** Ibid.

86 **As an arbitrage trader:** David Yaffe-Bellany, Lora Kelly, and Cade Metz, "She Was a Little-Known Crypto Trader. Then FTX Collapsed," *New York Times,* No-vember 23, 2022.

86 **"We Do Cryptocurrency Bitcoin Arbitrage":** Sylvie Douglas, "Sam Bankman-Fried and the Spectacular Fall of His Crypto Empire, FTX," *Planet Money,* NPR, November 16, 2022.

86 **about $500,000 in profits in November:** Approximate financial information from Alameda's early months provided by three anonymous sources.

87 **conference in Macau:** David Yaffe-Bellany, "A Crypto Emperor's Vision: No Pants, His Rules," *New York Times,* May 14, 2022.

Chapter Ten: Imagine a Robin Hood Thing

89 **FTX had raised $800 million:** Jamie Crawley, "FTX Reaches $32B Valuation with $400M Fundraise," *CoinDesk,* January 31, 2022.

89 **after raising $420.69 million:** Danny Nelson, "FTX Raises $420,690,000," *CoinDesk,* October 21, 2021.

89 **"it's important for people to think":** David Yaffe-Bellany, "A Crypto Emperor's Vision: No Pants, His Rules," *New York Times,* May 14, 2022.

89 **$210 million deal to sponsor:** Kellen Browning, "A Pro E-Sports Team Is Getting $210 Million to Change Its Name," *New York Times,* June 4, 2021.

89 **estimated cost of about $20 million:** Author's interview with Brett Harrison, former president of FTX US.

91 **He gave $5 million:** Sander Lutz, "White House Refuses to Answer Questions About Sam Bankman-Fried Donations," *Decrypt,* December 14, 2022.

91 **spread around at least $90 million:** Matthew Goldstein and Benjamin Weiser, "New Details Shed Light on FTX's Campaign Contributions," *New York Times,* February 23, 2023.

91 **One in three members of Congress:** Jesse Hamilton, Cheyenne Ligon, Elizabeth Napolitano, "Congress' FTX Problem: 1 in 3 Members Got Cash from Crypto Exchange's Bosses," *CoinDesk,* January 17, 2023.

91 **who'd received a $5,700 donation:** Cheyenne Ligon, "The 'SBF Bill': What's in the Crypto Legislation Backed by FTX's Founder," *CoinDesk,* November 15, 2022.

91 **"weird brand-building exercises":** Sam Harris, "Earning to Give: A Conversation with Sam Bankman-Fried," *Making Sense,* December 24, 2021.

93 **ultramarathon running record:** Mercury News, "Saratogan Nishad Singh Sets the World Record for Fastest 100-Mile Run by a 16 Year Old," *San Jose Mercury News,* September 10, 2012.

94 **"You could imagine":** It's possible that Singh did not know about any fraud at FTX at the time of this interview. At a court hearing in February 2023, when he pleaded guilty to criminal fraud charges, he said that he only started to learn what was going on in the summer of 2022, a few months after my visit.

Chapter Eleven: "Let's Get Weird"

97 **The hackers had been inside:** This account of the hack comes from a report commissioned by Bitfinex and obtained by the author.

98 **"Bitcoin had turned out":** Andy Greenberg, "Inside the Bitcoin Bust That Took Down the Web's Biggest Child Abuse Site," *Wired,* April 7, 2022.

99 **Friends remembered her being:** Cyrus Farivar, David Jeans, and Thomas Brewster, "Razzlekhan: The Untold Story of How a YouTube Rapper Became a Suspect in a $4 Billion Bitcoin Fraud," *Forbes,* March 17, 2022.

99 **"When she meets someone":** Author's interview with Amoniak.

100 **he was serving as a mentor:** Farivar, Jeans, and Brewster, "Razzlekhan: The Untold Story of How a YouTube Rapper Became a Suspect in a $4 Billion Bitcoin Fraud."

100 **One friend told a reporter:** Ibid.

100 **"This is Ilya":** Ibid.

100 **a high school classmate:** Kevin T. Dugan and Matt Stieb, "The Many Lives of Crypto's Most Notorious Couple: How the Accused Bitcoin Launderers Spent Their Time," *New York,* February 15, 2022.

100 **I'd written an exposé:** Zeke Faux, "How Facebook Helps Shady Advertisers Pollute the Internet," *Bloomberg Businessweek,* March 27, 2018.

101 **famed bank robber:** Willie Sutton said the quote was invented by a reporter and that he robbed banks because it was thrilling. Willie Sutton, Willie and Edward Linn, *Where the Money Was* (New York: Viking, 1976), 120.

101 **$600 million worth:** Chainalysis, "The 2022 Crypto Crime Report."

102 **a total of $3.2 billion:** Ibid.

102 **That's a hundred times more:** FBI, "Bank Crime Statistics," https://www.fbi .gov/investigate/violent-crime/bank-robbery/bank-crime-reports.

104 **In January 2017, about $22,000:** This figure comes from court records.

104 **died in prison:** Wassayos Ngamkham, "Canadian Drug Suspect Found Hanged in Cell," *Bangkok Post,* July 12, 2017.

105 **"We're picking up":** Nick Bilton, "The Ballad of Razzlekhan and Dutch, Bitcoin's Bonnie and Clyde," *Vanity Fair,* August 18, 2022.

105 **police were investigating:** Kenneth Garger, "NYC Man Charged with Helping Transport Nicole Flanagan's Body in Barrel to NJ," *New York Post,* August 24, 2021.

106 **As the agents started:** The search was described in filings in their criminal case.

108 **Roughly $70 million worth:** Tim Robinson, "Elliptic Follows the $7 Billion in Bitcoin stolen from Bitfinex in 2016," *Elliptic,* May 13, 2021.

109 **"importing urea from Russia":** Rob Guth, "Bandwidth Merchant?," *The Industry Standard,* January 25, 1999.

Chapter Twelve: "Click, Click, Click, Make Money, Make Money"

113 **According to its creator:** "Announcing C.R.E.A.M. Finance," *Medium,* July 16, 2020.

114 **Method Man:** "Cream Finance Theme—Method Man and Havoc," YouTube, https://www.youtube.com/watch?v=-SFPp7Gsycs.

115 **Among the first to arrive:** Neil Strauss, "Brock Pierce: The Hippie King of Cryptocurrency," *Rolling Stone,* July 26, 2018.

115 **"We're here to take":** Strauss, "Brock Pierce: The Hippie King of Cryptocurrency."

115 **Pierce liked to walk:** Ibid.

115 **He performed quasi-religious rituals:** Nellie Bowles, "Making a Crypto Utopia in Puerto Rico," *New York Times,* February 2, 2018.

115 **"So, no. No, I don't want to pay":** Ibid.

116 **"This is what our colonizers":** Coral Murphy Marcos and Patricia Mazzei, "The Rush for a Slice of Paradise in Puerto Rico," *New York Times,* January 31, 2022.

116 **At one point, protesters:** Ibid.

117 **Publicly, Mashinsky:** Joshua Oliver and Kadhim Shubber, "Alex Mashinsky, Celsius Founder Feeling the Heat," *Financial Times,* June 17, 2022.

Chapter Thirteen: Play to Earn

121 **"cheerful tube sock":** Steph Yin, "Seeking Superpowers in the Axolotl Genome," *New York Times,* January 29, 2019.

123 **It was founded:** Leah Callon-Butler, "Most Influential 2021: Trung Nguyen," *CoinDesk,* December 8, 2021.

123 **Even then, growth:** Darren Loucaides, "To Infinity and Back: Inside Axie's Disastrous Year," *Rest of World,* June 22, 2022.

123 **The game signed up:** Brandon Rochon, "Axie Infinity Growth Pt. 1—Approach to 10M Players," *Covalent,* December 1, 2021.

123 **By that October:** Aleksander Larsen. Interview. Patrick O'Shaughnessy, host. "Sky Mavis: The Builders Behind Axie Infinity," *Business Breakdowns,* September 15, 2021.

123 **Sky Mavis capitalized:** Yogita Khatri, "Axie Infinity Creator Announces $152 Million in Series B Funding Led by a16z," *The Block,* October 5, 2021.

123 **"It's actually the beginning":** Aleksander Larsen. Interview. Patrick O'Shaughnessy, host. "Sky Mavis: The Builders Behind Axie Infinity."

124 **"One of the main criticisms":** Packy McCormick, "Infinity Revenue, Infinity Possibilities," *Not Boring,* July 19, 2021.

124 **Sam Bankman-Fried's exchange:** Andrew Hayward, "FTX Sponsors Play-to-Earn 'Scholars' in Ethereum Game Axie Infinity," *Decrypt,* August 5, 2021.

124 **Cuban said in a quasi-documentary:** "PLAY-TO-EARN | NFT Gaming in the Philippines | English," YouTube, https://www.youtube.com/watch?v=Yo-Br ASMHU4&t=263s.

127 **North Korean hackers:** Nikhilesh De and Danny Nelson, "US Officials Tie North Korea's 'Lazarus' Hackers to $625M Crypto Theft," *CoinDesk,* April 14, 2022.

127 **weapons program:** U.S. officials estimate that digital heists including the Sky Mavis hack have been funding half of North Korea's ballistic missile program. Robert McMillan and Dustin Volz, "How North Korea's Hacker Army Stole $3 Billion in Crypto, Funding Nuclear Program," *Wall Street Journal,* June 11, 2023.

Chapter Fourteen: Ponzinomics

131 **Clinton was reportedly paid:** Lydia Moynihan, "How Sam Bankman-Fried's Ties with the Clintons Helped Him Dupe Investors," *New York Post,* January 19, 2023.

131 **Brady and Bündchen were paid:** Author's interview with SBF.

132 **accused in three lawsuits:** *Jules Vanden Berge v. Christopher Masanto, Andrew Masanto, Altitude Ads Limited, Blooming Investments Limited, and Amplify Limited,* 3:20-cv-00509-H-DEB (S.D. Cal. Mar. 17, 2020); *Socorro Lopo v. Christopher Masanto et al.,* 2:21-cv-01937-JAK-JEM (C.D. Cal. Mar. 2, 2021); *Widiantoro et al. v. Masanto et al.,* 1:21-cv-06941-KPF (S.D.N.Y. Aug. 17, 2021).

133 **at least five years:** I checked in with Michael Wagner in June 2023. By then, *Star Atlas* had released a playable demo, but the price of ATLAS tokens had

crashed to near zero. "Our philosophy, since inception, is to develop iteratively and release modularly," Wagner told me.

133 **A writer who visited:** Fisher, "Sam Bankman-Fried Has a Savior Complex—And Maybe You Should Too."

133 **was earning:** Shaurya Malwa, "Solana-Based STEPN Reports $122.5M in Q2 Profits," *CoinDesk,* July 12, 2022.

134 **an interview on a podcast:** SBF. Interview. Joe Weisenthal and Tracy Alloway, hosts. "Sam Bankman-Fried and Matt Levine on How to Make Money in Crypto," *Odd Lots* podcast, April 25, 2022.

135 **Kyle Samani, a crypto:** Hannah Miller, "Solana Generates $1 Billion in Returns for Multiple Early Backers," *The Information,* December 13, 2021.

138 **critical of his résumé:** Kadhim Shubber, Ryan McMorrow, Siddharth Venkataramakrishnan, "Tether's CEO: From IT Sales to Calling the Shots in Crypto Land," *Financial Times,* December 17, 2021.

138 **"If you dip the butt":** Nury Vittachi, "Doonesbury's Mr Butts Just Needs a Bath," *South China Morning Post,* March 27, 1996. Tether told the *Financial Times* that Van der Velde sold the company's other products.

139 **tens of billions of dollars' worth:** Pedro Herrera, "Dapp Industry Report—January 2022," *Dapp Radar,* February 3, 2022.

Chapter Fifteen: All My Apes Gone

141 **an appearance on *The Tonight Show*:** Paris Hilton. Interview. Jimmy Fallon, host. *The Tonight Show Starring Jimmy Fallon,* January 24, 2022.

142 **one ex–Goldman Sachs banker:** Yueqi Yang, "Wall Street Firms Make Crypto Push to Catch Up with 'Cool Kids'," Bloomberg, April 25, 2022.

143 ***The Wall Street Journal* featured:** Ben Cohen, "The Whales of NBA Top Shot Made a Fortune Buying LeBron Highlights," *Wall Street Journal,* March 9, 2021.

143 **"I look at my life":** Rosanna McLaughlin, "'I Went from Having to Borrow Money to Making $4M in a Day': How NFTs Are Shaking Up the Art World," *Guardian,* November 6, 2021.

143 **One collection, called Pixelmon:** Kate Irwin, "$70 Million Later, Pixelmon's Founder Calls Artwork Reveal 'Horrible Mistake,'" *Decrypt,* February 27, 2022.

144 **A woman known online:** The fart seller's name was Stephanie Matto.

144 **"Aping in":** Samantha Hissong, "How Four NFT Novices Created a Billion-Dollar Ecosystem of Cartoon Apes," *Rolling Stone,* November 1, 2021.

144 **suspected to be Sam Bankman-Fried:** Nate Freeman, "SBF, Bored Ape Yacht Club, and the Spectacular Hangover After the Art World's NFT Gold Rush," *Vanity Fair,* January 18, 2023.

144 **gold-colored fur:** Rosie Perper, "Rare Bored Ape Yacht Club NFT Sells for Record $3.4 Million USD," Hypebeast, October 26, 2021.

146 **while listing an ape:** Connor Sephton, "Collector Loses $391,000 as Bored Ape NFT Accidentally Sells for Just $115—How Did It Happen?," *CoinMarketCap Alexandria,* March 29, 2022.

146 **The actor Seth Green:** Sarah Emerson, "Seth Green's Stolen Bored Ape Is Back Home," *BuzzFeed News,* June 9, 2022.

146 **a Chelsea art-gallery owner:** Shanti Escalante-De Mattei, "Thieves Steal Gal-

lery Owner's Multimillion-Dollar NFT Collection: 'All My Apes Gone,'" *ART-News*, January 4, 2022.

Chapter Sixteen: It's the Community, Bro

153 **outed by *BuzzFeed*:** Katie Notopoulos, "We Found the Real Names of Bored Ape Yacht Club's Pseudonymous Founders," *BuzzFeed*, February 4, 2022.

154 **lifelike portrait of Charles Bukowski:** Jessica Klein, "Planet of the Bored Apes: Inside the NFT World's Biggest Success Story," *Input*, August 3, 2022.

154 **introduced Aronow and Solano:** Shirley Halperin, "From Maverick to Mogul, Madonna's Manager Guy Oseary Transcends the Music World to Take on NFTs," *Variety*, July 27, 2022.

154 **"white glove service":** Ryan Weeks, "MoonPay Has Quietly Set Up a Concierge Service to Help Celebrities Buy NFTs," *The Block*, November 25, 2021.

154 **MoonPay took advantage:** Paris Hilton was one of the investors in MoonPay. The deal was announced a few months after her appearance on Jimmy Fallon's show. Elizabeth Lopatto, "Thanks, Gwyneth! MoonPay Rides Celebrity Interest to $3.4 Billion Valuation," *The Verge*, April 13, 2022.

154 **about $1 billion worth:** Based on ApeCoin's public statements, there were 1 billion ApeCoins, and 15 percent went to Yuga Labs, and an additional 8 percent to the founders of the company—230 million ApeCoins. At the time of ApeFest, ApeCoins were worth about four dollars each.

154 **A presentation to venture capitalists:** Yuga Labs pitch deck was available on the website *Best Pitch Deck*. https://bestpitchdeck.com/yuga-labs.

156 **"It's extremely apparent":** Jessica Klein, "Planet of the Bored Apes: Inside the NFT World's Biggest Success Story."

156 **"Don't you think":** Interview. Damon Dash. Rashad Bilal and Troy Millings, hosts. "Dame Dash on Starting Rocawear, His Football League, NFTs, & More," YouTube, June 1, 2022, https://www.youtube.com/watch?v=Jnnmb5oiQNU&t=566s.

157 **Yuga Labs would later sue:** *Yuga Labs v. Ripps*, 22 Civ 4435 (C.D. Calif 2022).

157 **misquoting someone:** Lawyers for Yuga Labs said the quote was from *Forbes*, but it was from *Fortune*.

157 **a judge ruled:** Richard Whiddington, "Yuga Labs Has Won Its Lawsuit Against Artist Ryder Ripps for His Copycat Versions of Bored Ape Yacht Club NFTs," *Artnet News*, April 24, 2023.

158 **I later learned from a legal document:** *Yuga Labs v. Ripps*.

Chapter Seventeen: Blorps and Fleezels

162 **an obnoxious thirty-year-old South Korean:** Zeke Faux and Muyao Shen, "A $60 Billion Crypto Collapse Reveals a New Kind of Bank Run," *Bloomberg Businessweek*, May 19, 2022.

162 **Comedian John Oliver:** "Cryptocurrencies II," *Last Week Tonight with John Oliver*, HBO, April 23, 2023.

163 **Tether's tech chief, Paolo Ardoino:** Olga Kharif, "Tether Takes Victory Lap After Stablecoin Regains Peg," Bloomberg, May 12, 2022.

163 **more and more Tethers:** Ryan Browne, "World's Biggest Stablecoin Regains Dollar Peg After $3 Billion in Withdrawals," CNBC, May 13, 2022.

164 **But behind the scenes:** The details and internal communications were revealed in court filings. Celsius Network LLC, et al., 22-10964 (S.D. New York Bankruptcy).

164 **Mashinsky and his lawyers:** *The People of the State of New York v. Alex Mashinsky,* Index No.: 450040/2023 (Supreme Court of the State of New York, County of Westchester).

165 **"There are companies":** Steven Ehrlich, "Bankman-Fried Warns: Some Crypto Exchanges Already 'Secretly Insolvent,'" *Forbes,* June 28, 2022.

165 **When he founded Three Arrows:** Jen Wieczner, "The Crypto Geniuses Who Vaporized a Trillion Dollars," *New York,* August 15, 2022.

166 **"One of the last calls":** Interview. Kyle Davies. Hugh Hendry, host. "The Collapse of Three Arrows Capital: Part I with Kyle Davies," *The Acid Capitalist* podcast, December 3, 2022.

166 **The founders later said:** Joanna Ossinger, Muyao Shen, and Yueqi Yang, "Three Arrows Founders Break Silence Over Collapse of Crypto Hedge Fund," Bloomberg, July 22, 2022.

166 **filed for bankruptcy:** "Eastern Caribbean Supreme Court in the High Court of Justice Virgin Islands (Commercial Division), In re Three Arrows Capital Limited, Case No. BVIHCOM2022/0119," June 27, 2022.

167 **As crypto skeptics:** Amy Castor and David Gerard, "Crypto collapse: 3AC yacht 'Much Wow' back on the market, Celsius maybe-Ponzi, Voyager pays off the boys, Hodlnaut," AmyCastor.com, August 23, 2022.

167 **"You wouldn't normally show":** Madison Darbyshire, "Miami Nightclubs Mourn Absence of High-Rolling Crypto Entrepreneurs," *Financial Times,* November 26, 2022.

167 **"very fatty pork dishes":** David Yaffe-Bellany, "Their Crypto Company Collapsed. They Went to Bali," *New York Times,* June 9, 2023.

168 **Chappy didn't tell his son:** Author's interviews with "Chappy" and Zach Shallcross, May 31, 2023.

168 **"I think decentralization":** Freddy Brewster, "'Bachelorette' Contestant's Firefighter Dad Has Retirement Locked Up in Bankrupt Crypto Lender," *Los Angeles Times,* August 12, 2022.

169 **"a trading wunderkind":** Jeff John Roberts, "Exclusive: 30-Year-Old Billionaire Sam Bankman-Fried Has Been Called the Next Warren Buffett. His Counterintuitive Investment Strategy Will Either Build Him an Empire—Or End in Disaster," *Fortune,* August 1, 2022.

169 *The Economist:* "Crypto's Last Man Standing," *The Economist,* July 5, 2022.

169 **"I do feel like":** David Gura, "Crypto Billionaire Says Fed Is Driving Current Downturn," NPR, June 19, 2022.

169 **Bankman-Fried did say something ominous:** Steven Ehrlich, "Bankman-Fried Warns: Some Crypto Exchanges Already 'Secretly Insolvent,'" *Forbes,* June 28, 2022.

170 **might be less willing:** Tether has said it cooperates with all legal inquiries, but its history of fighting U.S. authorities gave it street cred.

170 **One of its most prominent:** *Protos* Staff, "China's Crypto King Pleads Guilty to Laundering $480M for Online Casinos, Report," *Protos,* May 12, 2021.

170 **When North Korea sent workers:** U.S. Department of Justice, Office of Public Affairs, "North Korean Foreign Trade Bank Representative Charged in Crypto Laundering Conspiracies," April 24, 2023.

170 **Transparency International Russia:** Transparency International UK, "From Russia with Crypto: Moscow-Based Exchanges Offering to Anonymously Convert Stablecoins for Cash in the UK." Available at: https://www.transparency .org.uk/news-and-events/press-releases/item/1936-from-russia-with-crypto -moscow-based-exchanges-offering-to-anonymously-convert-stablecoins-for -cash-in-the-uk.

171 **Russian money launderer:** *U.S. v. Orekhov et al.,* 22 Crim 434 (E.D. New York Sep. 26, 2022).

Chapter Eighteen: Pig Butchering

173 **nonsensical come-ons:** "Hi, Mike, I'm Dani, and this is my new number. My dog stopped eating dog food yesterday. Can you come and see him?" read another bizarre message I'd received from a random number.

175 **A project finance lawyer:** Alastair McCready, "From Industrial-Scale Scam Centers, Trafficking Victims Are Being Forced to Steal Billions," *Vice,* July 13, 2022.

175 **A divorced mother of three:** Brian Krebs, "Massive Losses Define Epidemic of 'Pig Butchering,'" *Krebs on Security* (blog), July 21, 2022.

175 **A twenty-four-year-old social media producer:** Kevin Roose, "Crypto Scammers' New Target: Dating Apps," *New York Times,* February 21, 2022.

177 **Once the mark was gone:** The con man's biggest challenge was getting rid of the victim after stealing their cash. Sometimes, they'd have a fake detective arrive and pretend to arrest the con man for stock manipulation, or one con man would pretend to shoot another, implicating the mark in a pretend murder. (This trick was employed by the con men played by Paul Newman and Robert Redford in the 1973 movie *The Sting.*)

177 **"a carefully set up and skillfully":** David W. Maurer, *The Big Con: The Story of the Confidence Man* (New York: Random House, 1940), 8.

178 **"I have never cheated":** Saul Bellow, *There Is Simply Too Much to Think About: Collected Nonfiction,* ed. Benjamin Taylor (New York: Penguin, 2016).

178 **required the cooperation:** Maurer, *The Big Con,* 218.

178 **often eventually arrested:** Shaffiq Alkhatib, "Jail for Money Mule Who Worked with Member of Nigerian Love Scam Group and Had Child with Him," *Straits Times,* February 23, 2023.

180 **IRS traced the funds:** Mitchell Clark, "A Cringe Rapper Slash Forbes Contributor Allegedly Found with Billions in Stolen Bitcoin," *The Verge,* February 8, 2022.

182 **U.S. Secret Service agent:** Brian Krebs, "Confessions of an ID Theft Kingpin, Part I," *Krebs on Security* (blog), August 26, 2020.

186 **string of suspicious deaths:** Mech Dara, "Spate of Violent Crimes Against Foreigners Nabs More Than 20 Suspects," *Voice of Democracy,* February 2, 2022.

186 **"If an ambulance doesn't go inside":** Husain Hader, "Sihanoukville's Dirty Secret: Dark Rumours and Inside Information Raise Questions About the China Project," *Khmer Times,* September 6, 2021.

Chapter Nineteen: "We Have Freedom"

190 **jailing opposition leaders:** "Cambodia: 51 Opposition Politicians Convicted in Mass Trial," *Human Rights Watch,* June 14, 2022.
190 **harassing union leaders:** "Cambodia: Rights Crackdown Intensifies," *Human Rights Watch,* January 12, 2023.
193 **arrested in his home country:** Jack Brook, "Scams, Human Trafficking Thrived at Bokor Mountain Behind Tycoon's Luxury Hotel," *CamboJA,* February 9, 2023.
195 **betting over livestreamed video:** Sangeetha Amarthalingam, "Sleepless in Sin City—Will Half-Sized, Outlawed Online Gambling Sector Persist Below the Surface in Cambodia?," *Phnom Penh Post,* September 2, 2021.
195 **generated as much as $5 billion:** According to Ben Lee, founder of IGamiX, a Macau-based consulting firm [quoted by the Japanese weekly magazine *Nikkei Asia,* January 10, 2020], gambling-related revenues in Sihanoukville reached between $3.5 billion and $5 billion a year—90 percent of which was generated by some four hundred virtual casinos, which Cambodian authorities are unable to control.
196 **a loan shark's lifeless body:** David Boyle, "Cambodia's Casino Gamble," *Al Jazeera,* 2019.
196 **more than 1,100 buildings unfinished:** Shaun Turton and Huang Yang, "Stuck in Sihanoukville: Projects Grind to Halt in Cambodia Resort Town," *Nikkei,* August 5, 2022.

Chapter Twenty: No Aceptamos Bitcoin

200 **Jack Dorsey said in an online talk:** BitcoinTV, "Interview with Jack Dorsey—by Michael Saylor," YouTube, February 1, 2022.
201 **and promptly lost half:** Bloomberg reconstructed Bukele's trading history from his tweets and calculated his losses. Sydney Maki, "El Salvador's Big Bitcoin Gamble Backfires to Deepen Debt Woes," Bloomberg, June 15, 2022.
201 **At least 150 people did die:** Bryan Avelar and Tom Phillips, "At Least 153 Died in Custody in El Salvador's Gang Crackdown—Report," *Guardian,* May 29, 2023.
201 **and flew out the next day:** Flight logs obtained by the author. Brock Pierce told me that in addition to throwing the party, he worked with Mayan elders to "reactivate" an ancient pyramid.
202 **El Zonte:** Sharyn Alfonsi, "Bitcoin Beach: How a Town in El Salvador Became a Testing Ground for Bitcoin," *60 Minutes,* CBS News, April 10, 2022.

Chapter Twenty-One: Honey Is Better

209 **An Italian judge:** His name was Giovanni Falcone. A colleague named Paolo Borsellino was also killed in a car bombing. Celestine Bohlen, "Fugitive Mafia Boss Arrested by the Italian Police in Sicily," *New York Times,* May 22, 1996.
209 **with Bernasconi's help:** John Parry, "Swiss Plan Law to Curb Laundering," *American Banker,* March 2, 1987.

209 **money laundering was finally made:** Alan Riding, "New Rule Reduces Swiss Banking Secrecy," *New York Times,* May 6, 1991.

Chapter Twenty-Two: Assets Are Not Fine

213 **Binance was reportedly under investigation:** Chris Strohm, "Binance Faces US Probe of Possible Russian Sanctions Violations," Bloomberg, May 5, 2023. Binance said in a statement quoted in the article that it complies with all U.S. and international financial sanctions and that it has a "zero-tolerance approach" to "obscure sources of money."

213 **Reuters called Binance:** Angus Berwick and Tom Wilson, "How Crypto Giant Binance Became a Hub for Hackers, Fraudsters and Drug Traffickers," Reuters, June 6, 2022.

213 **"we are operating":** *SEC v. Binance Holdings Limited, BAM Trading Services Inc., BAM Management US Holdings Inc., and Changpeng Zhao,* 1:23-cv-01599 (D.D.C. June 5, 2023), Complaint.

214 **whether there was any truth:** CZ told my *Businessweek* colleague Max Chafkin that a potential criminal prosecution was not why he avoided the United States. "I think I'm totally allowed in the U.S., no problem," he said. "But I don't want to give the perception that we're trying to solicit users there." Chafkin had flown to Dubai after being promised an office tour by CZ's public relations team. But when he showed up, all the giant company showed him was bare concrete floors, exposed ducts, and drywall—no computers or people at all. "We're doing a hot-desk system," the public relations person told him. Justina Lee and Max Chafkin, "Can Crypto's Richest Man Stand the Cold?," *Bloomberg Businessweek,* June 23, 2022.

215 **he needed a few billion dollars:** Joshua Oliver, "'Sam? Are You There?!' The Bizarre and Brutal Final Hours of FTX," *Financial Times,* February 29, 2023.

215 **Bankman-Fried reportedly told investors:** Gillian Tan, "FTX Warns of Bankruptcy Without Rescue for $8 Billion Shortfall," Bloomberg, November 9, 2022.

215 **U.S. regulators opened investigations:** Lydia Beyoud, Yueqi Yang, and Olga Kharif, "Sam Bankman-Fried's FTX Empire Faces US Probe into Client Funds, Lending," Bloomberg, November 9, 2022.

216 **many of FTX's top executives:** Tracy Wang, "Bankman-Fried's Cabal of Roommates in the Bahamas Ran His Crypto Empire—and Dated. Other Employees Have Lots of Questions," *CoinDesk,* November 10, 2022.

216 **"How is this guy not shackled?":** Jesse Watters, Jordan Belfort, *Jesse Watters Primetime,* Fox News, November 17, 2022.

Chapter Twenty-Three: Inside the Orchid

220 **U.S. Department of Justice scrutinized:** Katanga Johnson, Lydia Beyoud, Allyson Versprille, and Annie Massa, "Sam Bankman-Fried Facing Possible Trip to US for Questioning," Bloomberg, November 15, 2022.

221 **"So the ethics stuff, mostly a front?":** Kelsey Piper, "Sam Bankman-Fried Tries to Explain Himself," Vox, November 16, 2022.

223 **"If we named our company":** SBF. Interview. *Empire* podcast, "How Sam Bankman-Fried Made $10 Billion by the Age of 28," April 1, 2021.

224 **"As an individual":** Robert Wiblin, "Sam Bankman-Fried on Taking a High-Risk Approach to Crypto and Doing Good," *80,000 Hours* podcast, April 14, 2022.

224 **"Fifty-one percent you double the earth":** Tyler Cowen, "Sam Bankman-Fried on Arbitrage and Altruism," *Conversations with Tyler* podcast, January 6, 2022.

225 **"The way to really make money":** Caroline Ellison, Twitter, March 7, 2021.

225 **buying Dogecoin because Elon Musk:** Sam Trabucco, Twitter, April 22, 2021.

226 **and called for regulation:** Yueqi Yang, "FTX Chief Reminds Congress That 95% of Crypto Volume Is Offshore," Bloomberg, February 9, 2022.

226 **Ellison told her staff:** Two people with knowledge of the matter described Ellison's comments to me. The direct quotes come from the CFTC's case against her. Singh's allocution in the criminal case against him does not mention this meeting. In it, he claims he only learned the extent of the fraud later on.

227 **similar to the balance sheet:** Antoine Gara, Kadhim Shubber, and Joshua Oliver, "FTX Held Less Than $1bn in Liquid Assets Against $9bn in Liabilities," *Financial Times,* November 12, 2022.

Epilogue

233 **he got a call from his lawyer:** Steven Ehrlich, "Sam Bankman-Fried Recalls His Hellish Week in a Caribbean Prison," *Forbes,* January 26, 2023.

233 **His opening line:** Gillian Tan and Max Chafkin, "Sam Bankman-Fried's Written Testimony Is Called 'Absolutely Insulting' at House Hearing," Bloomberg, December 13, 2022.

233 **Around 6:00 P.M.:** Theodore Schleifer, "The Only Living Boy in Palo Alto," *Puck,* January 10, 2023.

233 **"It's not fit for humanity":** Lee Brown, "Sam Bankman-Fried's Bahamas Jail Infested by Rats and Maggots: 'Not Fit for Humanity,'" *New York Post,* December 14, 2022.

233 **He was assigned:** Ehrlich, "Sam Bankman-Fried Recalls His Hellish Week in a Caribbean Prison."

234 **"I was trying to pretend":** Ibid.

234 **a diplomatic cable:** Author's copy of document.

234 **Bankman-Fried realized this was Gary:** Ava Benny-Morrison and Annie Massa, "From Math Camp to Handcuffs: FTX's Downfall Was an Arc of Brotherhood and Betrayal," Bloomberg, February 15, 2023.

234 **His ankle restraints clanking:** Jacob Shamsian and Sindhu Sundar, "Sam Bankman-Fried to Be Released on $250 Million Bail and Will Be Required to Stay with Parents Ahead of FTX Trial," *Business Insider,* December 22, 2022.

234 **hunched over:** Benjamin Weiser, Matthew Goldstein, and David Yaffe-Bellany, "Sam Bankman-Fried Released on $250 Million Bond with Restrictions," *New York Times,* December 22, 2022.

236 **The Bankman-Frieds purchased:** Ehrlich, "Sam Bankman-Fried Recalls His Hellish Week in a Caribbean Prison."

236 **They hired armed guards:** Selim Algar, "Sam Bankman-Fried's Family Pays $10K a Week for Armed Security, Sources Say," *New York Post,* December 27, 2022.

236 **two chess sets:** Joshua Oliver, "'Sam? Are You There?!' The Bizarre and Brutal Final Hours of FTX," *Financial Times,* February 9, 2023.

236 **Galois Capital:** Laurence Fletcher, "Hedge Fund Galois Closes After Half of Assets Trapped on Crypto Exchange FTX," *Financial Times,* February 20, 2023.

236 **an NFT cockfighting game:** Molly White, "a16z-Backed Mecha Fight Club NFT Robot Cockfighting Game Put on Ice as Maker Pivots to AI," *Web3 Is Going Just Great,* May 13, 2023.

237 **"I think all that's been":** Jamie Dimon. Interview. Andrew Ross Sorkin, host. *Squawk Box,* CNBC, January 19, 2023.

238 **against Binance:** *Securities and Exchange Commission v. Binance Holdings Limited, et al.,* Civil Action No. 1:23-cv-01599 (U.S. District Court for the District of Columbia, filed June 5, 2023).

238 **and Coinbase:** *Securities and Exchange Commission v. Coinbase, Inc., et al.,* Civil Action No. 1:23-cv-04738 (U.S. District Court for the Southern District of New York, filed June 6, 2023).

239 **he posed with President:** Paolo Ardoino on Twitter, https://twitter.com/paoloardoino/status/1593298288568049664?s=20.

239 **"Every single token":** Vicky Ge, "Tether to Buy More Bitcoin for Stablecoin Reserves," *Wall Street Journal,* May 17, 2023.

240 **U.S. prosecutors were still investigating:** Tom Schoenberg and Matt Robinson, "Tether Bank-Fraud Probe Gets Fresh Look by Justice Department," Bloomberg, October 31, 2022.

240 **climbed to an all-time high:** "Between our battle-tested resilience in the face of market volatility and our industry-leading transparency practices, Tether has proven that it can be trusted," Paolo Ardoino, Tether's CTO, said in a celebratory statement. Tether, "Tether Reaches All-Time High, Surpasses Previous Market Cap High of $83.2B," June 1, 2023.

241 **which cost Celsius's customers:** Author's calculations based on hourly rates listed in court filings.

INDEX

ABOUT THE AUTHOR

ZEKE FAUX is an investigative reporter for *Bloomberg Businessweek* and Bloomberg News, and a former National Fellow at New America. and a former National Fellow at New America. He's a winner of the Gerald Loeb Award and the American Bar Association's Silver Gavel Award and a finalist for the National Magazine Award. He lives in Brooklyn with his wife and three children.

ABOUT THE TYPE

This book was set in Charter, a typeface designed in 1987 by Matthew Carter (b. 1937) for Bitstream, Inc., a digital typefoundry that he cofounded in 1981. One of the most influential typographers of our time, Carter designed this versatile font to feature a compact width, squared serifs, and open letterforms. These features give the typeface a fresh, highly legible, and unencumbered appearance.